A VENERABLE ASSEMBLY

The History
of Venable, Baetjer
and Howard
1900-1991

BY

Arthur W. Machen, Jr.

Library of Congress Card Catalog Number 91-67360

Machen, Arthur W. Jr. / A Venerable Assembly—The
History of Venable, Baetjer and Howard 1900-1991

ISBN 0-9631294-0-6

Published by the DeskTop Publishing Unit of Venable,
Baetjer and Howard under the supervision of Barton-
Gillet Company, Baltimore, Maryland.

**To my wife, Rose,
with love**

Table of Contents

CONTENTS

Preface

MOST HISTORIES OF law firms are notoriously dull and usually represent all partners as superlawyers and paragons of virtue. If dullness and exaggerations are the pitfalls of these histories, my only defense, if guilty of falling into them, is that I have done my best to avoid them.

Dullness may be overcome by the quality of the material and the ability of the writer to bring it to life in the written word. The protagonists on the stage at Venable, Baetjer and Howard over the last 90 years provide such a wealth of interesting material that no writer of its history can on this account find an excuse for failure. And as for bringing them to life, only the reader will decide whether this objective has been achieved.

With regard to deviations from virtue, there have, of course, been some in an operation of this size spanning nearly a century. Since I have served only one brief term as a rotating member of the Operating Committee and have had little involvement with firm management, it is likely that I have not become aware of most of them. I can only say that those which have come to my attention and which I considered newsworthy have been laid bare.

Believing that the soul of a law firm is revealed not so much by the statistics of its growth as the achievements of its members as advocates and counselors, I have endeavored to familiarize myself with the professional careers of the leading lawyers in the firm, particularly as set out in the reports of cases they tried or argued in the state and federal courts. For state decisions prior to 1937 this study has required an examination page by page of the Maryland Reports to cull from them the appearances by Venable, Baetjer and Howard attorneys; for post-1937 state decisions and all federal decisions the task has been made much simpler by use of the WESTLAW and LEXIS computers. Having thus compiled a list of cases and having perused them all, I have included in the text a precis of some of them but have tabulated most of the others in endnotes following each chapter, together, where appropriate, with an indication of the subject matter of the dispute. I have excluded almost all cases argued by attorneys while serving in public office and most where the particular lawyer was only "on the brief." I suspect that few readers will want to make any serious study of this catalogue of reported decisions, but the record is there for those who do. In the case of Charles McHenry Howard and H. Vernon Eney, however, at least a cursory perusal of these notes will be necessary to appreciate the dimensions of their careers as oral advocates.

To these litanies of decided cases in the endnotes there must be added a caveat lest the reader be misled into the belief that Venable, Baetjer and Howard has, over the years, been primarily devoted to litigation. Until the recent affiliation with Cook, Howard, Downes & Tracy, the firm had rarely represented casualty or life insurance companies in the defense of policy claims, nor until the last decade had it handled to any significant degree personal injury cases, domestic relations or criminal matters. Rather the primary thrust of its practice has been directed to commercial, financial, fiduciary and tax matters, as well as the management side of labor relations. The many appearances of its partners in the reports of decided cases have largely been an outgrowth of this business orientation of its practice.

Having sometimes criticized historical books for their inadequate or innaccurate indices, I have made up my own in this book. The professional indexer will doubtless find many shortcomings. I can only say that I have done my utmost to avoid errors and ommissions, but some must yet be there to be found. I have even included in the index an occasional citation to endnotes when I thought the references might have some personal or historical interest.

In the preparation of this history I have received advice, help and encouragement from so many sources that I could not begin to acknowledge them all. However, a special word of thanks must be extended to: Norwood B. Orrick, Richard W. Emory and the late Edmund P. Dandridge, Jr. for their firsthand recollections and helpful reviews of the early chapters; Mrs. John Henry Lewin for her perceptive comments on the chapter dealing with her late husband; Mrs. H. Vernon Eney, Dr. R. Donald Eney, Alexander Armstrong and Mrs. Nancy M. Looker for the assistance they provided on the chapter on Vernon Eney; John C. Cooper, III for his review of the chapter on his father; Edward C. Papenfuse, director of the Maryland Hall of Records, for his assistance with some aspects of Maryland history; Bradford Jacobs for his review of the Edwin G. Baetjer chapter and his helpful tips on Maryland political history; Robert J. Brugger for his constructive suggestions on structure and style; Ms. Margaret Colleluori, the firm's communications coordinator, for her capable editorial assistance; Ms. Laura Campbell, the firm's desktop publishing operator, for her transcription of the manuscript into publication form; a number of my partners, my former secretary of 29 years, Mrs. Joel Chewning, and especially Harold A. Williams, retired editor of the *Sunday Sun*, for their painstaking reading of the entire manuscript; and, finally, a special word of thanks to my present secretary, Mrs. Sharon U. Miller, and her word processing machine for their patience with my many mistakes and revisions. One wonders how it was possible to write a book, even one of this limited scope, without such personal dedication and electronic wizardry.

A. W. M., Jr.

PART I

The Founders

FROM THE TIME of its formation in 1900 until the year 1941, the character of Venable, Baetjer and Howard was shaped by Richard M. Venable, Edwin G. Baetjer and Charles McHenry Howard, here denominated as its "Founders." Although the surviving Founder, Edwin G. Baetjer, did not die until July 20, 1945, he was relatively inactive during the last four years of his life, as his youngest brother, Harry, emerged as the firm's unquestioned leader.

During its formative years the firm developed its reputation as a business-oriented group of practicing lawyers. Its principal clients were banks, trust companies, public utilities, commercial businesses and publishers, and it did a prodigious amount of free legal work for universities, schools, churches and hospitals. The Founders also established a tradition of involvement in the civic, charitable and political life of the community.

Part I of this history deals with the lives and careers of the three men who guided the fortunes of the firm for the first 41 years of its life. Part II, The Caretakers, covers a prosperous but relatively static period until the arrival of H. Vernon Eney in 1951; and Part III, The Innovators, deals with a period of explosive growth over the last four decades.

Richard M. Venable, 1839-1910.

PART I, CHAPTER 1

Richard M. Venable

Lexington Va
14 Nov'r 1868

My dear Colonel

Major Richard Venable, for whom I have a great esteem, goes to your City to practice Law. He gave to the South all the strength of his mind heart & body in her struggle for her rights, & since its close has by precept & example endeavored to train her youth for the performance of the whole duty imposed upon them by her condition. During the past session he was one of the assistant Professors of Mathematics in Washington College. It was there that he completed his Course of the Study of the Law. It was during this time that I became acquainted with the earnestness & integrity of his character.

I know of no better way of aiding him in the career that he has chosen, than of soliciting for him your advice and assistance, & through you, the kind consideration of other friends.

Very truly your friend

R E Lee

Col. Charles Marshall [1]

WITH THESE GRACIOUS words Major Richard Morton Venable was introduced to Baltimore by General Robert E. Lee. When the Major died 42 years later at the age of seventy-one, his admirers reflected on a career filled with contributions to the civic, political, cultural, and professional life of his adopted community.[2]

Venable was born on February 8, 1839 in Charlotte County, Virginia, the son of Richard N. and Magdalen McCampbell Venable. After graduation from Hampden-Sydney College in 1857, he entered the University of Virginia where he studied applied mathematics and engineering until the outbreak of the Civil War. While at the university, Venable displayed some of the swashbuckling propensities that later served him in good stead during the war. One night after having consumed too much corn whiskey, he rode up to Mr. Jefferson's rotunda and, in a display of marksmanship, shot the hands off the clock. For this he was suspended but was reinstated before the outbreak of hostilities.[3]

On April 21, 1861 he enlisted as a private in the Richmond Howitzers and fought in the Battle of Big Bethel, one of the first skirmishes of the war. He was later successively commissioned a Lieutenant of Artillery, Lieutenant of Engineers, Captain of Artillery and Engineers, and Major of Artillery and Engineers. He served in the Army of Northern Virginia until 1863 when he was transferred to the Trans-Mississippi Department.

After the war, Major Venable returned to Charlotte County to find his ancestral home in ruins and his family's wealth destroyed.

He then decided to enter the only vocation for which he was trained, the field of teaching, first as Commandant of Cadets and Professor of Engineering at the Military Academy and University of Louisiana, and then as Assistant Professor of Mathematics at Washington College at Lexington, now known as Washington and Lee University. While there, he studied law and received his LL.B. degree in 1868. On September 14 of that year he was admitted to practice before the courts of that commonwealth but immediately moved to Maryland, the land of opportunity on the border of a war-ravaged South.

Venable then hung up his shingle in Baltimore but, in accordance with prevailing custom in those days, was not admitted to practice before the Court of Appeals until his first appellate argument three years later.[4] Earlier in 1871 he had formed the firm of Venable & Packard, a partnership with Joseph Packard, a Confederate veteran who had served under Stonewall Jackson in the famous Stonewall Brigade.[5] The first appellate appearance of Venable & Packard is in *Lewis v. B. & O. Railroad*,[6] a case they lost. However, the firm continued and prospered for about 20 years, then broke up for reasons unknown.[7]

Venable had a long association with the faculty of the University of Maryland School of Law. He taught there from 1872 to 1906, lecturing on Real Property and Leasehold Estates, Constitutional and Statute Law, and General Jurisprudence. He was intimately exposed to the law students of the time, so that when his partnership with Joseph Packard was dissolved, it is not surprising that he decided to continue his practice in association with two of his best pupils, Edwin G. Baetjer who had graduated in 1890 and Charles McHenry Howard who had graduated in 1893. Baetjer was 29 years his junior and Howard 31.

The story is told that when Major Venable summoned Howard to his office to offer him a job, the latter after having accepted, observed that his father, McHenry Howard, a respected Maryland lawyer, had recommended Edwin G. Baetjer as a promising young attorney with whom the younger Howard would be well-advised to become associated. "Don't worry about that, young man," said Major Venable, "I engaged him last week."[8]

The two juniors joined their senior with offices at 206 North Calvert Street[9] for a few years before moving to the fourteenth floor of the Continental Building, now the Mercantile Trust Building, on the southeast corner of Calvert and Baltimore Streets, a structure which arose "phoenix-like" from the ashes of the Great Fire of 1904.[10]

The first case in which the names of Venable and Howard appear together in the decisions of the Court of Appeals is *Wethered v. Safe Deposit & Trust Co.*[11] in 1894, a will construction case eliciting the observation from the court, "The case was very ably argued."[12] Although Baetjer had graduated from law school three years before Howard, he was not admitted to the Court of Appeals until 1895, a year after the latter's admission. Baetjer's first case was *West Boundary v. Bayless*[13] in which he appeared by himself for the appellees; it was so well presented that the court refused to hear his oral argument, affirming the decision on the record. The first case in which Venable and Howard appeared together was *Hambleton v. Rhind*[14] which they had won in the lower court but lost on appeal.

Major Venable's name appears of record as oral advocate in a total of 29 cases in the Court of Appeals, but in only four after the firm was formed in 1900, and in four federal cases, only one of which was argued after 1900.[15] He was then in the twilight of his career, doubtless a reason for his formation of the partnership that still bears his name.

Some commentators have placed the birthdate of the firm of Venable, Baetjer and Howard as far back as 1894, the year after Howard had graduated from law school, while others have observed that the exact date is in doubt.[16] These speculations are dispelled by Volume No. 1 of the firm's docket which records the earliest entry date as July 7, 1900.[17] For at least six years before that Baetjer and Howard were practicing as Venable's associates.

After the formation of the partnership, Major Venable had only six more years of active practice before failing health compelled him to curtail his activities in 1906. A gradually worsening heart condition felled him on July 10, 1910.[18]

Major Venable is principally known in legal circles for his contributions to the law of real property. His treatise entitled *Syllabus of the Law of Property in Land*[19] was an invaluable tool of the trade for the Maryland real estate practitioner for many years. After the Great

Fire of 1904 he drafted the Burnt District Act regulating the reconstruction of devastated sections of the city, and it is said that the public improvements effected at the time, particularly the system of public docks, were largely due to his efforts.[20]

From 1903 to 1908 Venable served as president of the City Park Board. After studying the park systems of other cities and enlisting the help of qualified professional planners, he laid out a plan for the expansion of Baltimore's parks and, until two years before his death, expended boundless energies in its implementation and the improvement of the administration of the system. Deploring the practice of politicians who used public funds for transportation, even on public business, he bought a conspicuously colored light blue automobile which he dubbed *The Blue Goose* and used on his frequent inspections of Baltimore's parks, one of which was named after him.[21] Upon his death, and whether upon his orders or not, his ashes were strewn in Druid Hill Park.[22] This prompted the macabre observation from dowagers of the day as they were taking their outings that their carriages were driving directly over Major Venable.[23]

Major Venable is described by H. L. Mencken as "of great stature [with] a belly so vast that his waistcoat looked like a segment of a balloon. . . ."[24] He wore a large, bushy beard that gave his visage a forbidding look, yet his sense of humor and propensity for clowning belied the sternness of his countenance.

While serving in the City Council, he loved to chide a fellow councilman named George Howser by calling him "How, sir?," followed by a loud guffaw.[25] One night he entertained his fellow councilmen with a sumptuous feast at his house; after dinner he took them into the parlor where he took off his coat, lay on the floor and showed how he could balance chairs on his feet.[26] He was a member of the Maryland Club where he engaged in chess and conversation and was recognized as one of the best chess players in the city.[27]

Mencken also tells us that veteran newspapermen were wont to pull the legs of cub reporters by making them check out the story that

Major Venable was about to marry a prominent lady known for her good works. The Major's roars and bellows would send them reeling out of the house.[28]

Major Venable was a bachelor, a condition attributed by some to his innate misogamy, and, according to Mencken, his pet peeves were women and Christianity.[29] It is possible that Mencken was wrong on both counts.

As for women, a different impression is conveyed from a letter dated November 21, 1899 from the Major's first cousin twice removed, Mrs. W. Emmett (Louisa Venable) Kyle, who had visited him in Baltimore while on her honeymoon. She said in relevant part:

> Uncle Dick is as sweet and affectionate to me as if he had known me all my life. He never comes in the house that he does not call for "Bessie" and is always petting me. His friends here say that they never saw the Major so captivated. He won't hear of us going and says "the house is brighter than it has ever been, that I am the only person who has ever stayed here who seemed to realize that he was in need of a little attention."[30]

This account suggests a person of warmth and tenderness, one hungry for human affection, not a gruff and growling hater of women. Perhaps the Major was covering up this sensitive side of his psyche when he boasted of the joys of bachelorhood, maybe even making a virtue out of necessity.[31]

As for religion, there is no doubt that Venable was an agnostic but not the militant atheist suggested by Mencken. His personal library is said to have contained the largest private collection of books on religion in the city. Harry N. Baetjer referred to this paradox in these words:

> We spent hours talking. He would talk about everything from death — he claimed no one really feared it, because it was as natural

as being born — to religion. He certainly knew that subject. And because of his knowledge, or in spite of it, I don't know, he was an agnostic.[32]

Venable was much in demand as an after-dinner speaker and toastmaster. He was capable of turning a phrase in a gracious way, combining wit, charm and a clever use of the *double entendre*, as witness this toast to the ladies present at a banquet of the Maryland State Bar Association:

Fee simple and a simple fee
And all the fees entail,
Are nothing when compared to thee,
The best of fees—female.[33]

After the Major had become a prosperous lawyer, he generously shared his wealth with his less affluent Virginia relatives and also maintained a continuing financial interest in his alma mater, Hampden-Sydney College. When Union Theological Seminary was moved to Richmond, he bought its property near Farmville and donated most of it to the college. Another 152 acres became part of the campus at the death of the Major's sister-in-law. Irritated that the trustees prohibited dancing on school grounds, he bought some adjacent land on which a dance hall was constructed at his expense. His generosity also accounts for the football field, named to this day Venable Field.[34] Another athletic arena, Memorial Stadium, the long-time home of the Baltimore Colts and Baltimore Orioles, was built on part of Venable Park, now a small remnant of its original size because of the further encroachment (which Venable would have deplored) by Eastern High School.[35]

In 1890 Venable was awarded an LL.D degree from Hampden-Sydney and also elected a trustee, a post which he declined because of the pressure of legal business in Baltimore.[36] A lifelong Democrat, he was a delegate to the Democratic National Convention in 1896 that nominated William Jennings Bryan who was defeated by William McKinley in the general election.[37]

The senior partner among the three Founders laid down footsteps that many of his successors in his firm have followed.   Thus—

• He was president of the Bar Association of Baltimore City, as were later Edwin G. Baetjer, Charles McHenry Howard, J. Crossan Cooper, Jr., Norwood B. Orrick, and John Henry Lewin, Jr.

• He served on the board of trustees of the Johns Hopkins University, a post later filled by Edwin G. Baetjer, Charles McHenry Howard, Stuart S. Janney, Jr., Jacques T. Schlenger, and Benjamin R. Civiletti.

• He was a member of the board of trustees of the Johns Hopkins Hospital as were also in subsequent years Charles McHenry Howard, J. Crossan Cooper, Jr., Stuart S. Janney, Jr., Richard W. Emory, and William J. McCarthy.

• He was vice-president of the Johns Hopkins Hospital, and J. Crossan Cooper, Jr. later served as its president.

• His leadership of the Park Board has been emulated by service at the Baltimore municipal level by subsequent partners, including Francis D. Murnaghan, Jr., a member and president of the School Board and also a member and president of the board of trustees of the Walters Art Gallery; H. Vernon Eney and Jacques T. Schlenger on the Greater Baltimore Committee, the former also serving as its chairman; Neal D. Borden a member and president of the National Aquarium board; and Robert M. Thomas, a member and president of the board of trustees of the Baltimore Museum of Art. The Venable years were an auspicious beginning.

Endnotes to Part I, Chapter 1:

1. The original copy of this letter was exhibited to Norwood B. Orrick, a partner at Venable, Baetjer and Howard, by an elderly lady whose name he does not recall. With her permission, Orrick made a copy of the letter from which this transcript is taken. He advised her to give the original to the Maryland Historical Society, but this advice was apparently not followed. The present whereabouts of the original letter are unknown.

Col. Charles Marshall (1830-1902) was the grandnephew of Chief Justice John Marshall. A graduate of the University of Virginia, he was General Lee's military secretary and Chief of Staff during the Civil War. Present at Appomattox, he drafted Lee's acceptance of the terms of surrender. 4 Douglas Southall Freeman, *R. E. Lee*, New York, Scribner's, 1935 at 142. He then took up the practice of law in Baltimore, first with Thomas Hall and later with his sons and nephews, one of the latter being William L. Marbury, Sr., grandfather of Luke Marbury, a partner at Venable, Baetjer and Howard. Marshall was the sixth president of the Bar Association of Baltimore City. (Information compiled by Hon. James F. Schneider, Historian and Archivist of the Supreme Bench of Baltimore City, now the Circuit Court for Baltimore City, in *A Commemoration of the Centennial of the Bar Association of Baltimore City (1880-1980))*.

2. 15 *Transactions of Maryland State Bar Association* (hereinafter "*MSBA Transactions*"), 212 (1910).

3. Anecdote reported by Louisa Venable Kyle (Mrs. W. Emmett Kyle of Virginia Beach), the granddaughter of Major Venable's first cousin, Andrew Reid Venable in a memorandum entitled, *I Remember Major Richard Morton Venable*.

4. According to the records of the Supreme Bench of Baltimore City, Venable was admitted to practice before that court on September 28, 1868, only two weeks after his admission in Virginia. The records of the Court of Appeals of Maryland show his admission on December 21, 1871, shortly before his first appellate argument in *Hugg v. Baltimore and Cuba Smelting and Mining Co.*, 35 Md. 414, decided March 19, 1872. This was a case of maritime law (which Venable won) holding that when the captain of a damaged vessel lightens the load and transships part of the cargo, he is acting exclusively for the shipowner and the cost thereof cannot be passed along to the shipper under the doctrine of "general average."

5. 29 *MSBA Transactions*, 74 (1924). Packard had a distinguished ancestry, being a direct descendant on his mother's side of Richard Henry Lee, a signer of the Declaration of Independence, and also a cousin of General Lee. He was recognized as an outstanding lawyer and performed important civic service as president of the City School Board. A prominent Episcopal churchman, longtime vestryman at Emmanuel Church, Baltimore, and a many-time deputy to the General Convention of the Episcopal Church, this

staid and religious man made a strange bedfellow with the flamboyant and agnostic Venable.

6. 38 Md. 588 (1873), a personal injury case involving the defense of contributory negligence as an absolute bar to recovery. Venable & Packard were the unsuccessful counsel for the appellant.

7. The bill of complaint to construe the will of Arunah S. Abell was filed on July 2, 1890 by John I. Yellott and Venable & Packard as solicitors for the plaintiff, but by February, 1891 the pleadings were being signed by Richard M. Venable alone. In the decision of the Court of Appeals, *Abell v. Abell*, 75 Md. 44 (1891) counsel for the appellants were listed as Messrs. Yellott and Venable, individually. Thus, the break-up with Packard seems to have occurred in late 1890 or early 1891, although the names of the two lawyers appear individually as co-counsel in a federal case tried in 1893. *Clyde v. Richmond & D. R. Co.*, 55 F. 445 (Cir. Ct. E.D. Va. 1893).

8. Anecdote reported by Norwood B. Orrick.

9. J. Crossan Cooper, Jr., *Address to the Associates*, 4, (1976), places the original address as "in the 200 block of Calvert Street" and John Henry Lewin, *Richard M. Venable, Edwin G. Baetjer, Charles McHenry Howard and Harry N. Baetjer*, 3 (date unknown), pinpoints the site at 206 North Calvert Street.

10. *Id.*

11. 79 Md. 153 (1894).

12. *Id.* at 163.

13. 80 Md. 495 (1895), a contract case.

14. 84 Md. 456 (1897), a case involving business law, the fiduciary duty of one member of a syndicate to the others.

15. *Fisher v. Parr*, 92 Md. 245 (1901), involving the personal liability of directors for negligence in the conduct of corporate business, Venable appearing unsuccessfully with T. Wallis Blackistone for the appellees; *Baltimore City v. Gorter*, 93 Md. 1 (1901), involving the construction of the city charter and the powers of the Board of Estimates, Venable appearing with Bernard Carter and H. Arthur Stump for the appellees whose victory in the lower court was substantially reversed; *Morrison v. Barchtold*, 93 Md. 319 (1901), holding that corporate officers are not liable for activities shown by parol evidence to have been conducted in their representative capacities, Venable appearing

unsuccessfully with Col. Charles Marshall for the appellants; and *Baltimore City v. Steamboat Co.*, 104 Md. 485 (1906), Venable's last argument in the Court of Appeals in which he successfully appeared with Thomas F. Cadwalader for the appellee in a real estate case involving riparian rights. Venable's only federal case after 1900 was *Boston & A. R. Co. v. Parr*, 104 F. 695 (4th Cir. 1900) in which his demurrer to the bill of complaint was upheld. His opponents in this case were Bernard Carter and Charles J. Bonaparte, later Attorney General of the United States.

16. Cooper, *supra* note 9, places the date as 1894 while Lewin, *supra* note 9, says that the date is in doubt.

17. Volume 1 of the firm's docket ledger records under Case No. 16 the July 7, 1900 date.

18. *Supra* note 2, at 213.

19. Venable, *Law of Real Property and Leasehold Estates*, with Syllabus of Lectures on *Title To Real Property and Leasehold Estates*, Baltimore (1892).

20. *Supra* note 2, at 214.

21. William Stump: *Man in the Street, The Baltimore Sun*, hereinafter cited as *The Sun*, December 17, 1950. This article, one of a series on street names in Baltimore, recounts the origin of Venable Avenue and its nearby Venable Park intersected by 33rd Street west of Loch Raven Boulevard.

22. The report in *MSBA Transactions*, *supra* note 20, that the ashes were scattered "in accordance with directions which he had left" is inconsistent with Mencken's theory that Venable had directed the ashes to be deposited "into any convenient ashcan." H. L. Mencken, *Newspaper Days 1899-1906*, New York, Alfred A. Knopf, 1941 at 45. The iconoclastic Mencken may have been drawing the long bow. Mrs. Kyle (see *supra* note 3) recalls the explanation of cremation given her as a child and that ". . . he wished this done so that his ashes could be scattered in a Baltimore Park that he loved." By all odds that must be the accurate account.

23. The writer recalls this quip from the lips of his grandmother, Mary Gresham Machen, the first Mrs. Arthur W. Machen.

24. Mencken, *supra* note 22, at 44.

25. Lewin, *supra* note 9.

26. *Id.*

27. *Id.*

28. Mencken, *supra* note 22, at 45.

29. *Id.*

30. Mrs. Kyle, *supra* note 3.

31. Cooper, *supra* note 9, indicates that his bachelorhood was dictated "by a mortifying wound he received from a Union bullet."

32. Stump, *supra* note 21.

33. Baltimore *News-Post*, July 8, 1938.

34. Information taken from clippings and other data furnished by Mrs. Kyle. (See *supra* note 3).

35. *Supra* note 21. And see also Carleton Jones, *Streetwise Baltimore*, Chicago, Bonus Books, 1990, at 163, for more information on Venable Avenue and Venable Park.

36. The *Hampden-Sidney* (sic) *Magazine*, June, 1897, 377-378.

37. Id.

John Gill, President of Mercantile Trust Company,
W. W. Spence, Vice-President and Richard M. Venable, Counsel.

Reproduced from the archives of
Mercantile-Safe Deposit & Trust Co.

Edwin G. Baetjer, 1868-1945.

Edwin G. Baetjer

FOLLOWING THE DEATH of Major Venable in 1910 the firm of Venable, Baetjer and Howard entered into a long period of prosperity and increasing prominence under the guidance of the other two Founders, Edwin G. Baetjer and Charles McHenry Howard. This chapter deals with the career of Edwin G. Baetjer.

Born in Baltimore on June 25, 1868, the son of John G. and Mary A. Baetjer, "E. G." or "Mr. E. G." as he was referred to by his juniors (but never to his face), graduated from the University of Maryland School of Law in 1890. He practiced alone with offices at 10 East Lexington Street until his association with Major Venable some time after Howard's graduation in 1893. As already noted, the early records of the firm indicate that the three practiced law together for at least six years before the partnership was organized in 1900.

Edwin Baetjer and his four brothers, Charles, Howard, Walter and Harry, were all successful in their chosen fields of endeavor: Charles, an investment banker; Howard, an industrialist; Walter, a physician; and Harry, the second Baetjer to head the firm that still bears his brother's family name.

In a career at the bar that spanned 55 years, Edwin Baetjer was nationally recognized as one of the foremost lawyers of his day in the field of corporate finance and business law, yet he steadfastly maintained his status as a generalist, a luxury no longer available to lawyers practicing in major metropolitan firms. Only criminal and domestic relations cases were among the engagements that Edwin G. Baetjer and his firm were unwilling to accept.

He had a knack for reading financial statements as if their story had been written in plain English. Joseph C. France commented on this talent as follows:

> As a business lawyer, I do not believe he has a superior. Figures talk to him and tell him wonderful things, while I have to knock them down and trample on them before they will tell me anything.[1]

This talent was put to use in connection with the reorganization of the Seaboard Air Line Railway Company, an engagement in which the firm of Venable, Baetjer and Howard was embroiled as counsel for the Committee of Underlying Bondholders for over 15 years until it was concluded in 1946 after Baetjer's death the prior year. The institutional holders of a first lien on the most valuable part of the Seaboard system were faced with a dilemma: Unless they surrendered their right to foreclose they would receive no current interest, but if they gave up foreclosure rights they might wind up with receivers' certificates of questionable value. Accordingly, these holders of $32,000,000 of Seaboard bonds formed what was known as the Underlying Committee in order to protect their common interests. Edwin G. Baetjer was named chairman of the committee as well as its counsel.

From 1931 to 1938 Baetjer was assisted in this endeavor by his junior partner, Joseph France, the son of the Joseph C. France previously mentioned. In the concluding years of the life of the Underlying Committee, France assumed the leadership role assisted by Hunter H. Moss. (The latter had become a partner in 1939 when J. Crossan Cooper, Jr., John Marshall Butler, Stuart S. Janney, Jr., and Norwood B. Orrick were also admitted to the firm). Except for a fee of $20,000 paid in 1931, and $6,000 in each of the years 1933, 1934 and 1935, Venable, Baetjer and Howard had served without compensation on the Seaboard reorganization during its entire 15-year life.

When the reorganization plan had been finally approved and implemented, Judge W. Calvin Chesnut, sitting as a District Judge for the Eastern District of Virginia, appointed William L. Marbury of the Baltimore bar as special master to review the applications for compensation from the receivership estate and to make recommendations for their allowance.[2] By coincidence, H. Vernon Eney, later the managing partner of Venable, Baetjer and Howard, was appointed by Judge Chesnut as special counsel to the receivership estate to represent the creditors in connection with the allowances.[3] Hearings were held by Marbury in New York, Baltimore, Norfolk, and Jacksonville, and at all of them Eney was offered the opportunity to cross-examine the applicants.

The Marbury report, comprising 198 printed pages, is a fascinating account of one of the most significant and successful reorganizations to follow the Great Depression.[4] Marbury described Edwin Baetjer as "the outstanding lawyer in Maryland in the field of corporate reorganization," one whose reputation was "more than local," but rather a person "by many regarded as one of the ablest financial lawyers in the United States." He and Joseph France were said to have had "an influence in these proceedings at least equal to that of any other participant." Marbury recommended an allowance of $125,000 to the Underlying Committee "for the expenses of its counsel" and an additional $100,000 directly to the firm itself or $225,000 in all. This was $75,000 less than the $300,000 requested for the 15 years of labor on this engagement.

As a sidelight it should be noted that the firm maintained no accurate time records, this being a discipline imposed on it a decade or so later by none other than Vernon Eney. Instead, when put to the test to come up with something concrete in the way of time charges, they reconstructed an estimate of 2,850 hours for Baetjer, 6,700 for

France, and 1,300 for Hunter Moss. Multiplied by $37.50 per hour for Baetjer, $25 for France, and $13.30 for Moss, this came to $291,665 or a fair approximation of the requested $300,000.

Judging by the time charges posted by today's lawyers, one must conclude that this estimate was not just conservative but unrealistic. The total adds up to 10,850 hours, an average of 723 hours per year or only 241 per lawyer per year. In this day and age an eager associate can post 241 hours on a labor-intensive file in a few weeks. The Seaboard reorganization not only lasted for 15 years but required over 40 volumes of printed text to record its proceedings. There is no doubt that if the firm had maintained accurate time records, its requested allowance could have been much larger than $300,000, even at the low hourly rates then prevailing.

The court's award of $225,000 to Venable, Baetjer and Howard was the largest of any out of a total pool of about $2,500,000 allowed to a host of firms, including some of the most prestigious on Wall Street. In its day the Seaboard reorganization was a notable case.[5]

Another case, also with a happy ending, was nonetheless the most vexing of Edwin G. Baetjer's long career at the bar — the time he was named a defendant in a suit brought against him as a director of the Baltimore Trust Company instituted in August, 1936 by the bank's receiver, John D. Hospelhorn.

The largest bank in Maryland, the Baltimore Trust Company, lumbered through the market crash of October, 1929 but by mid-1931 was in deep trouble. Following a disastrous run in early September, 1931 a group of public-spirited citizens became apprehensive over the possible ripple effect of a crash of this bastion of the Maryland financial community. In hopes of bolstering public confidence they created almost overnight a guaranty fund of $7,755,400 in subscriptions from individuals and institutions with no assurance that the money could ever be repaid. The same group then asked Howard Bruce, one of the state's most respected financiers, if he would take over as chairman of the board and chief executive officer. He agreed on one condition: Edwin G. Baetjer must go on the board as well. At the time the latter was engaged in his favorite summer pastime of shooting grouse in Scotland.

No records have been found to document the exchange of cables that must have crossed the Atlantic that summer, but communications with Edwin Baetjer must somehow have been established. Both he and Bruce were elected directors on September 19, 1931 and served until the appointment of a receiver on January 5, 1935.[6] Bruce took office immediately, but Baetjer's acceptance was delayed until his return from Europe on September 28. Neither Bruce nor Baetjer had any previous experience in commercial banking, and their entry into this maelstrom can only be described as an act of self-sacrifice prompted by a sense of civic duty.

The Bruce-Baetjer stewardship of the affairs of the Baltimore Trust Company was effectively terminated on March 4, 1933 when, under the provisions of the Emergency Banking Act of 1933, its doors were closed, never to open again. It remained under the custody of the State Bank Commissioner until a new operating bank known as the Baltimore National Bank and a new liquidating corporation known as the Baltimore Trust Corporation were formed, whereupon the old bank was placed in receivership for the purpose of winding up its affairs.

After John D. Hospelhorn, the Deputy Bank Commissioner, had assumed the receivership under the jurisdiction of Judge Eugene O'Dunne of the Supreme Bench of Baltimore City, the latter appointed the following lawyers as counsel for the estate: at the suggestion of the Republican Governor Harry W. Nice, Alexander Armstrong and J. Purdon Wright, both distinguished members of the bar and prominent Republicans; on his own, Albert C. Ritchie, former Democratic Governor and Attorney General of Maryland; and, at the suggestion of Edwin G. Baetjer, Joseph C. France, then the undisputed dean of the Baltimore bar. Also named to the staff of the receiver's counsel was a bright young attorney, later destined to be Chief Judge of the Court of Appeals of Maryland, Solicitor General of the United States, and Chief Judge of the United States

Court of Appeals for the Fourth Circuit. His name was Simon E. Sobeloff.

The first bombshell to explode in the receivership proceedings was the release on December 31, 1935 of a 500-page report to the court, known thereafter as the Sobeloff Report.[7] It was a scathing attack on the directors and officers of the Baltimore Trust Company for their mismanagement of the bank over a long period of years, and, although it purported to apply a different standard to Bruce and Baetjer, nonetheless they were all accused of culpability for approving improvident loans and a general inattention to fiduciary duty before and after 1931. The report also used some purple prose, more likely to inflame the public and the press than to enlighten the court — such expressions as "a profligacy that now seems incomprehensible," "a reckless abandon that is perfectly shocking," "egregious follies," and "blunder after blunder."

When the receiver thereupon obtained leave of court to file suit against all directors, the infuriated Joseph C. France asked to be relieved as trial counsel. Unmoved, Judge O'Dunne publicly applauded the Sobeloff Report and appointed in France's place, and over his objections, none other than Simon E. Sobeloff.

To the complaint filed against them, Bruce and Baetjer responded with a vigorous answer, denying all charges, refuting one by one the allegations in the bill, demanding not only a speedy trial but an immediate one, and, in an extraordinary display of bravado, waiving the defense of limitations. Later, in a letter to the court, Charles McHenry Howard referred to this waiver as "heroic."[8] Applying today's standards one might call it stupid; who in this day and age would have sufficient confidence in the efficacy of the judicial system to waive a solid procedural defense to such a serious charge? Those, however, were the days when heroism and honor prevailed over pragmatism. *Sic transit gloria.*

As Baetjer kept bombarding the court and other counsel with a staccato of demands for immediate trial, Sobeloff became aware of the danger of an early and unfavorable resolution of the Bruce-Baetjer litigation before the suits against the other directors could be pursued. And so, he proposed an amendment to the complaint in the Bruce-Baetjer case to charge the defendants with negligence for not having brought suit against their fellow directors for their prior misconduct. If approved, this would have had the effect of telescoping all the cases into one. To prove the case against Bruce and Baetjer, the receiver would have had to prove the culpable malfeasance of the pre-1931 directors, and that, of course, was what the suits against them (very possibly barred by limitations) were all about.

Charles McHenry Howard screamed Foul! This was at best a belated attempt to stall the Bruce-Baetjer case until the others could be resolved, or at worst an attempt to try them all in a context in which the wrong parties would be the defendants.[9]

Judge Robert F. Stanton denied leave to amend, and, after extensive hearing, the case against Howard Bruce and Edwin G. Baetjer was dismissed. No appeal was noted. It was certainly a victory but more importantly a vindication of two honorable men. (The cases against the other directors were later dismissed or settled for modest amounts.)

A less known incident in Edwin Baetjer's life was his association with the Institute of Law at the Johns Hopkins University.[10] Not a law school in any sense of the term, this organization might today be referred to as a think tank —something akin to the Institute for Advanced Study at Princeton or the American Judicature Society. Its basic function was research. It had no curriculum and offered no degrees. The members of the faculty were to take turns at administration, and the organization was visualized as "a community of scholars engaged in scientific investigation in the field of law and related subjects."[11] The object of study was to be "the place of law as one of the instruments of social control, the administration of law, and the impacts of law on human life. . . . "[12]

In the fall of 1928 the institute opened its doors on the Homewood campus with a faculty of four distinguished scholars, Walter Wheeler Cook, formerly professor of law at Yale Law School; Herman Oliphant and Hessell E. Yntema, both from the law faculty at Columbia University, the former a prolific writer in the field of trade regulation, and the latter a Rhodes Scholar and authority on Roman law and comparative jurisprudence; and Leon C. Marshall, formerly professor of economics and business at the University of Chicago.

A trustee of Johns Hopkins, Edwin G. Baetjer injected himself with enthusiasm into the life of the institute, serving as chairman of a committee to raise a permanent endowment entirely from private sources. The noted lawyer and writer on corporation law, Victor Morawetz of New York, provided seed money to cover the cost of one professor of jurisprudence for two years; an anonymous donor pledged $450,000 for bricks and mortar, and Mrs. W. DeCourcey Thom of Baltimore gave $50,000 towards the cost of a library. However generous were these benevolences, they fell far short of the endowment necessary to put the institute on a sound financial footing.

Baetjer's file on the fund-raising effort fills a file drawer and his letterhead looks like a *Who's Who* of the legal, judicial, and political life of the nation in the late 1920's — Newton D. Baker, Carroll T. Bond, Wm. Cabell Bruce, Pierce Butler, Harry Flood Byrd, Benjamin N. Cardozo, Frederic R. Coudert, John W. Davis, John W. Garrett, B. Howell Griswold, Jr., Augustus N. Hand, Learned Hand, Charles Evans Hughes, Albert C. Ritchie, Franklin Delano Roosevelt, Elihu Root, Alfred E. Smith, George W. Wickersham, John H. Wigmore, and many more.

It is idle to speculate as to what might have been the future of the Institute of Law at Johns Hopkins University had it not been for the stock market crash of October, 1929 and the ensuing Great Depression, but these events surely spelled the doom of the institute and Baetjer's dreams for its success. It became impossible to secure new pledges and many already made proved uncollectible. In early 1933 the trustees, unwilling to underwrite further deficits for the institute, voted to suspend operations indefinitely.

Before its untimely death the institute had begun an ambitious survey of our judicial system with particular reference to the cost, delay, and uncertainty of litigation as well as in-depth analyses of the administration of justice in Ohio and Maryland. Other projects included an annual bibliography of current legal research, a survey of the effect of patent law on invention, and a series of studies on the economics of the practice of law.[13] It was a noble experiment.

Baetjer's other extracurricular activities were substantial. He was a director of the Central Savings Bank, Safe Deposit & Trust Company of Baltimore and of the Mercantile Trust Company, since merged and now known as Mercantile-Safe Deposit and Trust Company, and the Canton Company of Baltimore. He was chairman of the board and active in the management of Dun & Bradstreet Company, Incorporated. He was chairman of the commission that inaugurated the Baltimore Civil Service Commission, and acted for one term as chairman of the City Merit System. In World War I he was chairman of the Draft Appeals Board of Maryland and later served as Food Administrator for Maryland. He was a member of the original City Charter Commission and represented the city in controversies surrounding the introduction of natural gas into the metropolitan area. In addition to the Johns Hopkins University, he was a trustee of the Peabody Institute and McDonogh School. He was a co-founder of the Community Fund, now the United Way of Central Maryland.

In 1928-29 Baetjer served as special counsel to a blue ribbon committee (the Nelligan Committee) appointed by Governor Ritchie to investigate a substantial theft by 14 employees of the State Roads Commission who later went to prison, prosecuted by Herbert R. O'Conor, the state's attorney for Baltimore City. The governor and the commission chairman, John N. Mackall, were exonerated of any wrongdoing, but it was a major scandal in Ritchie's third term.[14]

Baetjer's appointment by Ritchie to such a sensitive post attests to their mutual admiration even though they were poles apart politically. The former was a lifelong Republican, the latter a leading candidate for the Democratic presidential nomination in 1932. Edwin Baetjer had himself a brief flirtation with politics in the 1920's when he was touted as a possible Republican candidate for governor and senator,[15] but it came to naught amid rumors that he had a lady friend. Such gossip, true or false, would have little effect on a candidacy in the 1990's, but in the post-Victorian era it was political dynamite. The result was probably just as well, for it is difficult to imagine this dignified gentleman playing the game of politics, and it is unlikely that he would have been good at it.

Edwin G. Baetjer's intellectual honesty is evidenced by an anecdote told by the late William L. Marbury. It seems that as a junior partner in Marbury, Gosnell & Williams, he had been participating in major litigation in the United States District Court for the District of Maryland in association with his senior partner, George Weems Williams. After a favorable outcome before Judge William C. Coleman in the trial court, Williams died, leaving young Bill Marbury in charge of the file for the appeal before the Fourth Circuit Court of Appeals. He describes the subsequent events as follows:[16]

> I was working on our brief when Edwin G. Baetjer of Venable, Baetjer & Howard came to see me and said that he had been asked by a leading New York law firm to become involved in the case with me.
>
> He asked me what the case was all about. With a sinking heart, I told him and explained the position which I planned to take on the appeal. I gave him a copy of Judge Coleman's opinion and a draft of my brief.
>
> About a week later, Mr. Baetjer called me to say that after reading those materials, he told New York counsel that the case was in good hands and that there was really nothing further he could contribute . . .
>
> My senior partners told me that Mr. Baetjer's action was just what they would have expected of him. It would be nice to think that such a thing could happen today, but of one thing I am sure — everyone would be surprised.

Edwin Baetjer's arguments before the Maryland Court of Appeals were not so numerous as those of his partner, Charles McHenry

Howard, but he still had a respectable career as an oral advocate in a total of 23 appearances. They covered a wide spectrum of legal issues, as evidenced by the following sampling:

One of his earliest cases involved the successful defense of a physician accused of mutilating a corpse during an autopsy.[17]

Six years later he argued two important cases dealing with the construction of the charter and ordinances of the city of Havre de Grace.[18]

In 1903 he successfully narrowed the preemption of state insolvency laws by the Federal Bankruptcy Act.[19]

He argued the *Atlantic Coast Line Dividend Cases*[20] involving the continued application of the Pennsylvania rule of apportionment in trust accounting practice. Like several other partners in his firm who followed him, he was unsuccessful in persuading the Court of Appeals to overrule its earlier decision in *Thomas v. Gregg*.[21] Baetjer tried once more, also without success, in the *Northern Central Dividend Cases*,[22] but he received the consolation prize in the court's observation that his "propositions were urged with great earnestness and ability."

He represented his regular corporate client, Nash Motors, Inc., in a contract case,[23] and the public utility, United Railways & Electric Company of Baltimore, in a rate case where his talent for numbers was once more displayed.[24]

Overall Edwin G. Baetjer acquitted himself well before the Court of Appeals, but he retired from oral advocacy in 1930, 15 years before his death.[25] By this time he was moving into the more esoteric field of corporate reorganizations where he had no peer at the bar of Maryland.

Among the firm's archives there have been discovered some undated handwritten notes by Norwood B. Orrick recounting his personal recollections of three episodes in Edwin G. Baetjer's career, The Dun & Bradstreet Matter, The Sugar Institute Case, and The U.S. Industrial Alcohol Case. The ensuing paragraphs under these subheadings, although extensively edited, borrow heavily from the Orrick manuscript without more specific attribution.

The Dun & Bradstreet Matter

E. G.'s wizardry in the field of corporate finance is illustrated by the circumstances giving rise to his longtime chairmanship of the board of Dun & Bradstreet, Incorporated. That company resulted from a merger that almost fell through when separate New York counsel for Dun and for Bradstreet could not agree as to how the new company's securities should be allocated among the existing security holders. At loggerheads, they referred the matter to E. G. as a disinterested expert. His recommendations were adopted by both sides as being demonstrably fair — so much so that the new board of directors named him their chairman.

The Sugar Institute Case

This was a suit brought by four sugar refining companies against the firm's client, C. D. Kenny Co., a local wholesaler and distributor of food products. Orrick worked on the matter as E. G.'s associate.

It seems that, following World War I, Kenny was caught with a large high-cost sugar inventory. At the same time sugar prices fell dramatically. In part settlement of unpaid bills presented by the refineries, the latter agreed to accept shares of Kenny's cumulative redeemable preferred stock. The years went by without the refineries' recovering a penny either in the form of dividends or a redemption of shares. Eventually, their patience failing, they filed suit, demanding compliance with the terms of their preferred stock.

Characteristically, Baetjer began his investigation of the facts by poring over Kenny's financial statements for the relevant years. He satisfied himself that although the company had remained marginally solvent, its profits would not have justified the payment of dividends or a redemption of shares — to do so would have been a violation of sound business practice. A proof of that point might have been enough to win the case, but Baetjer did not stop there. His study of the statements had aroused his curiosity as to why Kenny had lost money during a particular period in its history. The company's management could provide no answer.

At this point E. G. summoned Orrick into his office and explained the hunch that had occurred to him from a study of the numbers. Some years earlier the sugar refineries had formed a trust association known as the Sugar Institute Trust, an organization whose members had been enjoined against continued violations of the Sherman Antitrust Act.[26] Could it be, could it possibly be, he asked, that Kenny's losses had coincided with the period covered by the injunction and, if so, is there authority that would support a claim by Kenny against the refineries for treble damages? Orrick was directed to find out, and E. G. Baetjer left town for his annual grouse shooting in Scotland.

That summer Orrick spent hours in wading through the voluminous record of the *Sugar Institute* case in the Supreme Court and in the U.S. District Court for the Southern District of New York. Then, there followed more hours of research at the bar library. He established that Kenny's loss period had coincided with the period of the institute's illegal activities and that the items of loss which E. G. had spotted could be attributed to practices already found illegal under the antitrust laws. Next, he prepared a memorandum citing the authorities supporting the proposition that the injunction, standing alone, established the prima facie liability of the refineries for treble damages. The memorandum was presented to Mr. Baetjer upon his return from Scotland.

Years later Orrick recalled the "ah-ahs" coming from E. G.'s office as he began to read the report, culminating in roars of delight as he finished it. A few days later he mailed to plaintiffs' counsel a treble damage complaint which he proposed to file against the refineries unless their suit against Kenny was promptly dismissed. It was settled shortly thereafter by the refineries' surrender of their preferred stock in exchange for a sum that was even less than their accumulated unpaid dividends. This victory was the result of Orrick's diligent research, but it was Edwin Baetjer's understanding of numbers that made it possible.

The U.S. Industrial Alcohol Case

In 1934 the United States brought a civil action against Baetjer's client, United States Industrial Alcohol Company, seeking recovery of a so-called "tax" of $6.40 per gallon of distilled industrial spirits diverted to beverage purposes. This tax was one of the weapons used by the government in the enforcement of the 18th Amendment (Prohibition) which had been repealed by the 21st Amendment, effective December 5, 1933. Baetjer's first line of defense was that the tax was a penalty which the government was barred from collecting on the grounds of double jeopardy because the defendants had been previously indicted for a crime arising out of the same facts and their nolo contendre plea had been accepted. This contention was upheld by Judge Chesnut in the United States District Court for the District of Maryland[27] but was reversed by the Fourth Circuit Court of Appeals, Judge Soper dissenting.[28] Accordingly, the case came on for trial in the District Court.

The complaint charged that U.S. Industrial and its subsidiary had sold a lacquer thinner, consisting largely of anhydrous (i.e., 200 proof!) alcohol, knowing that thousands of gallons were being diverted into bootleg gin. The total tax claimed to be due aggregated $8,140,000, a considerable figure at the time.

The government embarked on a series of depositions to record the testimony of some of its key witnesses, including one Tommy Paradise, chief of the bootleg ring in Boston, and one Darwin (born Darbinsky), his New York counterpart. Together with Douglas Steimle of Shearman & Sterling of New York, Orrick attended all the depositions but Baetjer only two. His instructions to his associate were, "Mr. Orrick," [thus he addressed the younger lawyers in the firm], "don't cross-examine unless you have a definite objective in mind."

E. G. himself furnished an example of having a definite objective in mind in his cross-examination of Darwin. The witness admitted to purchasing from U.S. Industrial numerous batches of lacquer thinner in the names of fictitious companies, e.g., Broadway Paint Co., with delivery to an outfit in Buffalo which, under the direction of noted professors of chemistry from noted colleges, made the alcohol potable by removal of poisonous substances required by law to be added to industrial products. Baetjer went through the convoluted routes used by various carriers in the shipments of these orders, including interim or fake destinations and fake purchasers. For example, a steamship company operating out of Baltimore would deliver drums of alcohol from Industrial to a paint company in Florida. The latter would remove the plug on a drum, drain the contents, pour an unidentified red liquid into the drum, and replace the plug. Darwin described these techniques in detail but with suspicion that his inquisitor was after something. He was not sure what.

Baetjer then drew Darwin into an admission that the best way the ultimate user's identity could have been concealed would have been to use negotiable bills of lading so that title would pass from person to person by delivery of the paper. Next, Baetjer produced from the B. & O. Railroad the original bills of lading from U.S. Industrial, all of which were straight bills, not negotiable bills, the goods being deliverable only to the customer named in the instruments. If U.S. Industrial had been party to a conspiracy which was attempting, by convoluted shipping routes and fake purchasers, to conceal the identity of the ultimate user, why would it have used an instrument of transfer that positively identified that user? The witness could provide no answer.

Amos W. W. Woodcock, former United States Attorney for the District of Maryland and National Prohibition Commissioner, who was acting as special counsel for the government in this case, became disenchanted with the thugs on whose testimony he would have had to rely, and settlement discussions ensued. It was eventually disposed of for less than 3% of the government's original claim, the turning point being Baetjer's analysis of the bills of lading. In view of the result of the prior criminal proceeding, this result was satisfactory, to say the least.

Before Baetjer became a specialist in corporate reorganizations his appearance had been entered in a number of cases in the federal courts, including four in the Supreme Court of the United States. In two he appeared for the respondent on petitions for *certiorari*, and in each he prevailed.[29] The other two cases, both involving constitutional questions, were lost.[30]

He was the winner in a major antitrust case in the Fourth Circuit,[31] and appeared in several District Court proceedings involving the reorganization of United Railways & Electric Company of Baltimore, later the Baltimore Transit Company.[32] In an early case, Edwin Baetjer represented Major Venable as a member of the committee of bondholders of the insolvent Roanoke Street Railway.[33] His appearance is also entered in two patent cases[34] and two contract cases[35] in the federal courts.

In a case involving civil rights[36] Baetjer appeared as co-counsel with J. Wirt Randall, Edgar H. Gans, and Charles J. Bonaparte, the latter a former Attorney General of the United States, in successfully establishing the right of a black person to register to vote in Annapolis municipal elections. The statute that would have disqualified him was declared violative of the 15th Amendment to the Constitution. In this crusade on behalf of disadvantaged blacks Edwin G. Baetjer paved the way for Richard W. Emory, Norwood B. Orrick, Francis D. Murnaghan, Jr., and others in the firm who have been prominent advocates of civil rights. Parenthetically, however, it must be added that, as advocates, Venable partners have not always been on that side in civil rights litigation.

No profile of Edwin G. Baetjer would be complete without reference to his devotion to the great outdoors. A huntsman of note, he not only liked to shoot grouse in Scotland but also felled in New Brunswick a moose whose huge stuffed head once graced the wall of his firm's conference room — according to Crossan Cooper, the largest shot in New Brunswick up to that time.[37] It now adorns the Baltimore City Bar Library. He was a member of the exclusive Restigouche Salmon Club in Canada where the fishing is said to be unrivaled, at least in the eastern part of this continent. As a member of the Pineland Club in South Carolina, he had access to one of the finest game preserves in the country. In the fall and winter months he enjoyed hunting ducks and geese on his private preserve on Carroll's Island in the Chesapeake Bay, but his love of this sport was tempered by a concern, 40 years ahead of its time, for the ecology of the bay and the threats to its environment. Governor Ritchie appointed him a member of the Maryland Natural Resources Conservation Commission, and at the time of his death, according to an editorial in *The Sun*, he is said to have been writing a book about the natural resources of the Chesapeake Bay and the factors that threaten its viability.[38] The whereabouts of this unfinished work are unknown, but his interest in the preservation of the oyster bars of Maryland and its fishing industry is well established. He also owned and operated a quail farm in Tillman, South Carolina where he conducted experiments for the improvement of the breed.[39]

Edwin G. Baetjer's life-style has been described by Richard Emory as "all work or all play." When his workload reached peaks of intensity he would rent a room at the Belvedere Hotel, never to leave until the crisis had passed. His secretary, Joseph (Joe) Kerr, later the firm's office manager, would shuttle back and forth between Chase Street and Baltimore Street taking rounds of dictation at the hotel and typing it up at the office. At the time of his death Baetjer owned a farm in Stevenson as well as a downtown house at 16 West Madison Street which he used as a residence during winter months.[40]

Edwin Baetjer was a gourmet and connoisseur of fine wines. On one of their business trips to New York Norwood Orrick recalls Mr. E. G. ordering a bottle of champagne on the diner, explaining that his brother, Walter, "tells me it is good for my digestion." On another occasion they had dinner at the Vanderbilt Hotel on Park Avenue, his favorite after the old Waldorf had been torn down, and Mr. Baetjer ordered green turtle soup as a first course. Upon savoring it he tapped on his water glass with a spoon, whereupon the headwaiter appeared. Mr. Baetjer pointed out that the chunk of turtle required further attention. In due course, as he sipped his champagne, a parade emerged from the kitchen, first the chef bringing the refurbished bowl of soup, then the headwaiter, and last the waiter assigned to the table. According to Orrick, "They hovered anxiously as Mr. Baetjer probed with his spoon, put a piece of turtle in his mouth, chewed it thoughtfully, and swallowed it. 'Excellent,' he said. 'Excellent, thank you.' Then all smiles, the conference adjourned." As the entourage departed, Baetjer explained to his associate, "Mr. Orrick, the first bowl was quite good; but I'm very fond of turtle soup and this is the only place I've found in New York where they know how to make it. So, I want to keep them on their toes."

Another gourmet episode is reported by Dr. Alan C. Woods, Jr., a resident in surgery at Johns Hopkins Hospital at the time of Edwin Baetjer's terminal illness. He recalls one evening when he dined with Mr. Baetjer in his hospital room, two sumptuous meals on trays having been delivered by waiters from the Maryland Club. To Woods it was an unforgettable experience.

A long-time fixture at the Maryland Club was the doorman, Emmanuel Chambers, who greeted members as they arrived in their automobiles, summoned taxis for those needing transportation, and generally set the tone of decorum that typified the institution. When Chambers died, he stunned the community by leaving an estate in six figures, leading to speculation as to how he could have amassed such a fortune on the wages paid to domestics in those days. A popular theory was that he had bought heavily discounted railroad bonds during the Great Depression on tips from Edwin Baetjer. True or not, the latter was in his own right a successful investor; he left a personal estate valued at the time of his death at $3,163,000.

In his will, Baetjer bequeathed to his brothers, Howard and Walter, his share of the Pineland Club property, his shares of stock in the Restigouche Salmon Club, and all his shotguns, rifles, fishing rods, canoes, and other sporting equipment.[41] The youngest brother, Harry, was excluded from this bequest because he never displayed an interest in these forms of recreation. However, all his siblings shared equally in the division of the residuary estate.[42]

A bachelor, the second of the three Founders was survived by his four brothers, a sister, and three nephews. His namesake, Edwin G. Baetjer, II (Ned), the youngest son of his brother, Harry, had been killed in July, 1944 while on a combat mission in China as the flight engineer on a B-29 bomber. This tragedy prompted his uncle in a third codicil dated April 10, 1945, written only a couple of months before his death on July 20, 1945, to endow with a gift of $100,000 a lecture at Princeton University in the Department of Aeronautical Engineering in Ned's memory. The first lecturer, an engineer from Boeing Aircraft Company, speculated on the possible future use of jet propulsion in commercial transport aircraft.[43] Time marches on.

Endnotes to Part I, Chapter 2:

1. *The Sun*, February 18, 1921, quoted in H. H. Walker Lewis, *The Lawyers' Round Table And Its Charter Members*, Baltimore, Maryland Historical Society, 1978, at 23.

2. *Guaranty Trust Company of New York, et al., v. Seaboard Air Line Railway Company, et al.*, In Equity, Consolidated Cause No. 214 in the United States District Court for the Eastern District of Virginia, Order No. R.25 entered February 18, 1946, confirmed on March 1, 1946 in the Southern District of Florida.

3. *Id.*, Order of Court, April 10, 1946.

4. *Id.*, Report of Special Master, July 31, 1946.

5. The firm's income tax return for 1947 confirms the receipt in that year of the Seaboard fee of $225,000, less the $38,000 previously paid. The income averaging method was used to spread the fee over prior years.

6. Letter from H. S. Jackson, Secretary of the Baltimore Trust Corporation, to Alexander Armstrong and Simon E. Sobeloff, January 22, 1937.

7. A 13-page Summary of the *Sobeloff Report* is found in the archives of the Maryland Room of the Enoch Pratt Library, XHG 2613, B 24, B 2, V.3.

8. Letter from Charles McHenry Howard to Hon. Robert F. Stanton, January 12, 1937.

9. *Id.*

10. John C. French, *A History of the University Founded by Johns Hopkins*, Baltimore, the Johns Hopkins Press, 1946, at 243 et seq.

11. *Id.* at 246.

12. *Id.* at 247.

13. *Id.* at 247-8.

14. Harry W. Kirwin, *The Inevitable Success, A Biography of Herbert R. O'Conor*, Westminster, Md., the Newman Press, 1962 at 135-139 and note 51. The Committee, chaired by J. J. Nelligan, president of Safe Deposit & Trust Company of Baltimore, was appointed on April 19, 1928 and uncovered defalcations of $376,138.77.

15. *The Sun*, July 21, 1945.

16. *Daily Record*, March 14, 1988.

17. *Young v. College of Physicians*, 81 Md. 358 (1895). Baetjer was admitted to practice before the Court of Appeals on January 24, 1895, just before his argument in this case.

18. *Vanneman v. Pusey*, 93 Md. 686 (1901); *Hecht v. Coale*, 93 Md. 692 (1901).

19. *Old Town Bank v. McCormick*, 96 Md. 341 (1903). The headnotes list as co-counsel on the brief "Venable & Howard."

20. 102 Md. 73 (1903).

21. 78 Md. 545 (1894). See also Machen, *The Apportionment of Stock Distributions in Trust Accounting Practice*, 20 Md. L. Rev. (1960) for a catalogue of cases following *Thomas v. Gregg*.

22. 126 Md. 16 (1915).

23. *Godsol v. Nash Motors Company*, 139 Md. 395 (1921).

24. *Miles v. Public Service Commission*, 151 Md. 337 (1926).

25. Edwin Baetjer's last case in the Court of Appeals was *Douglass v. Safe Deposit and Trust Co.*, 159 Md. 81 (1930), which he argued with Joseph France for the appellees. It concerned the construction of a "trust agreement" for the management of a business.

26. *Sugar Institute Inc. v. United States*, 297 U.S. 553, 56 S. Ct. 629, 80 L. Ed. 859 (1936).

27. *United States v. United States Industrial Alcohol Company*, 15 F. Supp. 784 (D. Md. 1936).

28. *United States v. United States Industrial Alcohol Company*, 103 F.2d 97 (4th Cir. 1939).

29. *United Railways & Electric Company of Baltimore v. Consolidated Gas Electric Light & Power Company of Baltimore*, 300 U.S. 663, 57 S. Ct. 493, 81 L. Ed. 871 (1937); *Alexander Milburn Company v. Union Carbide and Carbon Corporation*, 273 U.S. 757, 47 S. Ct. 459, 71 L. Ed. 876 (1927).

30. *Mt. Vernon Woodberry Cotton Duck Company v. Alabama Power Company*, 240 U.S. 30, 36 S. Ct. 234, 60 L. Ed. 507 (1916) where the manufacture and sale of power was held to be a public purpose justifying the constitutional use of eminent domain; *Corry v. Baltimore*, 196 U.S. 466, 25 S. Ct. 297, 46 L. Ed. 556 (1905) where Baetjer unsuccessfully attempted to invalidate a Baltimore City property tax on stock of corporations having their principal place of business in the city.

31. *Alexander Milburn Co. v. Union Carbide & Carbon Co.*, 15 F.2d 678 (4th Cir. 1926), supra note 27, holding that in order to recover treble damages in an antitrust case, the plaintiff must establish a conspiracy.

32. See: *Consolidated Gas, Electric Light & Power Co. v. United Railways & Electric Co.*, 85 F.2d 799 (4th Cir. 1936); *In re United Railways & Electric Co.*, 15 F. Supp. 195 (D. Md. 1936); *In re United Railways & Electric Co.*, 11 F. Supp. 717 (D. Md. 1935).

33. *Fuller v. Venable*, 118 F. 543 (4th Cir. 1902) affirming 108 F. 126 (Cir. Ct. D. Md. 1901), Charles McHenry Howard appearing with E. G. Baetjer as counsel for their senior partner.

34. *Crown Cork & Seal Co. v. Brooklyn Bottle Stopper Co.*, 200 F. 592 (2d Cir. 1912) affirming 172 F. 225 (Cir. Ct. N.Y. 1909); *Standard Brewing v. Crown Cork & Seal Co.*, 190 F. 1022 (7th Cir. 1911), affirming 174 F. 252 (N.D. Ill. E. D. 1909).

35. *Norwood Paper Co. v. Columbia Paper Bag Co.*, 185 F. 454 (4th Cir. 1911); *Henry Paper Co. v. Columbia Paper Bag Co.*, 185 F. 454 (4th Cir. 1911).

36. *Anderson v. Myers*, 182 F. 223 (Cir. Ct. D. Md. 1910), affirmed *sub nom. Myers v. Anderson*, 238 U.S. 368, 35 S. Ct. 932, 59 L. Ed. 1349 (1915). Edwin G. Baetjer did not appear in the Supreme Court case.

37. Lewin, *Reminiscences*, 4.

38. *The Sun*, July 21, 1945.

39. *The Sun*, July 23, 1945.

40. *The Sun*, September 6, 1945.

41. *Id.*

42. *Id.*

43. *The Sun*, May 12, 1947.

CHARD M. VENABLE,
WIN G. BAETJER,
ARLES MCH. HOWARD.

KINS HENRY.

TELEPHONES:
C. & P. MT. VERNON 3830.
MD. COURTLAND 400.

VENABLE, BAETJER & HOWARD,
ATTORNEYS AT LAW,
1409 CONTINENTAL BUILDING,
BALTIMORE & CALVERT STS.,
BALTIMORE, MD.

February 10th, 1906.

Central Savings Bank of Baltimore,
    Thomas G. Potts, Esq., Treasurer,
      Baltimore, Maryland.

Dear Sir:-

    I write to acknowledge the receipt of your letter of February 7th, informing me of my election as a member of the Board of Directors of the Central Savings Bank, and to express to the Board of Directors my thanks and appreciation for its confidence.

    I accept the appointment and trust that I may be of service to your institution.

                Very truly yours,

Edwin G. Baetjer's letter of acceptance of his appointment as a director of Central Savings Bank. Observe the ampersand in the firm name, long since replaced by the word "and."

Another letterhead, used in August, 1906 records the name of Harry N. Baetjer as the junior associate below the name of Adkins Henry.

Charles McHenry Howard, 1870-1942.

Charles McHenry Howard

THE THIRD OF THE three Founders, Charles McHenry Howard, was born in Baltimore on May 8, 1870 and died 72 years later on May 19, 1942. His father, McHenry Howard, had been a successful Maryland lawyer after having served in the First Maryland Regiment of the Confederate Army. On his paternal side he was a great-grandson both of Colonel John Eager Howard of Revolutionary fame and of Francis Scott Key, the author of the lyrics to the *Star Spangled Banner*. His mother, Julia Douglas Coleman, came from a well-known Virginia family.

Howard graduated from the Johns Hopkins University in 1891 and from the University of Maryland School of Law cum laude two years later in 1893. Although the exact date of his first professional association with Major Venable has not been established, it must have been shortly after his graduation from law school since his first case in the Court of Appeals, with Venable on the brief, was decided on May 14, 1894.[1]

The ensuing 48 years before his death in 1942 witnessed the appearance of Charles McHenry Howard in 97 cases in the Court of Appeals, an achievement far short of the 295 appearances posted by John P. Poe between 1856 and 1909, but still remarkable considering that all of Howard's cases were derived from private practice whereas some of Poe's were argued during his years as Attorney General.

Howard's victories were also legendary. A widely told story, doubt-less apocryphal, is that on a given point of law there were two irreconcilable lines of authority in the Maryland decisions, their only common bond being that Charles McHenry Howard had won them both. It is certainly true, however, that whenever scheduled to argue a case he would draw a crowd to witness his skills in oral advocacy.

Like Edwin Baetjer, Howard was a generalist in his appellate practice and the only fields he did not enter were personal injury law and domestic relations. He even had one criminal case on behalf of his corporate client, the Whiting-Turner Contracting Company, which had been charged with a violation of the minimum wage law. Howard successfully established the invalidity of the indictment for its failure to identify the underpaid employees.[2]

The law of wills, estates and trusts provided him with the most state court cases,[3] while other fields involved such diverse issues (some of which would now be regarded as specialties) as real estate,[4] statutory construction,[5] contracts,[6] public utility law,[7] bondholders' and other creditors' rights,[8] libel,[9] corporation law,[10] taxation,[11] and partnership law.[12]

In addition to his many appearances in the state courts, Howard had a prodigious federal practice covering such fields as federal estate tax,[13] income tax,[14] contracts,[15] patents,[16] bankruptcy and creditors' rights,[17] public utility rates,[18] admiralty,[19] libel and slander,[20] federal jurisdiction,[21] federal regulation of package labeling,[22] and even one will construction case that found its way into the federal court system.[23]

The report of a skirmish before Judge Chesnut in 1940[24] tells a story about the enforcement of the Prohibition laws long after the 18th Amendment had been repealed by the 21st on December 5, 1933. It also tells something about Howard's ability to stall a case when it was to his client's interest to do so.

It seems that Title III of the National Prohibition Act had permit-ted manufacturers to secure a permit for making denatured alcohol, suitably doctored to prevent potability, if the application were sup-ported by a bond guaranteeing that it contained no misrepresentations as to the need of the product for legitimate commercial purposes. In an earlier encounter also before Judge Chesnut and argued by Edwin Baetjer, the court had sustained demurrers to the complaints against other sureties whose bonds were held distinguishable from those of United States Guarantee Co.[25] The amended complaint in the case at bar alleged that the assured's application had falsely represented that the alcohol was to be used for lacquer thinner, when in fact it made its way into the hands of bootleggers who rendered it fit for human consumption. (This same tactic was involved in Baetjer's *Industrial Alcohol* case, previously discussed). The surety was exposed on its three bonds in the penal sum of $50,000 each or $150,000 in all, but the importance of the case as a precedent is underscored by the appearance with Charles McHenry Howard of two partners from the Wall Street firm of Simpson, Thacher & Bartlett.

Howard's file was opened on May 31, 1934, the demurrer to the amended complaint was filed in 1936, and it came on for hearing before Judge Chesnut in September, 1940. This jurist had a reputation for speeding up the judicial process, and, in denying the demurrer, he observed dourly how long the case had been dormant. "Further progress in the case," he said, "will now be governed by the new Civil Rules . . . [and] counsel should now expedite the trial of the case on the merits."[26] This was bad news for Howard who, on this occasion, had no taste for trial. After his answer was filed on October 31, 1940 and the government's motion to strike on November 13, 1940, nothing happened for eight more months until the case was suddenly dismissed with prejudice on July 21, 1941, costs to be paid by the defendant.[27] Howard then sent his client a bill for $5,000, representing modest compensation for a favorable result after seven years of stalling.

Another Howard case, worthy of mention because of its notoriety at the time, is *Alfred Jenkins Shriver v. Druid Realty Co.*[28] It might be called *The Case of the Gentleman Moneylender.*

Shriver was a socially prominent man of means, later a benefactor of the Johns Hopkins University in whose memory Shriver Hall is named. His antagonist was Joseph Berman, a real estate operator who had built a large but unsuccessful apartment building. Berman's plan for avoiding financial ruin was to expand the facility and put the whole complex under one management in hopes of reducing overhead. For this he needed money, big money, and Shriver was known to have it or have access to it.

In furtherance of this plan, Berman formed a corporation, Druid Realty Company, to run the enterprise and on its behalf approached Mr. Shriver for a loan. The negotiated terms would have been subject to the defense of usury were it not for the statute prohibiting a corporation from setting up that defense. Eight years later the plaintiff became painfully aware that the terms to which he had agreed under the stress of impending financial disaster were exorbitant. Represented by distinguished counsel in the person of Alfred S. Niles, later a judge and the father of Judge Emory H. Niles, he brought a bill in equity to enjoin the transaction. Howard filed a demurrer and also asserted the defense of laches (limitations).

Judge George A. Solter overruled the demurrer and Howard appealed. The Court of Appeals reversed, pointing out that there was "no claim of actual fraud, misrepresentation, mistake, undue influence, fiduciary relation, or other common ground of equity jurisdiction," but only an allegation that the borrower's financial necessities were taken advantage of by the defendant "in compelling an extortionate and oppressive contract."[29] In these circumstances the courts would leave the parties as they had found them.

The decision is clearly correct, but Howard's client emerges from the scene with no more appeal than Shylock in *The Merchant of Venice*.

Another case handled by Charles McHenry Howard cannot be identified by citation because the story comes not from official records but from the personal recollection of Norwood B. Orrick, at the time one of Howard's juniors. It was a libel case in which Howard represented the A. S. Abell Company, publisher of *The Sun*. The paper had referred to a candidate for public office as "a wart on the body politic." During cross-examination Howard had brought out that the plaintiff had distributed within his district three different flyers in three different versions, each falsely purporting to have come from his opponent. One was calculated to be offensive to people of Jewish faith, the second to Protestants, and the third to Catholics. They were selectively distributed in those sections of the district where their negative impact would be strongest.

As the case was drawing to a close, the trial judge advised counsel in chambers that he would have to rule the published words libelous per se. Howard did not contest the ruling but in his closing argument to the jury said something to this effect:

> Gentlemen of the Jury: In a few moments His Honor will instruct you that as a matter of law you must return a verdict for the plaintiff. I have no quarrel with that instruction. But His Honor will also instruct you that the measure of damages is entirely within your discretion. The least you can award the plaintiff is one cent and the maximum is whatever dollars you feel will compensate him for the injury to his reputation caused by the published words, "a wart on the body politic." I say to you, gentlemen of the jury, that a man who will conduct himself as he has revealed himself to you on his cross-examination has no reputation at all, much less one that could be damaged by words in a newspaper. When you have completed your deliberations, I am confident that you will come to this conclusion.

The jury took only a few minutes to return a verdict for the plaintiff with damages fixed at one cent. This episode calls to mind another case of libel involving *The Sun*, the *Kirby* case, discussed *infra* in Part II, Chapter 3. The result in *Kirby* was not so favorable.

Howard came into national prominence as a member of the Council and vice-president of the American Law Institute during the years when the *Restatement of Trusts* and the *Restatement of Agency* were being drafted. On the former project he was thrown into contact with Professor Austin Wakeman Scott, a luminary of the Harvard Law School who later described Howard as having "about the best legal mind of any lawyer whom I have known."[30] Prof. Warren A. Seavey, the Reporter on the *Agency* project, said of him:

"His colossal knowledge of the law and keenness of intellect placed him in a class almost by himself among American lawyers."[31]

The scope of his mind had been manifested in law school days as he completed a three year course of study in two, receiving on graduation the highest prize for scholarship and also the award for the best thesis presented by the class.[32] He was fluent both in speaking and reading French, German, Italian, and Spanish and had some familiarity with Russian and Sanskrit.[33] He was widely read in history and the sciences and, according to Dr. William Henry Welch, the renowned pathologist of the Johns Hopkins School of Medicine after whom the Welch Library is named, Howard had more familiarity with medicine than any layman he had ever met.[34]

Further evidence of Howard's intellectual curiosity came to light as some of the firm's early files were being readied for the shredder — a file of letters to and from Howard and the noted antiquarian of the Maryland Historical Society, William B. Marye, dealing with the cartography of Maryland and a wealth of material concerning the Indians of this state, their names, language and settlements, their trading posts, paths and trails, their strange oyster shell mounds and many other details of their culture. As the repository of Marye's papers, the Historical Society already had the originals of Howard's letters, but since Marye maintained no copies of his holographic or typewritten letters, this represented only half of the correspondence. The firm's file has been given to the society, and the complete collection represents a remarkable record of scholarship.

Even to someone not versed in the arcane mysteries of Indian lore, the tribal and place names are intriguing — Tockwogh, Nantaquak, Wicomeses, Susquehannoughes, Shawanee, Assateagues, Choptank, Achawamp, and many others.

The Howard-Marye speculations even roamed into other fields, such as whether parakeets and panthers had ever been indigenous to Maryland.

The intensity of the correspondence is also a noteworthy facet. As a random example: replying to Howard's letter of August 25, 1938,

Marye responded on August 27th; Howard came back with another letter on August 30th to which Marye responded on September 2nd. Each of these letters was three or four pages long, dealing with the details of the Fry & Jefferson map, the location of Moravian mission-ary settlements, the Indian crossing of the Potomac at King Op-pessa's Town, later Oldtown, the location of the Warriors' Path, the causes of modern day pollution of the Potomac, etc. One wonders how a busy lawyer of Howard's stature would have found time to dictate letters of this length to be dispatched by return mail. Even more amazing is the fact that his mind had at instant recall the capacity to converse freely about these esoteric subjects.

Charles McHenry Howard married the former Ellen N. Carter on June 16, 1898, five years after graduation from law school and two years before the partnership of Venable, Baetjer and Howard was formed. Thirty years later Mrs. Howard died, leaving no children. Thereafter, Howard lived with his three unmarried sisters, the Misses Elizabeth, May, and Julia McHenry Howard,[35] sharing a house on St. Paul Street near Eager from which he walked to work every day — except during the month of July.

That was the month during which the Howards repaired to their vacation home, an old-fashioned frame house in Oakland, Garrett County. Although proficient in foreign languages, Howard was not a regular overseas traveller, generally preferring the rustic setting of Western Maryland for rest and relaxation. He owned a small waterfront lot on Deep Creek Lake with a pier and boathouse which he used as a starting point for prodigious bouts of swimming. He could alternate between breaststroke and backstroke, then float endlessly and effortlessly on his back as if lying on a mattress. Visitors were warned not to try to keep up with Mr. Howard in the water.

Shortly after their marriage in 1935, Norwood Orrick and his wife, Ruth, while visiting in the neighborhood at the home of Judge Stewart Brown, were invited to a midday Sunday dinner at the Howards. They were first given a tour of the environs in Mr. Howard's car, the driver having carefully timed the curves on the mountain roads so as to negotiate them without applying the brakes. To the passenger on the front seat, it was an unforgettable experience.

Then back to the house in Oakland, they were given a cocktail or toddy and shown around the establishment. Howard was always affectionate and courteous in dealings with his sisters, but he had a den that was off limits to the ladies. One of them observed, "Charlie has to have a place where he can get off by himself. He doesn't allow us to cross that threshold."

John Henry Lewin, Sr. presents this comparative description of Charles McHenry Howard and his partner, Edwin G. Baetjer:

> Mr. Howard was a short, stout, impressive man — melancholy looking — with a quiet, gentle, rather retiring bearing, every inch the scholar, every inch the gentleman. . . . He was a learned, technical lawyer. He and Edwin G. Baetjer complemented and supplemented each other completely — the latter independent, impetuous, sarcastic, mathematical, practical, and impatient of the precedents; the former calm, studious, informed of the decisions, and clear of statement. They were both extremely dignified, reserved in manners, and were indeed men of "infinite resource and sagacity."[36]

A revealing financial picture of Venable, Baetjer and Howard in the heyday of the Baetjer-Howard era results from an examination of the firm's federal income tax returns for the years 1928 and 1929.

In 1928 its gross receipts from professional fees aggregated $231,524, and its net distributable income to its three partners was $174,222. This reflected an expense ratio of 24.7%; i.e., of every dollar of fees billed, more than 75¢ turned up on the bottom line in net profits. By today's standards, such a record for a major law firm would be unheard of. As a result of this extraordinary efficiency, the partners received the following distributions:

Edwin G. Baetjer	(37%)	$64,462
Charles McH. Howard	(33%)	57,493
Harry N. Baetjer	(30%)	52,267

For the same year salaries paid to associates and staff were as follows:

Associates
Joseph France $15,120
J. Crossan Cooper, Jr.   2,833

Staff
Joseph Kerr, Secretary   4,575
Rudolph F. Bolard, Jr., Secretary   4,025
George S. Lynch, Secretary   2,083
Alan P. Longcope, Bookkeeper   3,225

Some points of interest emerge from the above figures: first, the draws of the three partners must be described as of the boxcar variety — in terms of purchasing power, Howard's translates into $446,037 in January, 1991 dollars on application of the Consumer Price Index, All Urban Consumers, All Items; second, the compensation of the highest paid secretaries exceeded that of the junior associates; and, third, since the files contain no 1928 information return for John Marshall Butler, his compensation for that year is not known.

In 1929, a year of business malaise culminating in the market crash in October, the three partners took substantial cuts and the expense ratio rose to 30%, still remarkably low by modern standards. They divided the profit in even one-third shares, each partner receiving $36,830.

In midyear 1929 Joseph France was elected a partner, the tax return showing that in that year he received $18,621 in salary as an associate and $12,277 in distributions as a partner, or $30,898 in all. France was thus impervious to the market crash, his total compensation increasing more than 100% over the prior year, doubtless in recognition of his new partnership status and the leadership role he was playing in the Seaboard Air Line reorganization and other engagements of importance.

Salaried staff personnel were also unaffected by the onset of the Great Depression, none suffering any salary cuts in 1929 and some receiving modest raises in the $200-$500 range. According to the information returns, the two associates, Crossan Cooper and John Marshall Butler, each received a salary of $3,900 for the year, a hefty raise for Cooper, and not at all bad when translated into $30,257 in 1991 dollars.

Howard's rewards from the practice of law were due to the success of the firm as a whole, for he himself was a notorious under-charger. Edmund Dandridge recalled occasions when Edwin Baetjer would chastise his partner for setting his fees too low, and also how generous Howard was with his time, especially in counseling other lawyers, both within and outside the firm. On one occasion, Howard gave Dandridge a lengthy explanation of the operation of the Statute of Uses, enacted by Parliament in 1535, because he perceived that his young associate had an inadequate grasp of the subject. Understandably, he was much revered and beloved by his juniors.

Charles McHenry Howard served as president of the Bar Association of Baltimore City in 1922, and in 1927-28 became the first of five members of his firm to hold office as president of the Maryland State Bar Association, the other four being H. Vernon Eney, Norwood B. Orrick, James H. Cook, and Roger W. Titus. An address by Howard to the Association in 1926, entitled *The Exclusive Use of Written Prayers and Instructions in Civil Cases in Maryland*, was a scholarly analysis which he modestly described as "not luminous but voluminous."[37] In 1912 he had been elected a member of the Lawyers' Round Table, the oldest of Maryland's law clubs, other members of Venable, Baetjer and Howard who followed in his footsteps being Harry N. Baetjer, J. Crossan Cooper, Jr., H. Vernon Eney, Richard W. Emory, Norwood B. Orrick, Francis D. Murnaghan, Jr., Benjamin R. Civiletti, James H. Cook, John H. Lewin, Jr., Roger W. Titus, and the author. At the time of his death Howard was a member of the Faculty Council of the University of Maryland School of Law and had earlier served as a part-time lecturer on Equity.[38]

On the civic side Howard was, like his father, a trustee of the Peabody Institute; he was also a trustee of the Johns Hopkins University, the Johns Hopkins Hospital and the Union Memorial Hospital. Mayor Howard W. Jackson appointed him chairman of two commissions charged with formulating plans for the financial welfare of Baltimore City. He had been president of the Criminal Justice Commission and served as legal counsel to the Grand Inquest of the Legislature that investigated the State Roads Commission scandals in 1928 and 1929.[39]

Shortly before his death Howard purchased two parcels of wooded land in Garrett County, aggregating 1,652 acres, to prevent their coming into the hands of a lumber company. The land was appraised in a supplemental real inventory for his estate at $9,300 or $5.63 per acre.[40] In his will he devised the two parcels to the State of Maryland for a forest and game preserve and, in accepting the gift for the state, Governor Herbert R. O'Conor acknowledged the donor's "generous action . . . from which great numbers of citizens of this and future generations will undoubtedly benefit."[41]

The residue of Howard's substantial estate was left in trust for his three sisters for their lives, thereafter to be divided into three shares: one for the Peabody Institute, one for the Johns Hopkins University and one for Emmanuel Episcopal Church.

A few months after Howard's death on May 19, 1942 a cloud of witnesses descended on the Supreme Bench of Baltimore City for memorial exercises in his honor.[42]

Mention has already been made of the presence of Professor Warren A. Seavey; other speakers were G. C. A. Anderson, president of the Bar Association of Baltimore City, the Brothers Baetjer (Harry and Edwin), James Clark on behalf of the Maryland State Bar Association, Judge John J. Parker, Chief Judge of the United States Court of Appeals for the Fourth Circuit, George Wharton Pepper of Philadelphia, one of the nation's most distinguished lawyers and president of the American Law Institute, William Draper Lewis, also of the American Law Institute, R. E. Lee Marshall, representing the

Baltimore bar, and Chief Judge Samuel K. Dennis, responding for the Supreme Bench. It was quite a ceremony. Few lawyers in Maryland's history have received such a send-off to posterity.

Coupled with the spinsterhood of his sisters, Howard's death without issue marked the end of his line of descent. Responding to a letter of condolence, Julia McHenry Howard commented poignantly on this circumstance:

> Charles McHenry Howard has never fallen below the standard his own father set. That knowledge and the reiterated statement of the fact by you and many others gives us a happiness in sorrow, and a pride in the very last of our race.[43]

Endnotes to Part I, Chapter 3:

1. *Wethered v. Safe Deposit & Trust Co.*, 79 Md. 153 (1894).

2. *State v. Lassotovitch*, 162 Md. 147 (1932). The corporate name is incorrectly stated in the opinion as The Whiting-Turner *Construction* Company.

3. *Wethered v. Safe Deposit & Trust Co.*, *supra* note 1; *Bentz v. Maryland Bible Society*, 86 Md. 102 (1897), holding that where a fund is bequeathed for distribution to a named legatee at the end of a specified period, coupled with a provision that if the legatee dies without issue it goes to other parties, the legatee is entitled to the fund absolutely if he is living at the end of the period — a victory for Howard and Edgar H. Gans; *Mercer v. Safe Deposit & Trust Co.*, 91 Md. 102 (1900), involving the early vesting of estates, a rare loss in this field for Howard; *Trinity M.E. Church v. Baker*, 91 Md. 539 (1900), upholding the validity of a charitable trust, a loss for Major Venable and Charles McH. Howard; *Stump v. Stump*, 91 Md. 699 (1900), an uninteresting case involving a claim of an executor as a creditor against his decedent's estate, a victory for Howard; *Ridgely v. Ridgely*, 100 Md. 230 (1905), involving the early vesting of estates, a loss for Howard and his father, McHenry Howard; *Marshall v. Safe Deposit & Trust Co.*, 101 Md. 1 (1905), a complicated will construction case in which Howard prevailed; *Lindsay v. Wilson*, 103 Md. 252 (1906), in which Howard successfully upheld the validity of a holographic will executed in France; *Bridge v. Dillard*, 104 Md. 411 (1906), holding that the Orphans' Court has no jurisdiction to try the question of a testator's residence until the will is offered for probate, a victory for Howard; *Johnson v. Safe Deposit & Trust Co.*, 104 Md. 460 (1906), involving the denial of a petition for the discharge of a committee for an incompetent, the first appearance of Harry Baetjer with Howard; *Baltzell v. Church Home*, 110 Md. 244 (1909), holding that a gift to a charitable corporation is not one to a religious corporation

requiring legislative consent under the Mortmain laws then in effect, a win for Howard; *Thiede v. Startzman*, 113 Md. 278 (1910), an undue influence case which Howard lost; *Schapiro v. Howard*, 113 Md. 360 (1910), where Howard upheld the validity of a conveyance of a contingent remainder; *Suman v. Harvey*, 114 Md. 241 (1911), another win for Howard involving a gift to "heirs"; *Maryland Casualty Co. v. Safe Deposit & Trust Co.*, 115 Md. 339 (1911), in which Howard successfully upheld the devolution of a trustee's powers to his successors; *Levenson v. Manly*, 119 Md. 517 (1913), a win for Howard in a case involving the Rule Against Perpetuities; *Foard v. Safe Deposit & Trust Co.*, 122 Md. 476 (1914), another win for Howard in a case involving the allocation to principal or income of dividends received during administration of a decedent's estate; *Safe Deposit & Trust Co. v. Carey*, 127 Md. 593 (1916), a win on appeal for Howard in a case construing a gift to next-of-kin; *Miller v. Safe Deposit & Trust Co.*, 127 Md. 610 (1916), another unsuccessful apportionments case; *Johns Hopkins University v. Garrett*, 128 Md. 343 (1916), a successful appeal by Howard in a case construing a devise of real estate; *Smith v. Diggs*, 128 Md. 394 (1916), a win for Howard on appeal in a case involving the admissibility of a will to probate; *Diggs v. Smith*, 130 Md. 101 (1916), another Howard victory in a case upholding the admissibility of a will; *O'Dunne v. Safe Deposit & Trust Co.*, 133 Md. 91 (1918), a dispute over a counsel fee which Howard lost to the tune of $250, the Court of Appeals deciding that $1,000 would be fairer than $750; *Krug v. Mercantile Trust & Deposit Co.*, 133 Md. 110 (1918), and *Lanahan v. Mercantile Trust & Deposit Co.*, 133 Md. 118 (1918), two more unsuccessful apportionments cases; *Geoghegan v. Smith*, 133 Md. 535 (1919), a win for Howard in a case defining the requirements for a valid declaration of trust; *Perin v. Perin*, 139 Md. 281 (1921), a complicated will construction case in which Howard's arguments, based on English authorities, did not prevail; *Iglehart v. Hall*, 140 Md. 293 (1922), a will construction case in which Howard unsuccessfully relied on the authority of *Perin, supra*, which he had lost the previous year; *Lee v. Waltjen*, 141 Md. 450 and 141 Md. 458 (1922), a loss for Howard in two cases holding that a gift to "children" vests in them an interest which is not divested by a child's death prior to the death of the life tenant; *Johns Hopkins University v. Uhrig*, 145 Md. 114 (1924), a win for Howard and his client, Johns Hopkins University, in a will construction case involving conflicts of laws; *Ball v. Townsend*, 145 Md. 589 (1924), involving the proper measurement of a remainder interest following an annuity, a win for Howard and his client, Johns Hopkins Hospital; *Manders v. Mercantile Trust Co.*, 147 Md. 448 (1925), a loss for Howard in a case deciding that an equity court may terminate a trust where all purposes inconsistent with absolute ownership have been fulfilled and where all interested persons are sui juris and consent; *Turner v. Safe Deposit & Trust & Deposit Co.*, 148 Md. 371 (1925), a victory for Howard in a case involving the Rule Against Perpetuities, holding that the invalidity of an ultimate remainder does not affect the validity of intervening estates; *West v. Sellmayer*, 150 Md. 478 (1926), a will construction case which Howard won below but was unable to sustain on appeal, the court ruling in favor of an equal division among children instead of a disproportionately favorable division for Howard's client; *Holloway v. Safe Deposit & Trust Co.*, 151 Md. 321 (1926), a significant victory for Howard in an interesting case holding that a child born out of wedlock but legitimized under the laws of her father's domicile is legitimate in

Maryland for purposes of determining her eligibility to share in an appointment to her father's "children"; *Sutton v. Safe Deposit & Trust Co.*, 155 Md. 483 (1928), a will construction case in which the majority of the Court of Appeals held the will in the case at bar a virtual clone of the will of Johns Hopkins, construed in *Mercer v. Hopkins*, 88 Md. 292 (1898), Judge Parke dissenting vigorously; *Blake v. Blake*, 159 Md. 539 (1930), holding that remote remaindermen lack status to file a caveat, a win for Howard; *Case v. Marshall*, 159 Md. 588 (1930), upholding the validity of an assignment of an interest in a trust for its duration, a victory on appeal for Howard; *Home For Incurables v. Bruff*, 160 Md. 156 (1930), a significant victory for Howard in a case upholding the corporate existence and capacity of the Maryland Bible Society to receive a legacy; *Newlin v. Mercantile Trust Co.*, 161 Md. 622 (1932), a will construction case involving the early vesting rule and an analysis of the difference between a gift "among" and "between" members of a class; *Gardner v. Mercantile Trust Co.*, 164 Md. 280 (1933), holding that a widow's statutory share includes that share of income during administration, a win for Howard; *Levin v. Safe Deposit & Trust Co.*, 167 Md. 41 (1934), holding that a widow's renunciation accelerates the remainder, a loss for Howard on appeal; *Wiesenfeld v. Rosenfeld*, 170 Md. 63 (1936), holding that a codicil takes precedence over a will in a case involving exceptions to an auditor's account distributing income during administration; *City of Baltimore v. Peabody Institute*, 175 Md. 186 (1938), a significant victory for Howard upholding the integrity of Leakin Park against the attempt of the city to use the Leakin trust funds for the establishment of small regional recreation centers; *Marburg v. Safe Deposit & Trust Co.*, 177 Md. 165 (1939), upholding a trustee's exercise of discretion, a win for Howard; *Bullen v. Safe Deposit & Trust Co.*, 177 Md. 271 (1939), confirming that proceeds of life insurance payable to third parties are not subject to a widow's statutory third, another win for Howard; *Hans v. Safe Deposit & Trust Co.*, 178 Md. 52 (1940), a leading case upholding the early vesting rule and the assignability of future executory estates, Howard appearing successfully for the trustee; *Revoc Company v. Thomas*, 179 Md. 101 (1940), upholding an implied power of sale in a trustee, another win for Howard.

4. *A. S. Abell Co. v. Firemen's Insurance Co.*, 93 Md. 596 (1901), a friendly suit, brought on a "case stated," to test the validity of title to real estate sold to the A. S. Abell Co., Bernard Carter and Charles McH. Howard appearing for the latter with Richard M. Venable and Edwin G. Baetjer on the brief; *Safe Deposit & Trust Co. v. Marburg*, 110 Md. 410 (1909), a win for Howard on appeal, holding that a ground rent unpaid for more than 20 years is barred by the statute of limitations and tenant owns the fee by adverse possession; *Kingan Packing Ass'n v. Lloyd*, 110 Md. 619 (1909), where Howard was successful in upholding the right of a trustee without power of sale to use the statutory procedure for redemption of ground rents; *Philpot v. Gelston*, 126 Md. 589 (1915), holding that a prior decision on the same issue between the same parties is the "law of the case," a loss for Howard; *Philipsborn v. Hutzler Bros.*, 128 Md. 337 (1916), construing a lease as requiring tenant to pay increase in taxes resulting from increase in assessment, a win for Howard's client as appellant; *Hammond v. Hammond*, 159 Md. 563 (1930), holding that where a deed in fee was immediately followed by a reconveyance in which

the granting clause conveyed a fee but the *habendum* clause only a life estate, the latter controls in order to give effect to the evident intent of the parties, thus reversing the usual rule that the granting clause prevails where only one instrument is before the court for construction, a loss for Howard on appeal; *Homewood Realty Corp. v. Safe Deposit & Trust Co.*, 160 Md. 457 (1931), a case in which Howard successfully brought a bill to quiet title to real estate so as to extinguish a neighbor's claim to an easement for light and air.

5. *Bond v. Baltimore*, 118 Md. 159 (1912), a loss for Howard in the field of statutory construction, the court holding that certain provisions of an enabling statute of the General Assembly to be directory rather than mandatory; *Minor Privilege Cases*, 131 Md. 600 (1917), construing the Baltimore City Charter provisions giving the Board of Estimates power to grant minor privileges in public highways as having no retroactive effect so as to permit the City to abrogate minor privileges previously granted; *Baltimore City v. Maryland Trust Co.*, 135 Md. 36 (1919), and *Safe Deposit & Trust Company of Baltimore v. Baltimore City*, 135 Md. 54 (1919), two companion cases construing charter provisions relating to the power of the City Court to review decisions of the Commissioners for Opening Streets, a loss for Howard; *Jenkins v. Continental Trust Co.*, 150 Md 416 (1926), construing the Uniform Stock Transfer Act as protecting a lender who accepts a stock certificate endorsed in blank with no notice of a wrongful endorsement and lends money on it in good faith, a win for Howard; *Frederick Iron & Steel Co. v. Page*, 165 Md. 212 (1933), a loss for Howard in a case involving an insolvent bank whose voluntary trust beneficiaries were held to be on a par with depositors and general creditors and not entitled to a statutory preference extending to the beneficiaries of court-appointed trusts; *Dvorine v. Castleberg Corp.*, 170 Md. 661 (1936), a case involving the statute regulating the practice of optometry in which Howard successfully defended the right of a jewelry store to employ a registered optometrist to provide optometric services to its patrons.

6. *Davison Chemical Co. v. Baugh Chemical Co.*, 133 Md. 203 (1918), an interesting case which Harry Baetjer and Charles McH. Howard won on appeal exonerating Davison Chemical from the performance of a contract which had been rendered impossible of performance because of war conditions; and see the sequel, *Davison Chemical Co. v. Baugh Chemical Co.*, 134 Md. 24 (1919) which Baetjer and Howard lost; *Godsol v. Nash Motors Co.*, 139 Md. 395 (1921), a victory for Edwin Baetjer and Charles McH. Howard in a case construing a contract for exclusive foreign country territorial rights as not precluding sales to the U.S. government during the war for resales abroad; *Hubbard Fertilizer Co. v. American Trona Corporation*, 142 Md. 246 (1923), involving Howard's successful defense of a charge of his client's breach of express and implied warranties of fitness in manufactured fertilizer alleged to have been harmful to Maine potatoes.

7. *Kelly v. Consolidated Gas. Electric Light & Power Co.*, 153 Md. 523 (1927), a case involving franchise rights for electric service in Havre de Grace, a win for Howard on appeal; *Public Service Commission v. United Railways Co.*, 155 Md. 572 (1928), and *United Railways v. Public Service Commission*, 157 Md. 70 (1929), two rate cases for United

Railways; *Susquehanna Power Co. v. State Tax Commission*, 159 Md. 334 (1930), and *Susquehanna Power Co. v. State Tax Commission*, 159 Md. 359 (1930), two cases involving the taxability of property of Susquehanna Power Co., a public utility, both losses for Howard.

8. *Pope v. Baltimore Warehouse Co.*, 103 Md. 9 (1906), involving the relative rights of creditors of an insolvent, Howard winning an affirmance for the appellee; *Mt. Vernon Woodberry Cotton Duck Co., v. Continental Trust Co.*, 121 Md. 163 (1913), involving the rights of bondholders of corporate mortgage bonds, Howard appearing successfully for the committee of bondholders; *Mercantile Trust & Deposit Co. v. Gottlieb-Bauernschmidt-Straus Brewing, Co.*, 122 Md. 502 (1914), a technical loss for Howard in a "case stated" to determine the powers of a corporate mortgage trustee in respect of the proceeds of sale of mortgaged property, Howard appearing for the trustee; *Frederick Iron & Steel Co. v. Page, supra* note 5; *Engle v. United States Fidelity & Guaranty Co.*, 175 Md. 174 (1938), a win for Howard in a case involving a surety's obligations when put on notice of a prospective default by a depositary which later became insolvent.

9. *Stannard v. Wilcox & Gibbs*, 118 Md. 151 (1912), a victory for Howard on demurrer to a suit for libel alleging slander of credit.

10. *Liquidation of George's Creek Co. (Scott v. Gittings)*, 125 Md. 595 (1915), involving the disposition of unclaimed dividends upon the dissolution of a corporation; *Mortgage Bond Association v. Baker*, 157 Md. 309 (1929), involving the rights of a stockholder in a building association, a win for Howard on appeal; *Alleghany Corp. v. Aldebaran Corp.*, 173 Md. 472 (1938), a significant win for Howard in an equity case resulting in an injunction against a corporate consolidation.

11. *Safe Deposit. & Trust Co. v. State*, 143 Md. 644 (1923), upholding the imposition of the collateral inheritance tax on income during administration, Howard appearing on the losing side along with Arthur W. Machen, the father of the author, opposed by the victorious Attorney General, Alexander Armstrong, later Machen's partner; *Downes v. Safe Deposit & Trust Co.*, 163 Md. 30 (1932), holding that the collateral inheritance tax is not to be imposed on property in trust subject to a power of revocation, a result later reversed by statute; *Downes v. Safe Deposit & Trust Co.*, 164 Md. 293 (1933), holding that the collateral inheritance tax is to be imposed on the value of an estate after re-appraisal, as are also the executor's commissions, Howard being denied the right to have his cake and eat it too; *State Tax Commission v. Allied Mortgage Companies*, 175 Md. 357 (1938), upholding Howard's contention that his client should be classified for Maryland tax purposes as a mortgage corporation, not an ordinary business corporation.

12. *P. T. George & Co. v. Morison*, 93 Md. 132 (1901), holding that a partnership of which an insolvent debtor was a member is not entitled to payment of its claim until after payment of the individual's creditors.

13. *Curley v. Tait*, 276 F. 840 (D. Md. 1921), a victory for Howard in a case holding that where a contingent remainder is reserved to the settlor, only the value of that interest and not the full estate is taxable (a result later reversed by statute); *Tait v. Safe Deposit & Trust Co.*, 78 F.2d 534 (4th Cir. 1935), affirming *Safe Deposit & Trust Co. v. Tait*, 8 F. Supp. 634 (D. Md. 1934), another win for Howard in a case holding that the reservation of a remote interest will not result in the taxability of the estate, another result that would not hold up today; *Helvering v. Safe Deposit & Trust Co.*, 95 F.2d 806 (4th Cir. 1938), involving the Estate of Henry Walters in which Howard successfully established the principle of a blockage discount for a large block of securities held in an estate; *Helvering v. Safe Deposit & Trust Co.*, 316 U.S. 56, 62 S. Ct. 925, 86 L. Ed. 1266 (1942), a loss for Howard in the Supreme Court in a case holding that proceeds of settlement in a will contest representing the agreed portion of the estate passing by appointment are includable in the gross estate.

14. *Magruder v. Segebade*, 94 F.2d 177 (4th Cir. 1938), holding that proceeds of settlement of threatened caveat to a will are not taxable as income to the recipients; *Safe Deposit & Trust Co. v. Magruder*, 34 F. Supp. 199 (D. Md. 1940), holding that the old Safe Deposit & Trust Co., now by merger Mercantile-Safe Deposit & Trust Company, qualifies as a "bank or trust company" under Sec. 117(d) of the Revenue Act of 1934.

15. *Bradlee & McIntosh Co. v. Frey & Son*, 280 F. 375 (4th Cir. 1922), a win for Howard in a case holding that where the contract calls for delivery in June or July, acceptance in September is not required; *Atlantic Coast Line Railroad v. Standard Oil Company of New Jersey*, 12 F.2d 541 (4th Cir. 1926), another win for Howard in a case holding that the interstate character of oil shipments was converted into intrastate by their interruption for storage and subsequent local reshipment; *Consolidated Gas, Electric Light & Power Company of Baltimore v. United Railways & Electric Company of Baltimore*, 76 F.2d 535 (4th Cir. 1935), a loss for Howard in representing United Railways (later Baltimore Transit Co.) in a dispute with the gas company over the construction of the contract for the delivery of electricity; *Martin v. Minerals Separation North American Corp.*, 29 F. Supp. 146 (D. Md. 1939), a win for Howard in a dispute between employer and employee over the former's obligation to pay the latter a percentage of profits on sales of his inventions.

16. *Wolf Minerals Process Corporation v. Minerals Separation North American Corporation*, 18 F.2d 483 (4th Cir. 1927), upholding Howard's defense of laches in an infringement case; *General Chemical Co. v. Standard Wholesale Phosphate & Acid Works*, 22 F. Supp. 332 (D. Md. 1938), and an earlier case under the same name in 8 F. Supp. 265 (D. Md. 1934), two wins for Howard in infringement cases; *Swan Carburetor v. Nash Motors Co.*, 25 F. Supp. 24 (D. Md. 1938), a loss for Howard.

17. *Fuller v. Venable*, 118 F. 543 (4th Cir. 1902), in which Baetjer and Howard represented their senior partner, Major Venable, as a member of a committee of

bondholders of the insolvent Roanoke Street Railway Company; *Scott v. Queen Anne's Railroad Co.*, 162 F. 828 (4th Cir. 1908), where Howard successfully argued that the expenses of a bondholders' committee are superior to the claims of the holders of mortgage debt; *In re Waite*, 223 F. 853 (D. Md. 1915), a bankruptcy proceeding where Howard succeeded in denying a discharge because the bankrupt had secured an audit on the basis of false statements; *In re United Railways & Electric Co.*, 11 F. Supp. 717 (D. Md. 1935), upholding a plan of reorganization, Howard representing the rustees.

18. *United Railways & Electric Company of Baltimore v. West*, 280 U.S. 234, 50 S. Ct. 123, 74 L. Ed. 390 (1930), reversing a decision of the Court of Appeals of Maryland reported in 157 Md. 70 (1929), *supra* note 7, Howard having successfully established that the rate fixed by the state court was unconstitutionally confiscatory; *West v. Chesapeake & Potomac Company of Baltimore City*, 295 U.S. 662, 55 S. Ct. 894, 79 L. Ed. 1640 (1935), affirming the decision of a three-judge panel of District Court judges that rates fixed by the Public Service Commission were unconstitutional [*Chesapeake & Potomac Telephone Co. v. West*, 7 F. Supp. 214 (D. Md. 1934)], Howard appearing successfully in both courts for the telephone company and besting John Henry Lewin for the P.S.C.

19. *Furness, Withy & Co. v. Louis Muller & Co.*, 232 F. 186 (D. Md. 1916), and *Furness, Withy & Co. v. Fahey*, 232 F. 189 (D. Md. 1916), companion cases representing victories for Howard on behalf of the respondent and holding that a charterer was not justified in refusing to load a vessel because of U-boat threats in World War I, it appearing that none of the named ports was blockaded and other vessels were carrying cargoes at the same time.

20. *Security Sales Agency v. A. S. Abell Co.*, 205 F. 941 (D. Md. 1913), Howard representing *The Sun* and successfully defending the proposition that A cannot hold B liable in damages by reason of injuries to A resulting from B's libel of C.

21. *De Bearn v. Safe Deposit & Trust Co.*, 233 U.S. 24, 34 S. Ct. 584, 58 L. Ed. 833 (1911), upholding the District Court's granting of Howard's demurrer for want of federal jurisdiction; *De Galard v. Safe Deposit & Trust Co.*, 196 F. 981 (D. Md. 1912), sustaining Howard's point that a federal court lacks jurisdiction over bonds already attached under writs issued by a state court; *Broderick v. American General Corporation*, 71 F.2d 864 (4th Cir. 1934), a partial loss for Howard in a case involving the New York Bank Commissioner's attempt to enforce a double liability assessment against Maryland stockholders of a failed New York bank, the court directing a dismissal of the complaint against all stockholders against whom claims were filed under the jurisdictional limit of $3,000, but remanding the case for further proceedings at law against other stockholders.

22. *United States v. Thirty Dozen Packages of Roach Food*, 202 F. 271 (D. Md. 1913), a loss for Howard in a case construing the language of the regulatory statute.

23. *Hinkley v. Art Students' League*, 37 F.2d 225 (4th Cir. 1930), affirming Howard's win

for the complainant in *Art Students' League of New York v. Hinkley*, 31 F.2d 469 (D. Md. 1929), dealing with the validity of the exercise of a power of appointment and the validity of a charitable trust, Judge Soper in the District Court writing a learned opinion on Maryland law.

24. *United States v. United States Guarantee Co.*, 34 F. Supp. 911 (D. Md. 1940). In *United States v. Mack*, 295 U.S. 480, 55 S. Ct. 813, 79 L. Ed. 1559 (1935), the Supreme Court had held that repeal of the 18th Amendmer' did not extinguish liability on bonds executed pursuant to the National Prohibition Act.

25. *United States v. Hartford Accident & Indemnity Co.*, 15 F. Supp. 791 (D. Md. 1936).

26. 34 F. Supp. at 913.

27. The dates in the text were procured from the docket entries on file with the federal archives in Philadelphia. The amount of the fee was found in the firm's ledger, File #17002. The bill was not sent out until November 6, 1941, four months after the case was dismissed, it being common practice in those days to bill almost everything during the final few weeks of the year.

28. 149 Md. 385 (1926).

29. Id at 389.

30. Letter dated February 3, 1962 from Prof. Austin W. Scott to the author.

31. Remarks of Prof. Warren A. Seavey at memorial exercises for Charles McHenry Howard on November 18, 1942 as reported in the *Daily Record*, November 23, 1942.

32. *Id.*, remarks of Harry N. Baetjer.

33. *Id.*

34. *Id.*

35. The obituary in the *The Sun* of May 20, 1942 incorrectly lists the third sister's name as "Frances." Harry Baetjer's remarks at the memorial exercises (*supra* note 31) and the *MSBA Transactions* (*infra* note 37) correctly state the name as "Julia McHenry."

36. Lewin, J. H., *Richard M. Venable, Edwin G. Baetjer, Charles McHenry Howard, and Harry N. Baetjer* (date unknown).

37. 31 *MSBA Transactions*, 120 (1926).

38. Obituary in 6 Md. L. Rev. 302, 303 (1942).

39. 47 *MSBA Transactions*, 136 (1942). The Grand Inquest, convened by the General Assembly and represented by Howard, was working in tandem with the Nelligan Committee, appointed by the governor and represented by Edwin G. Baetjer. See Harry W. Kirwin, *The Inevitable Success*, at 139, cited *supra* Pt. 1, Ch. 2 at note 14. According to today's standards this dual representation might raise questions as to a possible conflict of interest among partners, but at the time it was apparently not perceived as a problem.

40. *The Sun*, August 5, 1942.

41. *Id.*

42. *Daily Record*, November 23, 1942.

43. Letter from Julia McHenry Howard to Arthur W. Machen, May 24, 1941.

PART II

The Caretakers

From **1941** until the late 1950's when H. Vernon Eney became the de facto chief executive officer, Harry N. Baetjer remained the father figure at Venable, Baetjer and Howard. This era is notable for its prosperity but also its lack of change, the partners serving essentially as caretakers of the styles and traditions set by the Founders.

For more than two decades only eight new partners were admitted to the firm. Its ways of doing business remained in a static mold — even its checks were printed on white bond paper, this at a time when tamper-free bank stationery had long since come into common use. It was done this way because it had always been done this way, and it was not until the Innovators came upon the scene that such archaic business methods were changed. During this period the range of the firm's practice and client base also remained essentially the same, and it was an elitist assembly of lawyers, all its male members being to the manner born.

The lawyers comprising the Caretakers were Harry N. Baetjer, Joseph France, J. Crossan Cooper, Jr., John Marshall Butler, Hunter H. Moss, Stuart S. Janney, Jr., Norwood B. Orrick, Richard W. Emory, Edmund P. Dandridge, Jr., and John Henry Lewin. Vignettes on these partners appear in the ensuing chapters of this Part II.

Harry N. Baetjer, 1882 - 1969.
Reproduced from a group photograph of the Lawyers' Round Table at a formal 50th anniversary dinner
at the home of Judge William C. Coleman, April 1961.

PART II, CHAPTER 1

Harry N. Baetjer

Harry N. Baetjer was born on January 12, 1882, 18 years before the firm of Venable, Baetjer and Howard was formed. After receiving his B.A. degree from the Johns Hopkins University in 1903 and his LL.B. from the University of Maryland School of Law in 1906, he went to work as an associate in his brother's firm.[1] In a letter dated August 7, 1906, discovered among some of the earliest firm files, his name appears on an engraved letterhead below the name of the only other associate at the time, one Adkins Henry. Henry must have been the first casualty among the ranks of associates — the first among many — since he never made it to partner.

The date when Harry Baetjer became a partner has not been established, but he enjoyed that status at least as early as 1917, since he is shown as such in the firm's federal income tax return for that year, the earliest for which returns have been preserved.

At any rate, back in 1906 Charles McHenry Howard wasted no time in throwing his new twenty-four-year-old associate, Harry Baetjer, into forensic combat, as the two appeared together as co-counsel in a case argued in the Court of Appeals some time in the fall and decided on December 20 of that year. It was a simple case and they easily won an affirmance.[2]

Over the next 50 years Harry Baetjer's appearance was entered in 35 cases in the Maryland Court of Appeals, outstripping by an even dozen the record compiled by his more illustrious brother, not to mention many more cases in the federal courts. This may come as a surprise to those who regarded Edwin Baetjer as a superlawyer of outstanding brilliance and Harry as one of more modest talents who walked in his brother's shadow. Although there is some truth in this comparison, and while it is undisputed that Harry Baetjer was uncomfortable in oral advocacy, thus rarely appearing without the assistance of another partner or associate, it is undeniable from the decided cases that Harry Baetjer had an impressive career at the bar.

These decisions cover a wide spectrum of legal questions such as contracts,[3] trusts,[4] wills and estates,[5] inheritance tax,[6] creditors' rights and bankruptcy,[7] banking,[8] corporations,[9] real estate,[10] constitutional law,[11] and taxes.[12]

In *Kerr v. Enoch Pratt Library*,[13] Harry Baetjer successfully advanced before Judge Chesnut the contention that in refusing admission to a black applicant to the Enoch Pratt Library's training course, it was acting as a private, not a public institution since there was no "state action" to support plaintiff's claim to discrimination. John Henry Lewin argued the appeal and lost before a unanimous Fourth Circuit Court of Appeals.[14] The *Kerr* case was an early skirmish in the war against segregation.

A major bonanza befell the firm in 1942 when it was awarded a fee of $300,000 for services rendered over a six-year period in the estate of Zachary Smith Reynolds, and $90,000 for a three-year representation of the receiver of Chesapeake Corporation. These receipts gave rise to the firm's first use of income averaging techniques to spread their tax impact over the lives of the engagements.

The last case Harry Baetjer argued entirely by himself at the age of seventy-one was *Baker v. Standard Lime and Stone Co.*,[15] presenting complicated questions of corporation law.

His final appearance at the age of seventy-four was in *City of Baltimore v. DeLuca-Davis Construction Co.*,[16] the appellee, a client of

Richard W. Emory, having made a $589,880 mistake in bidding on a construction contract with the city. Emory won in the lower court, and brought in Baetjer on the appeal to add the prestige of his name and underscore the importance of the case. Emory bore the laboring oar, but the record shows that Harry Baetjer participated in the oral argument. Technically, they lost because the decree of the lower court in ordering reformation was reversed, but in fact they won a major victory because the remedy ordered by the Court of Appeals relieved Emory's client from a disastrous contract, the performance of which would have put it in bankruptcy. To compel such performance, the court held, would be "unconscionable." The city was given the option of awarding the business to the next lowest responsible bidder or throwing out all bids and starting the process over again. Twenty-one years later, Emory won another case for another contractor based on the same equitable principles.[17]

A piece of litigation in the federal courts in which Harry Baetjer participated in the twilight of his career was the *Penn Water* case, discussed more fully *infra* in the chapter on John Henry Lewin. The lead counsel in this complicated antitrust case were Lewin and Norwood B. Orrick from Venable, Baetjer and Howard and later Inzer B. Wyatt of Sullivan & Cromwell, but Baetjer made one of the oral arguments before the Fourth Circuit in 1951 at the age of sixty-nine.[18]

From earliest times it was understood that two classes of litigation in which Venable, Baetjer and Howard refused to engage were domestic relations and criminal cases. The exception to the latter during the days of the Founders was Charles McHenry Howard's successful defense of the Whiting-Turner Contracting Company against a charge of violating the minimum wage law.[19] Soon after his arrival at the firm in 1944, however, John Lewin teamed up with Crossan Cooper to defend a man accused of giving false testimony to the Draft Board resulting in the deferment of a fellow employee.

At first, Lewin refused the engagement, citing the firm's established policy of eschewing criminal cases. Nonetheless, the putative client persisted, finally reaching into his pocket to extract $20,000 in cash which he plunked down on Lewin's desk. John Lewin gazed at the wad of bills and asked to be excused for a minute.

Repairing to Harry Baetjer's office, Lewin made a fervent plea for permission to take the engagement. At first the senior partner said "No," but when told about the $20,000 retainer, his resolve was shaken. "Well," he said, "maybe we ought to make an exception just in this one case."

It came on for trial before Judge William C. Coleman in the federal district court, a jurist whose son had been killed in World War II and was known to be as tough on draft violators as he was lenient on duck hunters accused of baiting their blinds. Not surprisingly, Lewin asked for a jury trial, but to no avail. His client was convicted and the Fourth Circuit affirmed.[20] The defendant was sentenced by Judge Coleman to two years in prison. At this point the firm was batting .500 in its criminal practice, based on its record in the only two criminal decisions reported in the first 48 years of its history.

Harry Baetjer was of medium height and slender build, and like his brother, displayed a courtly, gentlemanly manner. He was an extremely kind, generous, friendly, and very shy man. A tragic turning point in his life occurred in 1923 when his wife, the former Katherine Bruce and the mother of their four sons, died of typhoid fever. For the next 46 years Harry Baetjer went into perpetual mourning, never taking a vacation and always wearing a black or dark blue suit and black necktie. He raised the four boys, Norman, Bruce, Howard II, and Ned, all of whom went on to successful business or professional careers except, of course, the youngest, Ned, who, as previously mentioned, was killed in China in World War II.

Unlike his brother, Edwin, who enjoyed outdoor recreational sports such as hunting and fishing, Harry Baetjer had no diversions from the office, although on rare occasions he would sneak off by himself to an afternoon baseball game at Oriole Park or Memorial Stadium. In the days before major league ball came to Baltimore he would sometimes go to Philadelphia to take in a Phillies game, and on one occasion, so the story goes, his picture appeared in the Baltimore papers sitting in the front row behind home plate in Shibe Park as the catcher was chasing a fly ball. Thus was exposed his cover story that he was going to Philadelphia on business.

Harry Baetjer had a gentle sense of humor as reflected in the following story recalled by his junior partner, Robert R. Bair. (Mr. Baetjer always referred to his juniors by their full first names; thus, it was Francis rather than Frank Murnaghan, Robert rather than Bob Bair.) On one occasion Bair was attempting to explain a complex solution he had devised for a corporate reorganization. After a few moments of reflection, Mr. Baetjer replied:

> Oh, no, Robert, I don't think we will bother with that. It reminds me of a story my brother, Ed, used to tell about the man who was asked if he could pee through a straw. He thought about it for a moment and then answered, "No, I don't think I can. Besides, it would be very difficult to do and wouldn't prove very much after I had done it."

Harry Baetjer was not so facile with numbers as his elder brother, Edwin. He once remarked, "Whenever I have a column of figures to add up, I do it three times and take the average."

He was also sometimes out of touch with reality in a strange and lovable sort of way. One Saturday morning with a skeleton force of secretaries on duty, he walked into the library where a stenographer was poised on a ladder replacing a book on the top shelf. Naturally, she had no pencil or pad at hand, but, nonetheless, Mr. Baetjer started dictating to her as if she were seated across his desk. "Please, Mr. Baetjer," she remonstrated, "Don't you see? I am not prepared." To which Baetjer responded, "A good secretary is always prepared." On Monday morning the story was all over the office.

Harry Baetjer's membership in the Lawyers' Round Table was one of his few social outlets. Some may have regarded his life as a sad and lonely one, but he would not have so described it.

His clients were men of property or managers of property, people such as his industrialist brother, Howard, George Pausch, one of the senior vice-presidents at the Safe Deposit & Trust Company of Baltimore, Hamilton Post and Fred G. Boyce, two of the top executives at the old Mercantile Trust Company, and prominent businessmen such as John M. Nelson, Sr., William G. Scarlett, Sr., Harrison Garrett, and Gilman Paul.

Harry Baetjer was immersed in the firm of Venable, Baetjer and Howard and extremely proud of his partners and their achievements. He rarely missed a day at his desk in the same small office in the Mercantile Building, formerly the Continental Trust Building, which he occupied for over 60 years. The walls of his office were literally papered with Maryland historical prints which he had collected over the years and which he bequeathed to the firm. They form the nucleus of a collection that graces the corridors, conference rooms and common areas of the firm's present quarters.

Harry Baetjer was not involved in bar association activities or civic affairs to any degree comparable with the participation of the Founders. His principal outside activities were as a member of the Draft Board in World War I, a member of the Bond Commission appointed by Governor O'Conor in 1941 to study the reorganization of the Court of Appeals, chairman of the Baltimore City Charter Revision Commission of 1944, trustee of Gilman School, and director of Baltimore Transit Co. and Maryland Casualty Co. He was frequently consulted by Governor Theodore R. McKeldin and other officials on matters of public importance, and was widely regarded as an elder statesman of the Republican Party in Maryland. He was an advocate of the sitting judge principle, and an editorial in *The Sun*, the day after his death, praised his leadership in the movement to free the judiciary from popular elections.[21]

The eighth codicil to Harry Baetjer's will contains a quixotic directive which in 1980, 11 years after his death on April 5, 1969, engendered a controversy between the firm and its former partner, Judge Francis D. Murnaghan, Jr. The testamentary provision read as follows:

If at any time, neither J. Crossan Cooper, Jr., H. Vernon Eney, Francis D. Murnaghan, Jr. or Norwood B. Orrick is a general partner of the Co-partnership Venable, Baetjer and Howard, then my name shall not be used as part of the firm name.

In all other respects, I hereby ratify and confirm my Last Will and Testament.

Murnaghan had resigned as a partner as of July 1, 1979 to go on the federal bench, and both Cooper and Eney had become Of Counsel on January 1, 1980. Orrick was slated to become Of Counsel on January 1, 1981 after reaching the age of seventy the previous October. Anticipating, therefore, that the circumstance described in the codicil would occur on January 1, 1981, Murnaghan, by letter dated January 21, 1980 and addressed to each of the active and retired partners, called attention to Baetjer's directive and concluded that "his wish must be complied with."

The letter caused resentment among the 27 younger partners who had never known Harry Baetjer and had not been employed by the firm in February, 1967 when he stopped coming to the office. To them it seemed as if the hand of an unknown decedent were reaching out of the grave to deprive them of a trade name they considered a proprietary right they had earned as part of the partnership selection process. A trade name used for many years in a business or profession takes on an institutional meaning of its own apart from the family names with which it may have been originally identified. The name, Venable, Baetjer and Howard, had been used for 80 years.

As to the other seventeen active partners, only nine had been a partner of Harry Baetjer's and a handful of them, possibly no more than three or four, had been aware of the eighth codicil. These seniors had consigned the oddity to an out-of-sight, out-of-mind limbo and were startled by Judge Murnaghan's mandate long after Mr. Baetjer's death.

At this point I was asked by the Operating Committee to advise the firm as to the legal effect of the controversial document. After research, I concluded that it had no legal effect. The name "Baetjer" in the firm name was not Harry Baetjer's, but that of his elder brother, Edwin, the former being in college when the firm was founded. More fundamentally, testamentary documents are to be used as a means of transmitting property interests at death and may not be used to direct or control the behavior of others after a person dies. Granted that the codicil may have reflected the testator's wishes at the time he wrote it, he could not in this manner impose his wishes on unrelated third parties.

Armed with this opinion Edmund Dandridge, as spokesman for the firm, laid the matter before Harry Baetjer's surviving sons. After consultation, they decided to take no action if the firm continued under the same name it had used for more than three-quarters of a century. This decision was reported to Judge Murnaghan who also took no action except to address the firm as Venable & Howard in subsequent correspondence.[22]

To those partners who were schoolmates or personal friends of the Baetjer sons it would have been most distasteful to have become involved in a dispute over their family name. Yet, it would also have been unfair to those partners who had never known Mr. Baetjer to have yielded to the whimsey of his eighth codicil. The peaceful resolution of this conflict was, as the Episcopal Prayer Book puts it, a happy issue out of all our afflictions.

In the celebration of the centennial of the Bar Association of Baltimore City in 1980, several firms claimed a longer lineage than Venable, Baetjer and Howard by adding to their lines of descent the lives of other firms with which they had merged over the years.[23] There were, however, none in existence in 1980 with the same name they had used continuously since 1900 except this one. It was then, as it is now, a venerable assembly of lawyers.

Endnotes to Part II, Chapter 1:

1. The dates in the text have been verified by the custodians of alumni records at Johns Hopkins University and the University of Maryland. They are at variance with dates given in J. Crossan Cooper's *Address to the Associates*, 1976; John Henry Lewin's *History of the Firm*, 1972; and William J. McCarthy's *Venable, Baetjer and Howard, Daily Record*, May 12, 1980.

2. *Johnson v. Safe Deposit & Trust Co. of Baltimore*, 104 Md. 460 (1906), decided December 20, 1906. The denial of a petition to discharge a committee for an incompetent was affirmed. Baetjer had been admitted to practice before the Court of Appeals almost a year before on January 30, 1906.

3. *Lohmuller v. Samuel Kirk & Sons*, 133 Md. 78 (1918); *Davison Chemical Co. v. Baugh Chemical Co.*, 133 Md. 203 (1918), and *Davison Chemical Co. v. Baugh Chemical Co.*, 134 Md. 24 (1919); *Jackson v. Davey Tree Co.*, 134 Md. 230 (1919); *Fidelity & Deposit Co. v. Sanford & Brooks Co.*, 158 Md. 525 (1930); *Hambleton & Co. v. Union National Bank*, 161 Md. 318 (1931); *Continental Milling & Feed Co. v. Doughnut Corp.*, 186 Md. 669 (1946), involving questions of arbitration and award.

4. *Safe Deposit & Trust Co. v. Ellis*, 136 Md. 334 (1920), involving the power of an equity court to approve a substituted trustee; *Zell v. Safe Deposit & Trust Co.*, 173 Md. 518 (1938), a "principal and income" case and a loss by Harry Baetjer, another in a long series of losses by partners of Venable, Baetjer and Howard in attempting to overturn the "Pennsylvania Rule of Apportionment" in trust accounting practice.

5. *Associated Professors of Loyola College v. Dugan*, 137 Md. 545 (1921); *Courtenay v. Courtenay*, 138 Md. 204 (1921); *Perkins v. Safe Deposit & Trust Co.*, 138 Md. 299 (1921), holding that the "legal age" of a female was eighteen, a loss for Harry Baetjer; *Goldberg v. Erich*, 142 Md. 544 (1923), a win for Baetjer in a case involving the Rule Against Perpetuities; *Syfer v. Fidelity Trust Co.*, 184 Md. 391 (1945), a will construction case in which Baetjer represented the executors.

6. *Good Samaritan Hospital v. Dugan*, 146 Md. 374 (1924), holding that the entire value of a charitable gift, not its net value after the inheritance tax is deductible for federal estate tax purposes. This is an interesting case involving the will of Thomas O'Neill, a wealthy Baltimore merchant who left an estate of $6,462,426.

7. *Philadelphia & Reading Coal Co. v. Willinger*, 137 Md. 46 (1920); *Chicago Bonding Co. v. State*, 137 Md. 132 (1920); *Goldsborough v. Tinsley*, 138 Md. 411 (1920), a win for Baetjer in a case involving an equitable lien arising out of a defective chattel mortgage; *Abell v. Safe Deposit & Trust Co.*, 192 Md. 438 (1949), another win for Baetjer together with John Henry Lewin, in a case involving an indenture to the A. S. Abell Co. In the

post-Depression era, Baetjer's appearance is recorded in a number of significant corporate reorganizations, *viz: In re Baltimore & Ohio R. Co.*, 63 F. Supp. 542 (D. Md. 1945); *In re Kelly-Springfield Tire Co.*, 10 F. Supp. 414 (D. Md. 1935); *In re Consolidated Coal Co.*, 11 F. Supp. 594 (D. Md. 1935); *T. H. Symington & Son v. Symington Co.*, 9 F. Supp 699. (D. Md. 1935); *Abercrombie et al. v. United Light & Power Co.*, 7 F. Supp. 530 (D. Md. 1934).

8. *National Union Bank v. Miller Rubber Co.*, 148 Md. 449 (1925); *Morse v. National Central Bank*, 150 Md. 142 (1926); *Perring v. Baltimore Trust Co.*, 171 Md. 618 (1936); *Dougherty v. Dougherty*, 175 Md. 441 (1938).

9. *Weiskittel v. Weiskittel*, 167 Md. 306 (1934), holding that a party has a right to use his own name in his business even if it incidentally interferes with another of the same name in the absence of artifice or a deliberate attempt to mislead the public. Compare Harry Baetjer's early victory in *Sprigg v. Fisher*, 222 F. 964 (D. Md. 1915), a trademark infringement case; *Warren v. Fitzgerald*, 189 Md. 476 (1948), involving the successful defense of the transit company's substitution of motor coaches for trolley lines over the objections of stockholders; *Brown v. McLanahan*, 148 F.2d 703 (4th Cir. 1945) involving the equitable rights of holders of voting trust certificates, a case lost on appeal by Baetjer and Lewin; *Todd v. Maryland Casualty Co.*, 155 F.2d 29 (7th Cir. 1946), involving questions of preemptive rights under Maryland corporation law in connection with the reorganization of Maryland Casualty Co.

10. *Lohmuller v. Samuel Kirk & Sons, supra* note 4; *Baltimore Trust Co. v. Canton Corn Products Co.*, 140 Md. 557 (1922); *Fetting v. Waltz*, 160 Md. 50 (1930); *Stieff v. Millikin*, 162 Md. 245 (1932).

11. In *Johns Hopkins University v. Williams*, 199 Md. 382 (1952), Mr. Baetjer graciously deferred to his young associate, the author, for the lead argument, his first appearance in the Court of Appeals. It was a significant victory, upholding the constitutionality of a bond issue to fund the construction of a new Engineering School building at the Homewood campus of Johns Hopkins.

12. *Burnet v. Sanford & Brooks Co.*, 282 U.S. 359, 51 S. Ct. 150, 75 L.2d 383 (1931) reversing *Sanford & Brooks Co. v. Commissioner of Internal Revenue*, 35 F.2d 312 (4th Cir. 1929). In this, Harry Baetjer's only case argued in the Supreme Court, he was unable to sustain his victory in the Fourth Circuit. It was an early case defining the meaning of "income" for tax purposes. Another tax case, this one a victory, was *Dugan v. Miles*, 292 F. 131 (4th Cir. 1923), involving federal estate taxes. And see *Mullikin v. Magruder*, 149 F.2d 593 (4th Cir. 1945), another estate tax case.

13. 54 F. Supp. 514 (D. Md. 1944).

14. *Kerr v. Enoch Pratt Free Library*, 149 F.2d 212 (4th Cir. 1945), cert. den. 326 U.S. 721 (1945).

15. 203 Md. 270 (1953).

16. 210 Md. 518 (1956).

17. *Baltimore County v. John K. Ruff, Inc.*, 281 Md. 62 (1977).

18. *Consolidated Gas, Electric Light & Power Co. of Baltimore v. Pennsylvania Water & Power Co.*, 194 F.2d 89 (4th Cir. 1952).

19. *State v. Lassotovitch*, 162 Md. 147 (1932). See Pt. I, Ch. 3, note 2, supra.

20. *Cataneo v. United States*, 167 F.2d 820 (4th Cir. 1948).

21. *The Sun*, April 6, 1969.

22. Orrick and the author of this history were the only two partners who were amenable to changing the name to Venable & Howard. They bowed to the consensus of the other forty-two active partners and the four retired partners (Cooper, Lewin, Eney and Emory), all of whom opposed any change. (See *supra* Pt. I, Ch. 2, note 19, for a citation to an early case that used the name Venable & Howard in the headnotes.)

23. *Daily Record*, May 16, 1980, Centennial Edition commemorating the 100th anniversary of the Bar Association of Baltimore City.

Edwin G. Baetjer encounters a friendly black bear, date and location unknown.

Reproduced from the family records of H. Norman Baetjer

PART II, CHAPTER 2

Joseph France

J OSEPH FRANCE, the son of Joseph C. France and the brother of Judge Robert France, appeared on the scene at Venable, Baetjer and Howard in 1919 following his graduation from Harvard Law School in 1917.[1] He was elected partner in 1929,[2] the gestation period for partnership development being somewhat longer in those days than at present. He was trained by Edwin G. Baetjer, and Richard Emory describes him as having "one of the best legal minds that I have ever been exposed to."[3] Like his mentor, France revelled in the joys of unravelling a knotty problem of corporation or tax law, and as previously noted, he played a leading role in the Seaboard Air Line Railway reorganization. He was counsel for the Baltimore Stock Exchange before its assimilation into the Philadelphia-Baltimore-Washington Stock Exchange and its eventual extinction, and numerous other corporate and financial in-stitutions were included in his list of clients.

France emulated Edwin Baetjer as an angler of note, having fished in rivers, streams and lakes all over the world, and having been consulted by the Shakespeare fishing equipment people to test and offer advice about their new products. He raised and handled German short-haired pointers, and one of his dogs won all the categories of competition for the breed in 1974. On his farm in

Upperco he raised and showed milk cows and beef cattle; he was also an expert on early American furniture and furnishings. He was consulted by the Metropolitan Museum of Art in New York as to whether and what American pewter to buy.

Joseph France made a fortune in real estate, and for a number of years was chairman of the board of the North Charleston Land Corporation. Towards the end of his career he would spend the winter months at the Yeamans Hall Club in Charleston, South Carolina, and a good part of the rest of the year on fishing expeditions hither and yon, all to the annoyance of Harry Baetjer and Crossan Cooper who resented the fact that a lawyer of such capacity did not devote himself 100% to the firm's business. They were right about his absenteeism but wrong in failing to appreciate his talents. According to Richard Emory who worked under his tutelage for fifteen years, "Joe France was a man of many interests, extraordinarily knowledgeable about everything he did."[4]

An unsung hero of Venable, Baetjer and Howard, Joseph France died on October 10, 1985 at the age of ninety-two, the first person in the firm's history to receive the title, Partner *Emeritus*. His wife, the former Julia McHenry, died in 1983, and he was survived by two daughters, Catherine F. Harrison and Pembroke F. Noble, five grandchildren and two great-grandchildren.

Endnotes to Part II, Chapter 2:

1. This Joseph France is not to be confused with Joseph I. France, a contemporary physician from Port Deposit who represented Maryland in the United States Senate from 1916-1922. A Republican, he was defeated by William Cabell Bruce in 1922 and in 1936 by George L. Radcliffe.

2. The date in the text is confirmed by the firm's federal income tax returns. France's obituary in *The Sun* of October 11, 1985 and various other histories of the firm have erroneously placed the date of his admission to partnership as 1930.

3. Letter from Richard W. Emory to the author, October 17, 1989.

4. *Id.*

EDWIN G. BAETJER
CHARLES MⁱᶠH. HOWARD
HARRY N. BAETJER
———
JOSEPH FRANCE
J. CROSSAN COOPER, JR.
JOHN M. BUTLER

TELEPHONE
PLAZA 6780

VENABLE, BAETJER AND HOWARD
ATTORNEYS AT LAW
1409 CONTINENTAL BUILDING
BALTIMORE & CALVERT STS.
BALTIMORE, MD.

December 1st, 1928.

John McHenry, Esq.,
        Secretary-Treasurer,
Mercantile Trust & Deposit Company,
        Baltimore, Md.

Dear Mr. McHenry:-

(text of letter omitted)

Very truly yours,

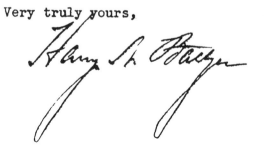

hnb-
jlk-
encs-

1928 Letterhead after the arrival of Cooper and Butler in 1927

*The typist, "jlk," was Joseph L. Kerr, long-time secretary to Edwin G. and
Harry N. Baetjer, later the office manager.*

J. Crossan Cooper, Jr., 1901 - 1980.

J. Crossan Cooper, Jr.

CROSSAN COOPER JOINED the firm of Venable, Baetjer and Howard as an associate in 1927, following his graduation from Yale Law School and a brief sojourn as an associate at Marbury, Gosnell & Williams.[1] He had attended Harvard Law School for one year but left for academic reasons when he attempted to apply at that institution the casual study habits he had acquired as an undergraduate at Princeton. His career at the bar is proof that he could, with proper application, have made the grade at any law school, even Harvard.

At the time of Cooper's arrival at the firm, Joseph France was the only associate, another, John Brewer, who might be called a "permanent associate," having recently died. Cooper later observed that Brewer "was born an associate, lived an associate, and died an associate."[2]

John Marshall Butler came on the scene at the same time as Cooper and both were paid $100 per month; however, as previously noted, they received $3,900 in compensation for 1929. This may seem a pittance compared with the salaries of junior associates in the 1980's and 90's, but to the author, who started as an associate at Armstrong, Machen & Eney in 1948 at $3,000 per year, the $3,900 paid to Cooper and Butler nineteen years before seems like heavy sugar.

In the late 1920's Venable, Baetjer and Howard had no female employees, the members of the staff consisting of Joseph Kerr who acted as secretary for Mr. Edwin Baetjer; Rudolph F. Bolard, Jr., who took care of Mr. Howard; George S. Lynch, later a Deputy Register of Wills of Baltimore County, who handled Mr. Harry Baetjer's work; Lewis Clark, the office boy; and a bookkeeper, Alan P. Longcope, the brother of Dr. Warfield Longcope, a leading internist at the Johns Hopkins Medical School. That line-up left no one to serve the needs of the associates. Cooper recalled, "We had to do our dictating to any male secretary whom we could prevail upon to listen to us. It was rough going."[3]

In 1931 the firm broke the all-male barrier by employing Miss Augusta Porsinger as switchboard operator. She remained on board, as it were, for about thirty years before leaving to get married. The employment of Miss Porsinger proved so successful that France and Cooper prevailed upon the hierarchy to let them engage their own female secretaries.

Cooper's was Miss Elaine Bell who arrived in 1932 and stayed with him for twenty-four years before she too left to get married.

In the ensuing years as the firm's business continued to grow despite the Great Depression, three more associates were added: Hunter H. Moss in 1931 and in 1932 Stuart S. Janney, Jr., and Norwood B. Orrick. Although Joseph France had been made a partner some time in mid-1929, he and Harry Baetjer had been the only additions to the partnership ranks in the first twenty years of the firm's history. Then, in 1939 five new partners were admitted: Cooper, Butler, Moss, Janney and Orrick, sometimes hereinafter referred to as the "Five Juniors." It had taken Cooper twelve years to cross the line, but Moss made it in eight and Janney and Orrick in six and one-half. This was a source of irritation to Cooper and for some years the firm's records showed his admission in 1937. To his credit, he set the record straight in his *Address to the Associates* in 1976.[4]

The Five Juniors were then asked to sign a written partnership agreement which had been, according to Orrick, drafted by Harry Baetjer. It divided the partners into two classes, the "Senior Partners" consisting of Edwin G. Baetjer, Charles McHenry Howard, Harry N. Baetjer, and Joseph France; and the "Junior Partners" consisting of the five new admittees. All management powers were vested in the Seniors, including even the power to dismiss any of the Juniors and to admit new partners. Each of the Five Juniors was entitled to 5% of the net profits, the remaining 75% to be divided among the Seniors in such shares as they might agree upon. Each Junior Partner was entitled to a salary of $5,000 per annum, but if his 5% share of net profits exceeded that amount, then the excess would be carried over as a prior charge against the next year's earnings. This effectively put a cap of $5,000 on the annual compensation of each Junior Partner.

Norwood Orrick recalls that Harry Baetjer presented this document for signature, and the five new admittees obediently signed it. Perhaps the seniors also signed it to humor the draftsman but, however that may be, it seems that its provisions were never honored. According to the tax returns, the Five Juniors each received a total of $13,004 in compensation in 1939 and $13,069 in 1940, many dollars more than the $5,000 cap. In subsequent years the harsh limitations of the 1939 agreement were also ignored.

On January 1, 1947 after the last of the Founders had died, a new "Agreement of Copartnership," also drafted by Harry Baetjer, was entered into, the eight signatories being Baetjer, France, John Henry Lewin (who had joined the firm in 1944), and the Five Juniors of 1939. This new edition provided succinctly: "The copartnership shall expire December 31, 1949." Despite this sunset provision, no replacement partnership agreement has ever been executed, although many of the firm's important policies and procedures, such as those regulating the election of new partners and payments on death, disability or retirement, have been reduced to writing and amended from time to time.

The 1947 agreement and the tax returns confirm that by this time Crossan Cooper had drawn away from the other four of the Five Juniors, all of whom had received identical compensation from 1938 through 1941. By 1942 Cooper had passed the others in total compensation, and in the 1947 agreement his draw was fixed at 14%, surpassed only by Baetjer's 23 ½%, and France's 16%. John Lewin was given 11%, and the percentages of the other Juniors ranged between Butler's low of 8% to a high of 9% for Moss. Cooper had established himself as the best business-getter or rainmaker in the firm and was being rewarded accordingly. Throughout his career he was adept in that aspect of the practice of law — now euphemistically dubbed business development. Cooper also had the advantage of several more years of experience at the bar than Moss, Janney, and Orrick.

Although never approaching the brilliance of Charles McHenry Howard, Crossan Cooper was an able lawyer whose primary attributes, according to Norwood Orrick, were "sound judgment and common sense."[5] As a case in point, he cites the decision of the U.S. District Court in *Hilgenberg v. United States*[6] where Cooper successfully attacked the constitutionality of a tax regulation making leasehold improvements taxable as income to the landlord. Cooper passed up the more tempting argument that the regulation was broader than the statute and instead went to the constitutional heart of the matter.

One case Cooper lost in the Circuit Court for Baltimore County was a *cause celebre* at the time, *A. S. Abell Co. v. Kirby*.[7] It was a libel case brought against the publisher of *The Sun* by one Edward Gordon Kirby who had served as acting sergeant in charge of the Rackets Squad of the Baltimore City Police Department and who had been characterized in an editorial as "infamous" and "a man with a motive." The plaintiff was represented by Alan H. Murrell, later the colorful Public Defender of Baltimore City and a noted trial lawyer, and the defendant by Crossan Cooper, assisted by his associate, Robert R. Bair, and Kenneth C. Proctor of the Towson bar, later a judge of the Circuit Court for Baltimore County. The question before the jury was whether the quoted words were privileged as "fair comment." The jury answered the question resoundingly in the negative with a $45,000 verdict. On the appeal Cooper stepped aside in favor of Proctor and Bair, appearing only as co-counsel with Venable, Baetjer and Howard on the brief. The verdict was affirmed, four to one, Judge Stedman Prescott dissenting vigorously.

In view of Kirby's prominence, his suspension from the police force, his association with unsavory characters, and the fact that he had been found guilty by the Police Commissioner of planting false evidence in an investigation, the result seems difficult to justify. It might be decided differently under the law now prevailing as a result of the Supreme Court's ruling in *New York Times Co. v. Sullivan*.[8] However, in view of the long history of the firm's representation of *The Sun* in libel cases and the successes achieved by Charles McHenry Howard, Francis D. Murnaghan, Jr., and Douglas D. Connah, Jr., the loss in *Kirby* stands out as an oddity.

A libel case for *The Sun* which Cooper won was *Pulvermann v. A. S. Abell Co.*,[9] involving a reprint from The New York *Herald Tribune* during the 1952 presidential campaign. Plaintiff's conduct had been represented in the story as "the biggest five percenter deal ever exposed in Washington" and General Eisenhower's speech was quoted as depicting "the sort of crookedness going on in Washington." The Court of Appeals for the Fourth Circuit held the offending language subject to a qualified privilege for which there would be no liability in the absence of a showing of express malice. It was a landmark First Amendment victory.

As counsel for Canton Railroad, Cooper developed an ingenious way of getting rid of small claims. Canton operated in street beds throughout the Baltimore downtown area numerous spur lines to various industrial complexes, and many accidents occurred at unprotected intersections. Some involved personal injuries, but for the most part they were fender bender property claims. Cooper's solution was to offer plaintiff's counsel the nuisance value of the suit plus a small sweetener with the proviso that unless accepted within 24 hours, the offer would decline so much per day. Thus, for example, he might offer $4,500 on Thursday, December 15, with the condition that unless accepted by the close of business on Friday, December 16, the offer would decline $200 per day. If plaintiff's counsel were to wait until Monday, December 19, to accept the settlement offer, he would find only $4,100 on the table.

At first, lawyers for the claimants could not believe what was happening to them, but after several had been forced to accept less than Cooper's original offer or else proceed to trial, the word got around that Crossan Cooper was not bluffing and that acceptance of his original offer, always reasonable in the circumstances, was the only way to get a settlement out of Canton Railroad. It is unlikely that this technique would work on large claims, but for small ones it was a useful device.

One of Cooper's most challenging cases in the Court of Appeals was *Johns Hopkins University v. Board of County Commissioners of Montgomery County*[10] in which he bested Hall Hammond, then deputy Attorney General and later Attorney General and Chief Judge of the Court of Appeals. Hammond had prevailed in the Circuit Court, but Cooper won on appeal. The issue was whether a substantial piece of real estate in Montgomery County entitled in the name of Johns Hopkins University was subject to real estate taxes. It had been acquired as an accommodation to the United States government for the erection of a research plant to promote the war effort in World War II. The agreement with the government provided that the property would be conveyed to the United States or its designee at the government's request. The court below had ruled in favor of the state on the theory that property held in a fiduciary capacity is taxable to the trustee as legal owner, without regard to the tax exempt status of beneficial owners.

In reversing and ruling in favor of Cooper's client, the Court of Appeals held that the lower court result would obtain in all cases except where the beneficial owner is the United States government. In that situation the Supreme Court holding in *United States of*

America and Mesta Machine Company v. County of Allegheny, Pennsylvania[11] was deemed controlling.

The decision in the *Johns Hopkins* case was, in fact, a much closer call than Judge C. Gus Grason's opinion would have the reader believe; Judge Hammond cited a number of cases that would have compelled a different result, but they were brushed aside by the majority. The case could have gone either way.

Other cases argued by Crossan Cooper in the Court of Appeals and in the federal courts covered a wide range of subjects such as will construction,[12] trusts,[13] corporation law,[14] banking,[15] taxes,[16] statutory construction,[17] mechanics' liens,[18] securities law,[19] and real estate.[20]

Because of his sound judgment, Crossan Cooper was much in demand as a business lawyer and served on the board of directors of Mercantile-Safe Deposit and Trust Company, Canton Railroad, and Penn Mutual Life Insurance Company. He was a long-time trustee of Gilman School and served on the board of the Johns Hopkins Hospital for 32 years, acting as its president from 1964 to 1972. Although not active in bar association activities, he was elected president of the Baltimore City Bar Association in 1954-55 and vice-president of the State Bar Association in 1952 in recognition of his stature in the profession and the community. He was also a fellow of the American College of Trial Lawyers and a member of the Rule Day Club and the Lawyers' Round Table.

Before the advent of Vernon Eney in 1951, Cooper applied his managerial skills to the operation of Venable, Baetjer and Howard and was sometimes referred to as its managing partner. This title would be a misnomer, however, to the extent that it might imply any erosion of the dominance of Harry N. Baetjer as the supreme authority in the firm until the onset of his last illness.

Crossan Cooper was a talented athlete. He was the star second baseman on the Princeton baseball team; the goalie on its soccer team; a one-time tennis champion of Maine; a consistent winner, with his friend Jack Ewing, of the Maryland Invitational Squash

Doubles Tournament; and a golfer who had a career total of three holes-in-one. Golf was a sport in which he excelled until a couple of years before his death when nerve damage from a broken arm plus an unsuccessful eye operation wrought havoc with his game. Yet he continued to play until a few weeks before his fatal heart attack on November 19, 1980.

In Norwood Orrick's *Reminiscences of Crossan Cooper* the author commented from first-hand observation:

> Crossan, also, in a quiet, unostentatious way, made many contributions of a charitable nature, using that term in its broadest sense. For example, he performed major legal services to the Boy Scouts in the acquisition of a large, wooded camp site and the establishment of a camping facility there. Crossan sent no bill. When the Scout organization insisted that he do so, they received a statement showing a substantial fee which his services fully justified. The statement was marked 'Paid'.

> Crossan was a stanch supporter of his Church. At his funeral services the priest made special reference not only to this fact, but also to the fact that Crossan had made many, many good works, most of which were publicly unknown.[21]

The Coopers lived in a spacious house on a multi-acre estate, named Windy Gates, off Lake Avenue on the southern border of Baltimore County, now the site of the Devon Hill condominiums. They had three children, a son, John C. Cooper, III, a second generation Baltimore attorney, and two daughters, Harriet C. Froth-ingham and Louisa C. Dubin. In addition to his children, Cooper was survived by his wife, the former Eleanor Chalfant.

Crossan Cooper was not only a successful lawyer but also a person of deep sensitivity and concern for the needs of others.

Endnotes to Part II, Chapter 3:

1. J. Crossan Cooper, Jr. in his *Address to the Associates* (1976), fixes the date of his arrival at 1927 and the alumni records at Yale confirm his graduation as June 22, 1927. However, the records of the Court of Appeals show that he was admitted to practice before that court on April 7, 1927. The explanation may be that he was able to transfer some credits from his first year at Harvard, thus enabling him to complete his legal studies at Yale in early 1927, even though his diploma was not delivered until June. Another possibility is that he took the bar examination and was admitted to the bar before graduation from law school, a practice permitted in those days. His son, John C. Cooper, confirms his father's brief tour of duty with the Marbury firm.

2. *Id.*

3. *Id.*

4. *Id.* Butler's obituary in *The Sun*, March 17, 1978, commits the same error in reporting that he became a partner in 1937. Both he and Cooper were, in fact, among the Five Juniors who made the grade on January 1, 1939.

5. Cooper also identifies Gerard F. Stickler as a male secretary in this era, but the tax records indicate that Stickler did not appear on the payroll until 1940. Later he was the long-time secretary for Norwood B. Orrick. Orrick, *Reminiscences of Crossan Cooper*, December 4, 1980.

6. 21 F. Supp. 453 (D. Md. 1937).

7. 227 Md. 267 (1961).

8. 376 U.S. 254, 84 S. Ct. 710, 11 L. Ed. 2d. 686 (1964).

9. 228 F.2d 797 (4th Cir. 1956), affirming 131 F. Supp. 617 (D. Md. 1955).

10. 185 Md. 614 (1946).

11. 322 U.S. 174, 64 S. Ct. 908, 88 L. Ed. 1209 (1944).

12. *Baker v. Baylies*, 231 Md. 287 (1963), submitted on brief for the trust company; *Smith v. Mercantile Trust Co.*, 199 Md. 264 (1952); *Inasmuch Gospel Mission v. Mercantile Trust Co.*, 184 Md. 231 (1945).

13. *Safe Deposit & Trust Co. of Baltimore v. Woodbridge*, 184 Md. 560 (1945).

14. *Shimko v. Eastern States Corp.*, 218 Md. 362 (1958).

15. *Fleishmann v. Mercantile Trust Co.*, 192 Md. 680 (1949).

16. *Western Maryland Railway v. State Tax Commission*, 195 Md. 206 (1950), a case argued and lost by John Henry Lewin with Crossan Cooper on the brief; *Mayor & City Council of Baltimore v. Canton Railroad Co.*, 186 Md. 618 (1946), a win for Cooper in a dispute with the city over its right to impose minor privilege charges on piers owned by Canton in navigable waters.

17. *United States v. Atlantic Coast Line Co.*, 99 F.2d 6, reh. den., 99 F.2d 932 (4th Cir. 1938), holding that Atlantic was "carrying on or doing business" for purposes of the capital stock tax imposed by the NIRA, a loss for Cooper.

18. *Canton Lumber Co. v. Cooper*, 75 F.2d 92 (4th Cir. 1935), upholding Cooper's contention that a retaining wall built to hold back dumped refuse is not a "wharf" within the meaning of Maryland laws relating to mechanics' liens.

19. *DiJulio v. Digicon, Inc.*, 339 F. Supp. 1284 (D. Md. 1972), a securities fraud case won by Cooper and Lewin, the prospectus being held adequate to disclose risk factors.

20. *Fetting v. Waltz*, 160 Md. 50 (1930), a case successfully argued with Harry Baetjer, *supra* Pt. II, Ch. 1, note 10 involving a wrongful holding over after termination of a lease.

21. *Supra* note 5.

John Marshall Butler

J OHN MARSHALL BUTLER graduated from the night school of the University of Maryland School of Law in 1926, following a two-year tour of duty in the army in World War I. He joined Venable, Baetjer and Howard as an associate in 1927,[1] and became a partner on January 1, 1939 as one of the Five Juniors of that year. His wife was the former Mary Louise Abell, a great granddaughter of A. S. Abell, the founder of *The Sun*. After eleven years as a partner he withdrew from the firm in 1950 to take his seat as a member of the United States Senate. Reelected in 1956, he retired from the Senate in 1962 at the age of sixty-four.

Butler had a pedestrian career as a practicing lawyer, mostly confined to routine civil litigation. One case that might not fall in this category is *Carey v. Howard*[2] in which John Marshall Butler represented Charles McHenry Howard as executor of Harriet B. Jones, deceased. Howard had brought suit in 1929 against his decedent's nephew, George Leiper Carey, Jr., for repayment of a $5,000 loan she had made to Carey before her death. The proceedings were instituted under the provisions of the Acts of 1886, Ch. 184, known as the Speedy Judgment Act, which permitted the entry of judgment in certain clear-cut cases on the fifteenth day after the "return day" (the measuring date for filing a response). For reasons that do not appear in the record, Howard did not avail himself of this "speedy" remedy but, instead, waited eleven years (yes, *eleven years*) before entering judgment in 1940. Carey's motion to strike the judgment was overruled, and the Court of Appeals affirmed over the objection of two dissenting judges. The majority construed the Speedy Judgment Act as permitting the entry of judgment after the expiration of fifteen days but as not requiring that it be entered within any time period thereafter, however extended or unreasonable. One wonders if Butler could have achieved this result if his client had been a lawyer of lesser stature than Charles McHenry Howard at the pinnacle of his career.[3] Even if technically right, the result seems unfair.

Butler had been a member of the Baltimore City Civil Service Commission from 1942 to 1949 but otherwise had held no elected or appointed office before his meteoric rise to the Senate. Russell Baker has described him as "a handsome, dim-witted Baltimore lawyer."[4]

His victory over Millard E. Tydings in 1950 was accomplished through application of the since discredited unit vote whereunder election results were determined by the majority vote of electoral units rather than the state-wide popular vote. It is also tarnished in memory by the dirty tricks used by his campaign managers. A political consultant from Chicago, the breeding ground of political shenanigans, engineered a negative campaign against Tydings, insinuating that he was soft on Communism and harsh in his criticism of Senator Joseph McCarthy, this at a time when the red scare was at its peak and McCarthy had not been exposed for the charlatan that he was. The innuendos reached a climax on election eve with the release of a four-page mock tabloid containing a composite photograph of Tydings and Earl Browder, the leader of the Communist Party in the United States, with the caption, "Tydings Promised Probe, But Gave Whitewash."[5]

Herbert R. O'Conor, the junior senator from Maryland and former governor, called the anti-Tydings effort "the most deplorable resort to mud-slinging and character assassination this state has witnessed in many years."[6]

In 1956 Butler came on for reelection but this time had no need to resort to dirty tricks, for he was the beneficiary of God's gift to the Republican Party in the person of George P. Mahoney. This successful paving contractor, turned politician, had the knack of winning Democratic primaries and losing the general election, or losing the primary with such bloodshed that the victor was too wounded to wage an effective campaign against his Republican opponent. In 1956 Mahoney arrived at the general election by the back door, having won the popular vote but having lost the nomination to Tydings by the unit vote. He was nonetheless named the Democratic candidate after Tydings was forced to withdraw because of a debilitating case of shingles. Butler defeated Mahoney handily. Other Republicans who have been the recipients of Mahoney's largesse have included Theodore R. McKeldin, J. Glenn Beall and, last but not least, Spiro T. Agnew, President Nixon's vice-president who resigned his office after pleading *nolo contendere* to charges of tax evasion.

During his twelve years in the Senate, Butler established himself as an arch-conservative, in modern parlance a constitutional strict constructionist. He was a stanch advocate of Robert A. Taft of Ohio for the Republican nomination for president in 1952, opposing Governor McKeldin who supported the more liberal "Ike" Eisenhower. On the floor of the Senate he was a spokesman for the port of Baltimore and opponent of the St. Lawrence Seaway. By the end of his second term he was the ranking Republican member of the Foreign and Interstate Commerce Committee. He was a supporter of the armed services and on at least one occasion gave them credit for a greater capability than they enjoyed — when asked what he thought about the first Russian satellite, Sputnik, he replied in all seriousness, "We should shoot it down." He did not say how. He eschewed a run for a third term on the grounds of ill health but lived happily thereafter for sixteen years in retirement.

John Marshall Butler died on March 14, 1978 at the age of eighty. He was an affable, courtly, gentlemanly man, in appearance and manner the very quintessence of a United States senator.

Endnotes to Part II, Chapter 4:

1. Cooper's *Address to the Associates* says that he and Butler started at the same time on July 5, 1927. The alumni records at the University of Maryland School of Law confirm Butler's graduation in 1926, and the records of the Court of Appeals show his admission on December 14 of that year. Strangely, it appears that he did not start working as an associate for a year after graduation and six months or so after his admission.

2. *Carey v. Howard*, 178 Md. 512 (1940).

3. Butler made the argument, accepted by the court, that Carey was better off being an obligor on his note at 5% interest than being a judgment debtor at 6%. This argument could have been turned around to suggest that Howard might have been surcharged for allowing the 1% differential to go by the board for eleven years.

4. Russell Baker, *The Good Times*, New York, William Morrow and Company, Inc., 1989, at 132.

5. Robert J. Brugger, *Maryland, A Middle Temperament*, Baltimore, the Johns Hopkins University Press, 1988, at 572-3.

6. *Id.* at 572.

Hunter H. Moss

UNTER MOSS BECAME associated with Venable, Baetjer and Howard in 1931 after graduation from the University of Virginia Law School where he had served as editor-in-chief of the *Law Review*. He had previously undergone two years of academic studies at the University of Virginia. Except for a brief tour of duty in the Merchant Marine during World War II, Moss practiced law continuously with the firm until his death on October 3, 1948. He had been made a partner on January 1, 1939 as one of the Five Juniors of that year. He was a member of the Rule Day Club.

Moss was known not only for his scholarship but also for his warm, friendly manner and keen wit. He was a practical joker but always good-natured and full of fun. His death at the age of forty-two brought to an untimely end what had promised to be an outstanding career at the bar.

Stuart S. Janney, Jr., four-time winner of The Maryland Hunt Cup, astride his winning mount, Winton.

Reproduced from the family records of Stuart S. Janney, III

Stuart S. Janney, Jr.

S TUART S. JANNEY, JR., whose father, Col. Stuart S. Janney, was a law partner of Governor Ritchie, graduated from Gilman School in 1925, from Princeton University in 1929 where he earned a Phi Beta Kappa key, and in 1932 from Harvard Law School where he was a member of the board of editors of the *Law Review*.

After graduation, Janney became an associate at Venable, Baetjer and Howard and was admitted to practice before the Court of Appeals on November 15, 1932. Except for service as a captain in the First Division of the Marine Corps during World War II, participating in some of the bloodiest battles of the South Pacific conflict, he practiced law with the firm until his retirement in 1959 at the age of fifty-one. He had been made a partner on January 1, 1939 as one of the Five Juniors of that year.

Janney was an authority in the field of trusts, estates, and related tax matters. He might have gone down as one of the firm's ablest lawyers had he continued in practice, his major weakness being that he did not suffer fools gladly, even if they were valued clients. Perhaps this impatience reflected his growing dissatisfaction with the daily grind at the office, intensified by his love of horses and the diversion they provided. He had been a four-time winner of the

Maryland Hunt Cup, retiring from competition at the age of thirty-nine, a former chairman of the Maryland Racing Commission, and a successful breeder of race horses in his own right. He decided to devote himself full time to that vocation.

In this endeavor he was also successful. Before his thoroughbred, Ruffian, suffered a broken leg in a match race with Foolish Pleasure at Belmont Park in 1975 and had to be destroyed, she had been hailed as the best filly to run in the United States. In 1988, the year of his death, Janney had produced Private Terms and Finder's Choice, two of the top three-year-olds of the year, the former being one of the favorites in the Kentucky Derby.

Janney was a director of Mercantile-Safe Deposit & Trust Company and a trustee of Johns Hopkins University and Johns Hopkins Hospital. He left a million dollar bequest to the Johns Hopkins Oncology Center.

Stuart Janney died on September 22, 1988 in an automobile accident resulting from a heart attack. He was predeceased by his wife, the former Barbara Phipps, a granddaughter of Henry Phipps who endowed the Johns Hopkins psychiatric center that still bears his name. He was survived by three daughters, Sheila Janney Williams, Barbara Janney Trimble, and Sarah Janney Rose, and a son, Stuart S. Janney, III, a third generation member of the Maryland bar.

Stuart Janney had been an ornament to the ranks of lawyers at Venable, Baetjer and Howard and a distinguished Maryland citizen.

PART II, CHAPTER 7

Norwood B. Orrick

NORWOOD **B. ORRICK** was the youngest of the Five Juniors admitted to partnership at Venable, Baetjer and Howard on January 1, 1939.

Born in Cumberland, Maryland on October 5, 1908, he attended the Episcopal High School in Alexandria, Virginia and went on to undergraduate studies at the University of Virginia and from there to the Virginia Law School. He graduated with his LL.B degree in 1932 having served as editor-in-chief of the *Law Review*.

In the fall of 1931 in the depths of the Great Depression, Orrick applied for a job at Venable, Baetjer and Howard. Joseph France seems to have been the partner in charge of what we would now call recruiting — although in those days the task entailed little more than signing a form letter informing applicants that no openings existed. These letters were then routinely dumped into a file with the caption "Law Students Looking for Jobs."[1] Orrick was one of the few whose application was not thus summarily dismissed, for a memorandum dated November 20, 1931 bearing the initials "J. F." records Orrick's address in Charlottesville and the fact that his father was Jesse Lewis Orrick of Cumberland.

As subsequent events have established, Orrick had much more going for him than ancestry, notably a keen legal mind. France, perceiving this capability, offered him a job, at least tentatively, and suggested an interview. Orrick's response of May 16, 1932 was as follows:

Dear Mr. France:

Many thanks for your letter of May 14th. I will be only too delighted to come to Baltimore to see you. I can be there all day, Saturday, May 21st. However, if either Friday the 20th, or Monday the 23rd would be more convenient to you, please wire me collect at the Phi Psi House, University of Virginia to that effect. If I do not hear from you, I will assume that Saturday will be satisfactory.

From the way things look now, I doubt if I could start work before June 24th.

Sincerely yours,

Norwood Orrick

France replied laconically by letter, not collect telegram, that Saturday morning the 21st would be satisfactory. The interview must have been productive, since Orrick started working for Venable, Baetjer and Howard as an associate on July 5, 1932, thus allowing him a week's vacation plus the Independence Day holiday. It took him only six and one-half years thereafter to make partner as one of the Five Juniors of 1939.

Over the next 57 years until July 5, 1989 when he retired, he was active in the civic and cultural life of the Baltimore community in addition to holding down an active legal practice and participating widely in bar association activities. Among his accomplishments was his service on the board and as president of the Baltimore County Library trustees when this organization was in the fledgling stage; it later became the public library with the largest *per capita* circulation in the country. He served on the Mayor of Baltimore City's Civil Rights Committee and also as a member of the Lawyers' Committee on Civil Rights under Law.

Few Maryland lawyers have been more active in service to the profession and in the improvement of our laws. He was president both of the Bar Association of Baltimore City and the Maryland State Bar Association. He was a member of the State Commission to Study the Bankruptcy Laws and a similar Committee to Study the Uniform Consumer Credit Code. He was a perennial member and often chairman of bar association committees and also a member of two law clubs, the Wranglers and the Lawyers' Round Table.

Orrick entered the profession at a time when general practice was the order of the day, but as the years went by he became more and more known as a specialist in corporation law, banking law and the law dealing with creditors' rights.

His first appearance in the Court of Appeals occurred only five years after his admission to the bar — a wrongful death case in which he represented a Captain James C. Sammon, the pilot of a biplane which collided, fatally, with a young boy on a bicycle who crossed the path of the descending aircraft as it made its final approach to landing.[2] The scene was at the old Curtiss-Wright Airport off Greenspring and Smith Avenues in the Mount Washington area. The occasion was an air show complete with parachute jumping and other daredevil aerobatics. It was to be preceded by a toy balloon contest sponsored by the local department store, Hochschild, Kohn & Co. Counsel for the parents of the deceased boy, true to form for plaintiff's counsel, sued everyone in sight — not only the pilot (Orrick's client), but also the owner of the airport, the owner of the plane, and Hochschild, Kohn. The case against the owner of the airport was dropped after its demurrer had been sustained and the plaintiff elected not to amend. Judge Solter in the Court of Common Pleas of Baltimore City granted a directed verdict for all other defendants.

The Court of Appeals (5-3) affirmed the dismissal as to Hochschild, Kohn but reversed as to the other defendants, i.e., the owner and operator of the plane. The court held that jury questions remained as to whether the pilot should have "fishtailed" his aircraft in order to eliminate the blind spot caused by his lower wing. In the primitive days of aircraft navigation "fishtailing" was a technique of wiggling the forward direction of the plane so as to afford the pilot a visual line of sight to objects that might be in his way on the runway below. The appellate court also ruled Judge Solter in error in declaring as a matter of law that the boy on the bicycle was guilty of contributory negligence, and the case was remanded for further proceedings in accordance with the opinion. Three judges, among the most respected at the time (Bond, Parke, and Sloan, J. J.), dissented and would have affirmed Orrick's victory in the lower court.

Sammon was a case filled with drama and human interest, the majority opinion by Judge Urner reading like a well-written short story. The archives of the Court of Common Pleas at the Hall of Records confirm the anticlimax that on remand the case was settled for an undisclosed sum.

During World War II, Orrick served as an officer in the United States Naval Reserve, joining ranks with Janney and Dandridge who also left the firm to fight the war. Like other firms, it must have been left seriously shorthanded.

In addition to the *Sammon* case, Orrick's appearance is entered in 18 other cases in the decisions of the Court of Appeals, eight of which were argued while he served as Assistant Attorney General of Maryland. In private practice his cases covered a wide variety of subjects, including the scope of application of the Maryland Use Tax,[3] wills, trusts, and estates,[4] torts,[5] construction of a percentage lease,[6] the validity of an assignment of an expectancy,[7] and establishing title by adverse possession.[8] He also played an active role in the *Penn Water* litigation in the federal courts, as described in the chapter on John Henry Lewin, and his other federal appearances involved wrongful death,[9] contracts,[10] admiralty,[11] patent infringement,[12] antitrust,[13] federal procedure,[14] a court appointment for a petitioner in a *habeas corpus* case,[15] representation of the Maryland Bankers Association as *amicus curiae* in a case involving methods of concern to the banking industry,[16] and civil rights.[17]

One of Orrick's most prestigious clients was International Telephone and Telegraph Company (ITT), which had been incorporated in Maryland in 1920. Every year it would engage in some transaction such as a new issue of preferred stock or convertible securities, an acquisition, or articles of amendment that would compel its Wall Street counsel, Davis, Polk, Wardwell, Sunderland & Kiendl, to consult Maryland counsel on the local law aspects. Not exactly a major piece of rainmaking, this was, nevertheless, what Harry Baetjer would describe as a "ground rent" — a reliable source of regular revenue. Eventually, ITT lost patience with the state legislature's delays in bringing the Maryland General Corporation Law into the twentieth century, particularly provisions dealing with short form mergers and the indemnification of officers and directors. ITT reacted by moving its corporate situs to Delaware. It was a loss to Maryland's reputation as a hospitable domicile for big business, and also a loss for Orrick and the firm.

Another client and personal friend was Robb Tyler. Shortly after World War II, Tyler went into the trash disposal business with the motto "We Never Refuse Refuse" emblazoned on his dumpsters. Tyler was always in trouble with the zoning officials and complaining neighbors as his sanitary landfills erupted into flames. Putting Tyler's fires out became both a literal and figurative assignment of duty for Orrick. Yet, despite Tyler's difficulties with the authorities and the neighbors, his business flourished over the years and was sold in 1970 at a handsome price to Browning-Ferris Industries, Inc., a national concern. Thereafter, Orrick and others at Venable, Baetjer and Howard represented Browning-Ferris as a continuing and valued client.

Orrick was a trout fisherman of note, his favorite stream being the Cowpasture River in Virginia. One summer he visited the Seven-D Ranch near Cody, Wyoming and could be seen working the pools and eddies of Sunlight Creek with his fly rod. While duffers snarled their lines in tree branches by the stream, Orrick would deftly place his lure exactly where he wanted it. The rest was history. Trout for breakfast.

He was also artistically gifted, and some of his oil paintings of Baltimore scenes, notably Tyson Street on a snowy night and the Washington Monument, have been much admired.

He was married on June 12, 1935 to Ruth Hughes and they had three children, Bentley, William, and Phyllis. The younger son, Bill, was killed in an automobile accident in February, 1970. For most of their married life the Orricks lived in a charming rambling house on Club Road in Ruxton. Following Ruth's death in 1986, Orrick moved into Roland Park Place, a retirement community, and the Ruxton residence was sold.

Norwood Orrick was a lawyer's lawyer and dean of the corporate bar. When he closed his office on July 5, 1989, exactly 57 years after his arrival in 1932, the firm lost one of its ablest members.

Endnotes to Part II, Chapter 7:

1. Venable, Baetjer and Howard File No. 15586 (9/25/31).

2. *State to the use of Birckhead v. Sammon*, 171 Md. 178 (1936).

3. *Comptroller of the Treasury v. American Can Co.*, 208 Md. 203 (1955).

4. *Rippon v. Mercantile Bank & Trust Co.*, 213 Md. 215 (1957), upholding the validity of an *inter-vivos* trust; *Mercantile Safe-Deposit & Trust Co. v. Apponyi*, 220 Md. 275 (1959), another unsuccessful effort by a partner at Venable, Baetjer and Howard to overturn the Pennsylvania Rule of Apportionment in trust accounting practice.

5. *Buczkowski v. Canton Railroad Company*, 181 Md. 377 (1943).

6. *Walker V. Associated Dry Goods Corporation*, 231 Md. 168 (1963).

7. *Scott v. First National Bank*, 224 Md. 462 (1960), applying Connecticut law.
8. *Ridgely v. Lewis*, 204 Md. 563 (1954).

9. *Goldsmith v. Martin-Marietta Corp.*, 211 F. Supp. 91 (D. Md. 1962); *United States v. Guyer*, 218 F.2d 266 (4th Cir. 1954), affirming with modifications *Snyder v. United States*, 118 F. Supp. 585 (D. Md. 1953).

10. *Morse v. Arthur H. Richland Company*, 272 F.2d 183 (4th Cir. 1959), affirming *Richland v. Morse*, 169 F. Supp. 544 (D. Md. 1959).

11. *Atlantic Steamer Supply Company v. The Ss. Tradewind*, 153 F. Supp. 354 (D. Md. 1957), supplementing 144 F. Supp. 408 (D. Md. 1956).

12. *Cummins Engine Company v. General Motors Corporation*, 424 F.2d 1368 (4th Cir. 1973) affirming 299 F. Supp. 59 (D. Md. 1969); *Technograph Printed Circuits, Ltd. v. Martin-Marietta Corp.*, 474 F.2d 798 (4th Cir. 1973), affirming 340 F. Supp. 423 (D. Md. 1972).

13. *Lanier Business Products v. Graymar Company*, 342 F. Supp. 1200 (D. Md. 1972). See Part III, Ch. 3 at note 3, *infra*, for a discussion of the significance of this case in the career of Benjamin R. Civiletti.

14. *Moore v. Firedoor Corporation of America*, 250 F. Supp. 683 (D. Md. 1966).

15. *Bowler v. Warden of Md. Penitentiary*, 219 F. Supp. 25 (D. Md. 1963).

16. *United States v. Bland*, 159 F. Supp. 395 (D. Md. 1958). Orrick also filed briefs as amicus for the Bankers Association in two state court cases, *B. F. Saul Co. v. West End Park North, Inc.*, 250 Md. 707 (1968) and *Falcone v. Palmer Ford, Inc.*, 242 Md. 487 (1960).

17. *Dobson v. Mayor and City Council of Baltimore City*, 330 F. Supp. 1290 (D. Md. 1971), an unsuccessful attempt to overturn a redistricting plan on the ground that it discriminated against black voters.

EDWIN G. BAETJER
CHARLES McH. HOWARD
HARRY N. BAETJER
JOSEPH FRANCE
————
J. CROSSAN COOPER, JR.
JOHN M. BUTLER
HUNTER H. MOSS
STUART S. JANNEY, JR.
NORWOOD B. ORRICK

TELEPHONE
PLAZA 6780

VENABLE, BAETJER AND HOWARD
ATTORNEYS AT LAW
1409 MERCANTILE TRUST BUILDING
BALTIMORE & CALVERT STS.
BALTIMORE, MD.

June 17, 1936

Charles B. Reeves, Esq.
Garrett Building
Baltimore, Maryland

Dear Charlie:

(text of letter omitted)

Very truly yours,

J. Crossan Cooper, J.

JCC:EB

1936 Letterhead after the arrival of Moss, Janney and Orrick. The addressee, Mr. Charles B. Reeves, was the father of Charles B. Reeves, Jr., currently a Venable partner. The typist, "E.B." was Miss Elaine Bell, long-time secretary to J. Crossan Cooper, Jr.

Richard W. Emory

THE ARRIVAL OF Richard W. Emory as a lateral entry associate in 1945 was a significant event in the life of Venable, Baetjer and Howard. He became one of its leading litigators and served for many years as a member of the Operating Committee.

Born in Baltimore on August 20, 1913, he attended Gilman School and Harvard University. His father, German H. H. Emory, a war hero in World War I, was killed in action in France on November 1, 1918, ten days before the armistice. He had been a prominent Baltimore lawyer, a partner in the firm of Frank, Emory & Beuwkes, forerunner of Frank, Bernstein, Conaway and Goldman.

After graduating in 1938 from Harvard Law School where he was on the *Law Review*, Richard Emory spent one year as a clerk to Judge Morris A. Soper of the Fourth Circuit Court of Appeals.[1] He then sought a job in Baltimore but found that Venable, Baetjer and Howard had just taken on Raymond S. Clark as an associate, and Semmes, Bowen & Semmes had recently engaged William A. Fisher, Jr. Although those firms had been his first two choices, he had to settle for a job with Hershey, Donaldson, Williams & Stanley. He worked there for a few months in the fall of 1939 and winter of 1940 until wooed away by Hunton, Williams, Anderson, Gay & Moore (now Hunton & Williams) in Richmond with an offer of $200 more per month. After the eruption of the war in December, 1941, he entered the U.S. Navy.

Following three years' service as an intelligence officer in the South Pacific on the staffs of Admiral Nimitz and Admiral Towers, rising to the rank of Lt. Commander,[2] Emory returned to Baltimore to visit his mother. As he was walking to the train station after the visit, he encountered Stuart Janney whom he had met in the Pacific. Janney asked whether Emory would be returning to practice in Richmond. He replied that Richmond did not appeal to him, and he thought he might look around in Baltimore. Janney then said, "Why don't you come with me to see Mr. Baetjer? I am sure he will offer you a job."

So, instead of going to the train station, they reversed directions and came back to the office where Janney made the introductions to Harry Baetjer. Emory's service on the Harvard *Law Review* followed by four years of practice made him an attractive lateral entrant, and Baetjer wasted no time in concluding that Emory should be employed. It being late Friday afternoon, Baetjer asked if it would be all right if he deferred the offer until Monday after consultation with his partners. Emory was amused at Baetjer's diffidence but elated at the prospects of employment. Shortly thereafter he began working at Venable, Baetjer and Howard and became a partner on January 1, 1951.

In a career at the Maryland bar that spanned 45 years until his last case in the Court of Appeals in 1983,[3] Emory participated in a wide variety of litigation in the state and federal courts. From January 1, 1947 to June 15, 1948 he also served as Deputy Attorney General of Maryland under Attorney General Hall Hammond.

In the chapter dealing with Harry Baetjer mention has been made of the *DeLuca Davis* and *John K. Ruff*[4] cases in which Emory made new law in the field of competitive bidding for government contracts. An interesting sequel to those cases is the U.S. District Court holding in *President and Council of St. Mary's College v. Aetna Casualty & Surety Co.*[5] where Judge Roszel Thomsen, in obvious disagreement with the result in *DeLuca Davis*, reluctantly followed it after having exerted heroic efforts to force a settlement. Emory stuck to his guns, and Judge Thomsen had to yield to the clear Maryland precedent.

Emory was also active, and for the most part successfully, in the fields of condemnation,[6] public utility law,[7] administrative law,[8] bankruptcy,[9] insurance,[10] libel,[11] real estate,[12] wrongful death,[13] fiduciary relations,[14] banking,[15] patents,[16] real estate taxation,[17] corporations,[18] retail sales tax,[19] and attorney grievance.[20]

Three constitutional law cases merit special mention, one of which Emory won and the other two he lost.

In 1949, shortly after leaving the Attorney General's office, Emory was engaged by the County Commissioners of Calvert County to represent them in a dispute with the State Tax Commission over assessment procedures.[21] The Legislature had divided Baltimore City and each County into five districts and had directed the commission to reassess the real estate in each district one by one, year by year. Thus, the property in District One would be assessed on the basis of 1944 sales prices, building costs and rents, while the other four districts would continue to be assessed on the basis of 1941 standards. Worse yet, District One would always lag behind the others and would never catch up. The Calvert County Commissioners refused to send out the notices of reassessment based on these procedures, whereupon the Attorney General instituted a *mandamus* action against them to compel compliance.

Ruling in Emory's favor, Judge John B. Gray of the Circuit Court for Calvert County held these reassessment procedures violative of the Equal Protection Clause of the 14th Amendment. The State appealed.

Emory recalls the opening words of Hall Hammond's argument for the Appellant:

> May it please the Court. For the last two years Mr. Emory has distinguished himself as a General for the State. Today, he appears before the Court as the General for the Insurrection.

Without a second's wait Judge Markell interrupted, "You couldn't have described the situation more accurately!"

From this repartee Emory sensed that the case was lost before he was given a chance to open his mouth. It was. However, to the loser went the spoils as Emory became counsel for the Tax Revision Commission of 1951, and a year later, the legislature, by the Acts of 1952, Ch. 34, reversed the system of reassessing real property on an intra-county district basis. In effect, the result in *Rogan v. State Tax Commission* was overruled.

In *Howard County Metropolitan Commission v. Westphal*,[22] Emory dealt with the much litigated construction of the provision in Article 35 of the Declaration of Rights that "no person shall hold, at the same time, more than one office of profit, created by the Constitution or Laws of this State." The court held that a county commissioner could not, in the light of this prohibition, sit as a member of the Howard County Metropolitan Commission, but that two subordinate state employees were not disqualified. One was the chief of the Alcoholic Beverages Division of the Comptroller's Office and the other the chief of the right-of-way department of the State Roads Commission. Neither of these positions was found to be an "office for profit" within the meaning of the Constitution. Emory prevailed both in the lower court and the Court of Appeals.

In Emory's last case in the Court of Appeals, *Hornbeck v. Somerset County Board of Education*,[23] he was unable to uphold at the appellate level a decision in his favor by Judge David Ross of the Circuit Court for Baltimore City holding it a violation of Article 24 of the Declaration of Rights for the state to grant lower per capita funding of public school education in Baltimore City and in Somerset, Caroline, and St. Mary's Counties than in the more opulent jurisdictions with greater property wealth behind each pupil. Applying a strict constructionist attitude, Chief Judge Murphy reversed the lower court, while the dissenting Judge Cole insisted that the prevailing funding practices were in violation of the constitutional requirement that a "thorough and efficient system of Free Public Schools" be maintained by the state. It is difficult to believe that the majority result in *Hornbeck* would obtain today.

One of Emory's most publicized victories was in a *nisi prius* case that was never appealed but has been recognized as a landmark in its field.[24] Carter Products, Inc., having been for many years privately owned by the Hoyt family, went public with a prospectus which announced that after the secondary offering it expected to list its shares on the New York Stock Exchange. This it did, but later its board of directors recommended and the stockholders approved a charter amendment for the creation of a new class of non-voting common stock which would be issued as a stock dividend to existing stockholders. A majority of shares not held by the Hoyt family and their affiliates voted against the amendment. Under then prevailing rules of the exchange, an issuance of non-voting stock would have resulted in a delisting of all the company's shares, a fact which had been disclosed in the prospectus.

Several mutual funds which had bought Carter stock in the offering or in the aftermarket brought suit to enjoin the transaction arguing, through the advocacy of Richard Emory, that (1) the delisting would be a violation of the representation in the prospectus that the Carter shares would be listed on the exchange; and (2) the issuance of non-voting shares was motivated by no legitimate corporate purpose but only by the private purpose of enabling the family members to dispose of their stock without losing control.

Judge Reuben Oppenheimer, later a judge of the Court of Appeals, ruled in favor of Emory's clients. Listing on the exchange, he held, was a valuable corporate asset belonging to all stockholders. Also, the directors owed a "fiduciary obligation" to the minority stockholders that would be violated by sanctioning the "private purpose" of perpetuating family control. The issuance of non-voting stock would serve no useful corporate purpose not served by the issuance of voting shares, and, accordingly the injunction was ordered. The nub of the case was the loss of the listing privilege and, despite Judge Oppenheimer's rhetoric about fiduciary relationships and the need to find a corporate purpose, it may be that the injunction might not have been issued, absent this critical factor.

Carter Products is a remarkable case. Although only a lower court decision in the Circuit Court of Baltimore City, it received nation-wide publicity, including several references in Louis Loss's classic treatise, *Securities Regulation*.[25] Judge Oppenheimer's ruling was never appealed because it made multi-millionaires of the defeated defendants; Carter stock soared on the exchange after the decision was announced.

Emory's major contribution to the development of the law of Maryland was in the field of public utility rate-making. From his many appearances on behalf of Potomac Electric Power Co. (PEPCO), he came to be recognized as an authority in this highly specialized area.[26]

He was active in the civil rights movement long before it became popular. In 1956 he was named the first chairman of the Maryland Equal Employment Opportunity Commission (the EEOC) and for seventeen years, between 1950 and 1967, was a member of the board of trustees of Morgan College (now Morgan State University), serving from 1965 to 1967 as its chairman. He was a trustee of Gilman School from 1946 to 1965 and president of the board for the last nine years of that period during which time the school was integrated. Following the footsteps of Edwin G. Baetjer, Emory was an early conservationist, having served as a member of the Governor's Commission on Maryland Conservation Laws (the Bowman Commission) in 1948. He was a member of the Maryland Board of Natural Resources from 1949 to 1951.

Emory's other extracurricular activities included the chairmanship of the board of directors of Columbia Bank & Trust Co. from 1967 to 1982, and membership on the board of trustees of Johns Hopkins Hospital from 1967 to 1983.

A long time member of the Lawyers' Round Table, Emory succeeded Judge Emory H. Niles as its secretary from 1962-1969.

Richard Emory's first wife, the former Elizabeth A. Burke, died in 1969 survived by her husband and two sons, Richard W., Jr. and John B., both members of the bar. In 1970 Emory married Lila Jones Boyce, the widow of C. Meredith Boyce, and they have enjoyed many years of happiness.

After arguing the *Hornbeck* case, Emory remained for a time an elder statesman on the Operating Committee but retired from the active practice of law. As Harry Baetjer would have put it, "He was a lawyer of capacity."

Endnotes to Part II, Chapter 8:

1. Judge Soper had been a devoted friend of Richard Emory's father, German H. H. Emory, and the latter's younger son, Morris Soper Emory, was named after him. They were not related by blood.

2. See W. J. Holmes, *Double Edged Secrets*, Annapolis, U.S. Naval Institute, 1979 at 113, where the author describes Emory as "a tall, good-looking, Harvard-educated lawyer, whose keen legal mind enabled him to become an outstanding naval air intelligence officer." Emory's naval rank as Lt. Commander was on a par with Venable's military rank of Major in the Confederate Army; both were surpassed by John Pavlick, a retired Lt. Colonel in the Army and by F. Dudley Staples, Jr., a Captain in the U.S. Naval Reserve.

3. *Hornbeck v. Somerset Board of Education*, 295 Md. 597 (1983).

4. *Supra*, Part I, Ch. 1, notes 16 and 17.

5. 237 F. Supp. 787 (D. Md. 1964); aff'd 344 F.2d 331 (4th Cir. 1965).

6. *Smith v. Potomac Electric Power Co.*, 236 Md. 51 (1964); *Duvall v. Potomac Electric Power Co.*, 234 Md. 42 (1964); *Ligon v. Potomac Electric Power Co.*, 219 Md. 438 (1959); *Jeweler v. Potomac Electric Power Co.*, 217 Md. 458 (1958); *Potomac Electric Power Co. v. Birkett*, 217 Md. 476 (1958).

7. *Gainesville Utilities Dept. v. Florida Power Corp.*, 402 U.S. 515 (1971), 91 S.Ct. 1592, 29 L. Ed. 2d 74 (1971); *Florida Power Corp. v. Federal Power Comm.*, 425 F.2d 1196 (5th Cir. 1970); *Montgomery County v. Public Service Comm.*, 203 Md. 79 (1953).

8. *Mahoney v. Byers*, 187 Md. 81 (1946).

9. *David v. Annapolis Banking & Trust Co.*, 209 F.2d 343 (4th Cir. 1954); *Columbia Foundry v. Lochner*, 179 F.2d 630 (4th Cir. 1950).

10. *Coppage v. Insurance Company of North America*, 263 F.Supp. 98 (D. Md. 1967).

11. *Smith v. Esquire, Inc.*, 494 F. Supp. 967 (D. Md. 1980).

12. *Gulf Oil Corporation v. Clark*, 169 F. Supp. 717 (D. Md. 1959).

13. *Manaia v. Potomac Electric Power Co.*, 165 F. Supp. 486 (D. Md. 1958); *Manaia v. Potomac Electric Power Co.*, 163 F. Supp. 671 (D. Md. 1958); *Snyder v. United States*, 118 F. Supp. 585 (D. Md. 1954), reversed in part and affirmed in part in *United States v. Guyer*, 218 F.2d 266 (4th Cir. 1954), reversed by the Supreme Court in *Snyder v. United States*, 350 U.S. 906, 76 S. Ct. 191, 132 L.Ed. 796 (1955), the District Court's judgment being reinstated.

14. *Skeen v. McCarthy*, 46 Md. App. 434 (1980).

15. *Savings Bank of Baltimore v. Bank Commissioner*, 248 Md. 461 (1968); *University National Bank v. Wolfe*, 279 Md. 512 (1977).

16. *Toy Ideas, Inc. v. Montgomery Ward & Co.*, 172 F. Supp. 878 (D. Md. 1959); *Brock v. Brown*, 138 F. Supp. 628 (D. Md. 1956).

17. *Maryland State Fair & Agricultural Society v. Supervisor of Assessments*, 225 Md. 574 (1961).

18. *J. I. Case Credit Corp. v. Insley*, 293 Md. 483 (1982), *Southern Maryland Agricultural Association v. Magruder*, 198 Md. 274 (1951).

19. *Comptroller of the Treasury Retail Sales Tax Division v. Maryland Specialty Wire, Inc.*, 282 Md. 538 (1978), affirming 37 Md. App. 528 (1977).

20. *Attorney Grievance Commission v. Brewster*, 280 Md. 473 (1977), a victory for Emory in disciplinary proceedings against former Senator Daniel B. Brewster, the panel's sanction of reprimand being upheld.

21. *Rogan v. County Commissioners of Calvert County*, 194 Md. 299 (1949).

22. 232 Md. 334 (1968).

23. *Supra* note 3.

24. *United Funds, Inc. v. Carter Products, Inc.*, CCH Federal Securities Law Reporter ¶91,288, Circuit Court for Baltimore City (1963). It is questionable whether the views of Judge Oppenheimer, a liberal jurist, on the subject of a majority stockholder's "fiduciary obligation" to the minority would be upheld today.

25. 5 Loss, *Securities Regulation*, Boston, Little, Brown and Co., 1969 Supp., at 2204, 2767, 2806, 2808 and 2809.

26. See the cases collected *supra*, note 7.

HARRY N. BAETJER
JOSEPH FRANCE
J. CROSSAN COOPER, JR
JOHN HENRY LEWIN
JOHN M. BUTLER
HUNTER H. MOSS
STUART S. JANNEY, JR.
NORWOOD B. ORRICK

RICHARD W. EMORY
RAYMOND S. CLARK
EDMUND P. DANDRIDGE, JR.

VENABLE, BAETJER AND HOWARD
ATTORNEYS AT LAW
1409 MERCANTILE TRUST BUILDING
BALTIMORE & CALVERT STS.
BALTIMORE-2, MD.

RICHARD M. VENABLE
1839-1910
CHARLES McH. HOWARD
1870-1942
EDWIN G. BAETJER
1868-1945

October 14th, 1946.

Mr. Howard Baetjer,
5th Floor, Mercantile Trust Bldg.,
Baltimore, Md.

Dear Howard:

(text of letter omitted)

Yours

HNB:rfb.
encs-

1946 Letterhead after the election to partnership of The Five Juniors of 1939.
The typist, "rfb" was Rudolf F. Bolard, secretary to Harry N. Baetjer, before he succeeded
Joseph L. Kerr as office manager.

Edmund P. Dandridge, Jr.

E DMUND **P. DANDRIDGE, Jr.** was born on February 5, 1912, the son of Bishop Edmund P. Dandridge, the Episcopal Bishop of Tennessee. He was a Virginia gentleman with a genial personality and sense of humor. He was also an aggressive litigator.

Dandridge graduated from the Episcopal High School in Alexandria, Virginia in 1930 and from the University of Virginia in 1933, receiving intermediate honors in college and election as vice-president of his graduating class. He then attended the University of Virginia Law School from which he graduated with honors in 1936. He was also a member of the *Law Review*.

Dandridge thereupon entered the practice of law with Ritchie, Janney, Ober & Williams in Baltimore, becoming associated with Venable, Baetjer and Howard in 1940. He served as Enforcement Attorney for the Baltimore Office of Price Administration from 1942 to 1943 and then received a commission in the United States Naval Reserve, holding the rank of Lt. (j.g.) at the end of World War II. He served in Air Combat Intelligence in the South Pacific.

After the war he returned to Venable, Baetjer and Howard, becoming a partner in 1952 and specializing in litigation. He retired in 1983 and became Of Counsel to the firm.

Following the tradition of the Founders, Dandridge was active in civic and charitable enterprises. He was a member of the Draft Board from 1941 to 1943 and the State Board of Social Services from 1963 to 1969, acting as chairman for the last four years of his term. He was a member for many years of the board of managers of the Family & Children's Society (now Family & Children's Services of Central Maryland) and its president from 1965 to 1967. He was a member of the Wednesday Law Club.

He was secretary and trustee of the Robert Garrett Fund for the Surgical Treatment of Children, founded by Mary Frick Jacobs, the widow of Robert Garrett and later the wife of Dr. Henry Barton Jacobs. The income from this fund is dedicated to the pediatric surgery unit at the Johns Hopkins Hospital and over the years has been a major source of funds for that institution.

Dandridge also was a trustee of St. Timothy's School and the Episcopal High School. As counsel for St. Timothy's he was a principal architect in the merger of that institution with Hannah More Academy.

The most hotly contested case of Dandridge's career was *Johns Hopkins University v. W. E. Hutton & Co.* on which he and John Henry Lewin worked as a team for over ten years. This case is discussed fully in the next chapter dealing with Lewin. It was an exhausting piece of litigation that came to a successful conclusion after two hard-fought battles in the Court of Appeals for the Fourth Circuit.

Another case in which Dandridge represented Johns Hopkins was *McElroy v. Mercantile-Safe Deposit & Trust Company*,[1] involving the construction of the will of Walter L. Clark, a prominent Baltimore trial lawyer and professor of law at the University of Maryland School of Law. A better example could not be found for the corollary to the cliché that a lawyer who tries his own case has a fool for a client: so is a litigator who writes his own will. Clark's testamentary document was a model of ambiguity. Its major defect was its lack of a residuary clause, although an ultimate remainder appeared to have been left to three charities, one of which was Hopkins.

The case was first argued before a panel consisting of Judges Horney, Sybert, Hammond, Marbury, and Prescott. Apparently unable to agree, the court called for reargument before an enlarged panel of seven judges, the original five being joined by Chief Judge Frederick W. Brune and Judge Emory H. Niles, Chief Judge of the Supreme Bench of Baltimore City, specially assigned. In a lengthy and scholarly opinion by Judge Niles, speaking for a unanimous court, the will was virtually rewritten to create a residuary clause and obviate an intestacy, thus enabling the three charities to take their interests upon the death of the widow.

Another victory is recorded in *Cunningham v. A. S. Abell Co.,*[2] involving a long and bitter contract dispute between *The Sun* and its carriers. A jury award of $37,500 for the plaintiffs was set aside on motion for judgment notwithstanding the verdict, a result which Dandridge sustained on appeal for his newspaper client.

One of his last appellate appearances was in *Resnick v. Kaplan,*[3] involving a dispute over the disposition of earnings of the law firm of Kaplan, Heyman, Engelman & Resnick, particularly earnings realized after the firm had been disbanded. Dandridge replaced Benjamin R. Civiletti as counsel for the Kaplan group after Civiletti had withdrawn from Venable, Baetjer and Howard to join the Department of Justice in the early days of the Carter administration. The Kaplan group was opposed by Resnick, represented by Benjamin Lipsitz. Judge Karwacki of the Circuit Court for Baltimore City awarded the Kaplan group $207,872, a sum which was reduced only slightly by the appellate court to $200,728, Resnick receiving only $29,862. The rationale of the decision was that the division should be based on the terms of the partnership agreement without regard to the amount of work done and fees produced by individual partners after the break-up of their firm. This attests to the forensic skills of Edmund P. Dandridge, Jr. but leaves open some questions as to the fairness of the result.

Other cases tried or argued by Dandridge in the Maryland appellate courts and in the federal district and circuit courts dealt with will construction,[4] torts,[5] ejectment,[6] creditors' rights,[7] domestic relations,[8] procedural questions,[9] contracts,[10] antitrust,[11] compromise and settlement,[12] banking,[13] and easements.[14]

Long active in the affairs of the Episcopal Church, Dandridge had been a vestryman, lay reader and chalicist at St. Thomas', Garrison Forest, and also a frequent delegate to the Convention of the Diocese of Maryland. For many years the Dandridges lived in the Green Spring Valley, not far from their parish church, in a rented house on the Shoemaker property known as Burnside.

After a two-year fight with cancer, Dandridge succumbed on November 21, 1989, survived by his wife, the former Ann Davis, and their three children, Ann D. Hartman, Sarah D. Lemco, and Edmund P. Dandridge, III. A memorial tribute in *The Voice*, the weekly "company newspaper" of Venable, Baetjer and Howard, of November 27, 1989 concluded:

> Ed was a litigator who had the gift of being able to disagree without being disagreeable. When it was time to be tough, he could be tough, and when it was time to relax, to laugh and to play, he could do all these things with a glad heart and infectious sense of humor. In his work habits he was thorough and painstaking. In his relationships with his partners, associates, secretaries and staff, he was always considerate of others. And in his understanding of the ethical and moral values that guide our conduct as lawyers, he epitomized the best of being a member of a learned profession.... [H]e will be sorely missed at Venable, Baetjer and Howard.

Missed, indeed, he has been.

Endnotes to Part II, Chapter 9:

1. 229 Md. 276 (1962).

2. 264 Md. 649 (1972).

3. 49 Md. App. 499 (1981).

4. *Marty v. First National Bank*, 209 Md. 210 (1956); *Davis v. Mercantile Trust Co.*, 206 Md. 278 (1955); *Black v. Gary*, 199 Md. 354 (1952); *Hitchens v. Safe Deposit & Trust Co.*, 193 Md. 62 (1949).

5. *Buczkowski v. Canton Railroad Co.*, 181 Md. 377 (1943).

6. *Berlinsky v. Eisenberg*, 190 Md. 636 (1948), a victory for Dandridge in securing a judgment evicting a tenant, followed by another victory in *Berlinsky v. Eisenberg*, 196 Md. 290 (1950) awarding damages to the landlord for the tenant's failure to vacate.

7. *Central Savings Bank v. Post*, 192 Md. 371 (1949).

8. *Hitchens v. Safe Deposit & Trust Co.*, 193 Md. 53 (1949).

9. *Hamburger v. Standard Lime & Stone Co.*, 198 Md. 336 (1951).

10. *Holder v. Maaco Enterprises*, 644 F.2d 310 (4th Cir. 1981); *Westinghouse Electric Company v. Garrett Corp.*, 601 F.2d 155 (4th Cir. 1979).

11. *A. S. Abell Co. v. Chell*, 412 F.2d 712 (4th Cir. 1969); *Neugebauer v. A. S. Abell Co.*, 474 F. Supp. 1053 (D. Md. 1979).

12. *Nalle v. First National Bank of Baltimore*, 412 F.2d. 881 (4th Cir. 1969).

13. *Lee Construction Co. v. Federal Reserve Bank of Richmond*, 558 F. Supp. 165 (D. Md. 1982).

14. *Armiger v. Lewin*, 216 Md. 470 (1958), an interesting case in which Dandridge represented John Henry Lewin in a dispute with his next-door neighbor. Fashioning new Maryland law, the Court upheld Lewin's right to dedicate to public use part of a driveway over which his neighbor had a right-of-way for egress and ingress.

John Henry Lewin arguing the Socony-Vacuum Oil *case in the United States District Court for the Western District of Wisconsin, 1938*

While on a vacation trip to New York, John Lewin and his wife, Janet, observed this sketch by John Steuart Curry in the window of an art store on Madison Avenue. The likeness and style of the protagonist being unmistakable, they bought the sketch, now owned by John Henry Lewin, Jr.

John Henry Lewin

ONE OF THE MOST colorful and capable lawyers to grace the halls of Venable, Baetjer and Howard was John Henry Lewin. He devoted 60 of his 85 years to a career at the bar of Maryland.

Born in Parkton in upper Baltimore County in 1898, Lewin graduated from the Maryland Line Public School in 1912 and in 1916 from Tome School for Boys, located in Port Deposit. Tome, now disbanded, was for many years the archrival of Gilman School in Baltimore.

Thereafter, Lewin attended the Johns Hopkins University, graduating in 1920, and Harvard Law School from which he received his LL.B. degree *cum laude* in 1923. While in college he was editor of the *News Letter* and also participated in dramatics and debating. In law school he served as an editor of the *Law Review*.

Lewin's first legal position was as an associate with the Baltimore firm of Hershey, Machen, Donaldson & Williams and later with Armstrong, Machen & Allen. He also served part-time as an assistant city solicitor and in 1929 was appointed by Governor Ritchie as special counsel to the Public Service Commission. He argued one rate case in the Supreme Court[1] and worked on the brief in another,[2] both of which were lost to Charles McHenry Howard.

John Lewin was a Democrat with a flamboyant manner and keen sense of humor. He was sometimes heard to say in his inimitable way of speaking: "Of course, there are exceptions. But by and large, yes by and large, Republicans are a *dreadful* lot."

Stricken by Potomac fever at the onset of the New Deal, he left Baltimore in 1933 to join the ranks of bright young men of liberal bent who swarmed to Washington. He first served as general counsel to the securities administrator in the Federal Trade Commission, then chief of the litigation section of the Agricultural Adjustment Administration (the AAA), one of the many New Deal agencies declared unconstitutional by the "nine old men" of the Supreme Court, as President Roosevelt called them.

From 1935 to 1944 Lewin achieved stature as a federal litigator, first serving as assistant to the attorney general in the antitrust division of the Department of Justice and becoming first assistant in 1942. He appeared as lead counsel for the government in two major antitrust cases in the Supreme Court and on the brief in a third[3] and won them all.

The most significant was the *Socony-Vacuum Oil* case in which 27 oil companies and 56 individuals had been indicted for a criminal conspiracy to fix oil prices in violation of Section 1 of the Sherman Act. The case was tried in the District Court for the Western District of Wisconsin, the jury returning a verdict of guilty as to 16 corporations and 30 individuals. As a result of new trials and judgments *non obstante veredicto* granted by the trial court,[4] the list of convicted parties was pared down to 12 corporations and 5 individuals. The corporate defendants were each fined $5,000 and each individual defendant $1,000, obviously nothing more than a slap on the wrist dollar-wise. The parties nonetheless stood branded as convicted criminals. The Seventh Circuit Court of Appeals reversed the remaining convictions[5] and the case came on for argument before the Supreme Court on a writ of *certiorari*. John Henry Lewin and Thurman Arnold presented the case for the government.

The Supreme Court reversed the Seventh Circuit, reinstating the convictions in the District Court.[6] By this time the nine old men had been largely replaced by new appointees (Justices Black, Reed, Frankfurter, Douglas, and Murphy), and the court's outlook was decidedly more liberal than in the early days of the New Deal. Mr. Justice Douglas wrote an 89-page majority opinion in which he was joined by Justices Stone, Black, Reed, and Frankfurter. Justices Roberts and McReynolds, two of the survivors of the old court dissented, and Justices Hughes and Murphy took no part in the case.

The Douglas opinion was a ringing victory for Lewin and his colleagues. Agreements to fix prices in interstate commerce were held illegal *per se* under the Sherman Act. There was no formal contract among the conspirators; the conspiracy was instead "pieced together from the testimony of many witnesses and the contents of over 1,000 exhibits, extending through 3,900 printed pages of the record."[7] The indictment, drafted by Lewin, was used as a model by the Department of Justice in future price-fixing cases.

Dissenting, Mr. Justice Roberts argued that trial counsel for the government (a lawyer from Superior, Wisconsin who described himself as intimately familiar with the perambulations of the Mississippi River) had been guilty of improper and prejudicial conduct in his closing arguments. One incident, said to be prejudicial, was a reference to John Lewin and his associates as the "crusaders" and "boys" who had come from distant climes to present a case of such importance to the United States government. The lawyer said to the jury:

> Now, just between yourselves, do you honestly think that these boys here (indicating counsel at government table) fired with the enthusiasm of crusaders, as I say, and having given to the case every ounce of mental and physical strength they have, and I myself have contributed, also, would be trying to convict these men unless that was the wish and the desire of the highest officials in the Government of the United States?[8]

Later, still addressing the jury, the same Wisconsin counsel added this touch of cornball humor:

> You know, we lawyers have to depend — most of us are kind of tough guys. We have our own way of talking about witnesses. And one thing that we very often say and talk about is the three classes of liars. There is the plain liar, the damn liar and the expert witness. And of all of them, the expert witness is the worst.[9]

Sitting at the trial table, John Lewin may have cringed at the possibility that these remarks might constitute reversible error resulting in years of trial preparation going down the drain. As it turned out, there was nothing to fear. The somber Justices Roberts and McReynolds saw these acts of "clowning" as fatal flaws, but Mr. Justice Douglas was painting the picture with a broader brush. Granting that some of the statements were "highly improper," he yet held them nonprejudicial.[10]

Another case in which Lewin served as lead counsel was *American Medical Association v. U.S.*, upholding the convictions of the AMA and the Medical Society of the District of Columbia for conspiring to restrain trade or commerce in violation of Section 3 of the Sherman Act.[11] Some government employees had formed a nonprofit cooperative known as Group Health, designed to provide medical care and hospitalization to its members on a risk-sharing prepayment basis. The two medical associations had conspired to coerce individual practitioners from accepting employment by Group Health or from consulting with its doctors who might desire such dialogue. The societies had also endeavored to induce hospitals to refuse admission to patients of the Group Health physicians.

The argument in the Supreme Court resulted in a 7 to 0 opinion by Mr. Justice Roberts, two of the newer appointees, Murphy and Jackson, taking no part in the case. It was a stellar victory.

In 1944 John Lewin left government service and was admitted as a partner in Venable, Baetjer and Howard. Twenty-one years before he had applied to that firm, which at the time was not in a hiring mode, although he had been received "courteously but cooly" in an interview with Mr. Howard.[12] Accordingly, he accepted a position with Hershey, Machen, Donaldson & Williams, later moving to Armstrong, Machen & Allen. These associations, he later said, were ones he "never regretted."[13]

His new association with Venable, Baetjer and Howard in 1944 provided him with an intellectually stimulating environment necessary for the continued practice of his profession, and also the opportunity to establish a household in suburban Baltimore with his charming and artistic wife, the former Janet Gordon Keidel, and their two sons, John Henry, Jr., and Richard Carmichael (Mike).

The ensuing 30 years of practice as one of the firm's foremost litigators were filled with many civil cases of public importance and others involving millions of dollars. Big or small, important or trivial, John Lewin threw himself into each with boundless energy. Invariably, he regarded his opponent with scorn. Many of his engagements could be singled out for analysis, but in the interests of brevity only a few will be mentioned here.

The *Penn Water* litigation[14] ranked among the most important of his cases in the early 1950's. The firm represented the Consolidated Gas, Electric, Light and Power Company of Baltimore (now known as Baltimore Gas and Electric Company) in a bitter dispute with Pennsylvania Water and Power Company (Penn Water) over contracts regulating the distribution of energy from dams on the Susquehanna River, with exposure to treble damages running into enormous numbers. The case went to the Fourth Circuit Court of Appeals three times and was denied a writ of *certiorari* twice by the Supreme Court. At one time or another every associate in the firm was involved in some aspect of the case, Harry N. Baetjer, Norwood B. Orrick, and John Henry Lewin being the partners most actively participating.

In the third and final round before the Fourth Circuit Court of Appeals, the case was argued for Consolidated by Inzer B. Wyatt of Sullivan & Cromwell with Lewin, Baetjer, and Orrick on the brief, a team which achieved total victory. Despite the prior holdings that the contracts were violative of Section 1 of the Sherman Act, the Court held that Penn Water, having operated under those contracts without objection for 17 years, was estopped under the doctrine of *in pari delicto* (i.e., being equally guilty) from recovering treble damages. This vindicated Harry Baetjer's prediction from the outset that Penn Water's position was not sustainable. Given the high stakes in the litigation, this was a bold prediction. Norwood Orrick recalls having shuddered when seeing in the Consolidated proxy statement a report to the effect: "In the opinion of Venable, Baetjer and Howard, the position of Penn Water is without merit." Few lawyers would express such an opinion today, even as to litigation which seems frivolous on its face.

The *Hutton* case[15] must be listed among Lewin's most gruelling cases, one that was brought into the firm by Edmund P. Dandridge, Jr. as counsel for the Johns Hopkins University. Dandridge enlisted the help of Lewin and they operated as a team for ten years on this one engagement.

Hopkins had purchased through the brokerage firm of W. E. Hutton & Co. some $1,300,000 of oil and gas production payments which went sour, and the University thereupon filed suit against Hutton under Section 12 of the Securities Act of 1933 and Rule 10b-5 under the Securities and Exchange Act of 1934. Lead counsel on the other side was a contentious Wall Street litigator, John A. Wilson of Shearman & Sterling.

The Lewin-Dandridge team secured two summary judgments, and the case was pending on appeal when settlement discussions opened. To this point Hopkins had been pressing for rescission, but a sharp increase in oil prices in the 1970's made the production payments more valuable and their rescission less attractive. Dandridge recalled the silence that greeted his announcement: "We are no longer interested in rescission; we want money damages."

And that is what they got. Hopkins kept the oil and gas production payments and received a substantial money settlement to boot.

One of John Henry Lewin's most colorful cases was *Mark Jennings Hammett v. The Times Herald*[16] in which he represented the defendant newspaper in a libel case in the U.S. District Court for the District of Maryland.

Hammett had been named after Mark Hanna, a prominent Republican politician and William Jennings Bryan, an even more prominent Democrat. He aspired to political office even though his background and attainments had been modest. For years he had been a clerk in the Bureau of the Budget and his higher education seems to have been limited to some correspondence courses. Nonetheless, he threw his hat into the ring in the Republican primary for nomination to Congress. To bolster his candidacy he released a self-laudatory brochure describing his extensive educational experience and other achievements in glowing terms. Lewin put it this way:

> The contents, written in heroic style, in which he extravagantly extolled his merits were almost beyond belief. He claimed in addition to great learning and experience, to be the world's greatest authority on finance and taxation. His brochure ended with this paragraph:

> Possessed as I am of pleasing personality, vast erudition, social punctilio and physical pulchritude of highest order, I recommend myself to the electorate.[17]

Lewin's own report continues:

> One can imagine the glee with which the *Times Herald* columnist found a copy of this brochure. Successful work on his column was practically done for that day. He had only to make many quotations from the brochure, introducing them sarcastically with phrases like "This paragon goes on...; But this is not all . . . " etc.

> He ended the column with the quotation about physical pulchritude which I have given you plus the pungent punch line:

> Anybody like to go with him steady?[18]

The initial proceedings in the case were conducted by Hammett *pro se* during which he continued to delight John Lewin with one misspelling or malaprop after another. In an early exchange he explained that the offensive words had accused him of being a homosexual, or "ferry" — yes, "F-E-R-R-Y," or, as John Lewin later put it, "You know, the old side-wheeler kind."

In an early skirmish before Judge Chesnut, the Judge asked Lewin to be so kind as to explain precisely what innuendo plaintiff claimed to attach to the words "Anybody like to go with him steady?" The following colloquy ensued:

> *Mr. Lewin*: Your Honor, hold tight to your seat and I will tell you. Plaintiff actually contends that the term connotes homosexuality.

> *The Court*: Oh, indeed, that had not occurred to me. Fortunately, here in Baltimore we have no homosexuality. I understand, from hearsay, of course, that the phenomenon has arisen in the District of Columbia.[19]

The case came on for trial before Judge Roszel Thomsen and a jury. After two weeks of courtroom hilarity, including Lewin's display of a Capital Transit placard reading, "Anybody like to go steady with us?" and testimony by Dr. Kemp Malone, professor of English at the Johns Hopkins University and expert on dirty words, the jury rendered a verdict in favor of the newspaper. The Fourth Circuit affirmed in a per curiam opinion which said that the only error in the record was the failure of the trial judge to direct a verdict in the defendant's favor.[20] The court could thus have cut short the proceedings, but that would have taken all the fun out of the case. A case that was fun personified was *Hammett v. Times Herald*.

John Lewin was a lawyer not intimidated by the judicial robe and did not hesitate to call a spade a spade even if the remark might strike a judge's sensitive nerve. A case in point occurred when a federal judge was endeavoring to work out with counsel a trial date for an important case. Lewin's request to eliminate from consideration the period of his vacation was turned down by the judge, but a few minutes later the latter ruled out another period which was said to conflict with his vacation. Thereupon Lewin remarked, "Oh, I see. It all depends on whose vacation is being gored." It would be an understatement to say that the jurist, like Queen Victoria, was not amused.

For three weeks during the cold winter of 1961 Lewin was engaged in one of the most hotly contested trials of his career. He represented the International Brotherhood of Electrical Workers (IBEW) whose president, having revoked the charter of Local 28 for persisting in an unauthorized wildcat strike, had set up a new Baltimore local in its place. The displaced local sued for reinstatement, claiming that the revocation was taken in bad faith and constituted an unreasonably severe sanction. The courtroom was packed each day with crowds of striking workers and their families. Local 28 was represented by Patrick A. O'Doherty, a Baltimore attorney noted for his panache.

Judge Roszel Thomsen, the presiding judge, showed early irritation with O'Doherty, particularly when he would respond to the court's questions on intricate labor law issues by saying: "I don't know anything about that, Judge; I'm just a TRILE LARW-YEAR." Wisely, Local 28 engaged Melvin J. Sykes to assist O'Doherty. An outstanding scholar and advocate, Sykes anticipated the court's questions and soon had the judge's ear. From then on, the rulings began to favor the local union to the cheers of the striking multitude. The exchanges between counsel and between counsel and the court were at times tumultuous. Judge Thomsen found that IBEW's president had acted with "mixed motives" tantamount to legal malice.[21]

The argument on appeal was heard by Chief Judge Sobeloff and Judges Bell and Soper. Lewin was well known to these judges as an able lawyer, but one given to the use of vocal volume as a means of persuasion. Only a minute or so into the argument Judge Sobeloff, with customary charm, inquired whether the noise level could be "turned down by a few decibels." Although not in accordance with his style, Lewin obliged.

In a 40-page opinion,[22] Judge Soper dissenting, the Fourth Circuit reversed Judge Thomsen's findings of fact and conclusions of law, prompting Lewin to utter a phrase he often repeated, "Thank God for the Court of Appeals!"

At another time Judge Thomsen got the better of John Lewin. During one of the early skirmishes in the *Hutton* case he and his opponent, William L. Marbury, were flailing away, each oblivious to everything else in the courtroom. Amused by the intensity of the debate, the judge signaled the bailiff to remain seated as he quietly slipped into his chambers without either protagonist realizing that he was gone. According to some reports (which may be apocryphal) Judge Thomsen actually returned to the courtroom in his business suit and seated himself in the well to watch the argument continue. Whether or not this embellishment be true, it is agreed that several minutes elapsed before the warring lawyers realized no one was on the bench to hear their bellicose exchanges.

Judge Chesnut was another federal judge with whom John Lewin had many encounters, and no one was a better mimic of the judge's clipped manner of speech and use of the broad "a." Lewin loved to tell the story of the only time he had gotten a summary judgment out of Chesnut who explained the decision as follows:

> Ordinarily, I do not grant summary judgments because I'm a great believer in the jury system. However, in this case I'm constrained to grant Mr. Lewin's motion because I honestly do not see how the plaintiff can possibly prevail.

Then there was a reflective pause and Judge Chesnut continued:

> Of course I use the word "honestly" purely for purposes of emphasis.[23]

Another incident in Judge Chesnut's court occurred at a time when John Lewin, having broken his leg while stamping down a molehill on the lawn of his home in Ruxton, was hobbling around on crutches and sporting a plaster cast. He was seated on the front row with other lawyers waiting their turn to argue motions while Judge Chesnut presided over the arraignment of a defendant of Chinese extraction named Wan Duck who was charged on three counts of selling dirty noodles in interstate commerce. The defendant spoke no English and the colloquy with the bench took place through an interpreter. The dialogue went something like this:

The Court: Ask the Defendant Duck if he has counsel.

Translator: (After consultation in Chinese): No.

The Court: Ask the Defendant Duck if he desires counsel.

Translator: (After consultation in Chinese): No, can't afford counsel.

The Court: Inform the Defendant Duck that he may have counsel appointed by the Court for him free of charge if he desires counsel.[24]

At this point an attorney seated next to Lewin and perceiving what was about to happen, whispered in his ear, "John, you'd better get on your crutches and get the hell out of here or you're going to get yourself a case." Lewin was, however, so transfixed by the proceedings that he was glued to his seat.

His own description of the rest of the story is as follows:

Sure enough, after a quantity of Chinese, Duck elected counsel and Judge Chesnut graciously gave me the assignment, at the same time offering no compensation but the facilities of the Court library for consultation and research. Because of the quantity of rat dirt and hair in the shipment, which Duck admitted, we decided to plead guilty, to one count only, in full settlement; and we were duly fined $100.

I left the Courthouse but was summoned back when the Clerk, Mr. Zimmerman, interpreted the sentence as being $300 — $100 on each count. When I got to the Courthouse, Duck was in a rage, threatening to take the building apart.

We repaired to Judge Chesnut's chambers with the problem. He resolved it by summoning Clerk Zimmerman and stating: "The judgment of the Court amerced the Defendant Duck in the precise and exact sum of $100 *and no more*."[25]

Then, to the astonishment of all, Duck pulled out of his pocket a wad of $100 bills and extracted one for delivery to Mr. Zimmerman, and in perfect English with a Chinese inflection, said "Where do I pay? Where do I pay?" Even the taciturn Chesnut broke into a grin. John Lewin hobbled out of the courthouse unpaid but revelling in a story he could tell the rest of his life.

So ended the strange case of *United States v. Wan Duck*.

In a speech delivered to the partners and associates of Venable, Baetjer and Howard on November 21, 1977 Lewin described an earlier appearance before Judge Chesnut in a case in which he championed a federal regulation of bacon, his adversary on that occasion being Senator George Wharton Pepper. He said:

> Judge Chesnut was the best trial judge I've ever practiced before, but in all things he was exceedingly *precise*. One characteristic penchant was his desire to have the subject matter of the case exactly defined. Here he was confronted with the word "bacon," and he questioned us as follows:

> Let us at the outset define our terms. We should know precisely what we are talking about. Now, in my house, my wife, Mrs. Chesnut, prepares (or rather has prepared) for me each morning for breakfast (or at least on many mornings) two thin slices of a pork product, rather fatty in consistency, I may say, perhaps having a width of one inch and I should estimate as long as (or perhaps a trifle longer) than this pencil. These strips or portions are then cooked (or subjected to heat) and are served after becoming rather brown in color and fairly rigid or crisp.

Now, gentlemen, in our house we call that "breakfast bacon." In this case are we talking about a substance such as I have described?[26]

Between 1959 and 1964 Lewin was engaged in three bitter battles, designated in the decisions of the Court of Appeals as *Armco I, Armco II,* and *Armco III.* Like World Wars, they merited their Roman numeral designations. In each of these engagements, Lewin was assisted by his junior partner, Robert M. Thomas.

In *Armco I*[27] Lewin and Thomas were successful in knocking out a personal property tax assessment in excess of $13,000,000 levied against their client, Armco Steel Corporation, for the year 1957. Their case rested on a statutory construction of a Baltimore City ordinance granting an exemption for certain raw materials used by refiners of metal products.

In *Armco II*[28] the Lewin-Thomas team upheld a claim for refund of the same taxes for the years 1958 and 1959. The city had attempted to nullify the prospective effect of *Armco I* by enacting an ordinance declaring that the original legislative intent was at variance with the appellate court's construction. The ploy did not work. Speaking for the Court of Appeals, Judge Hammond said that the city could not escape the exemption "by ordaining that the earlier ordinances had not intended what we said they intended." In other words, the Court of Appeals means what it says howsoever the City Council says what it meant.

In *Armco III*[29] the city finally prevailed in its attempts to tax Armco's unrefined ores, having by this time amended the exemption to limit it to "ores and unrefined metals shipped into the city for refining *by others than the owners thereof.*" This language had the effect of preserving the exemption for the competing Asarco, a toll refiner which did not own the ores in its possession but denied the exemption to refiners such as Armco which admittedly did. Lewin's attack on the constitutionality of the amended exemption was rejected, the court observing that Armco had "'bearded the lion' on two previous occasions to the tune of some one million or more dollars." In effect, the court was saying, "Enough is enough." However that may be, the loss in *Armco III* could not take away the sweet taste of victory in *Armco I* and *Armco II*.

As a raconteur, John Lewin had no peer. He loved to recite poetry and passages of prose from the classics. One of his best was from Moby Dick. "Thar she blows! — And sparm it is!" he would exclaim with dramatic gesture and blazing eyes.

Another specialty was Casey At The Bat. No one who has heard these renditions could forget them.

Lewin enjoyed poking fun at those who act pretentiously. One of his favorites was Wendell Willkie's opening gambit in an argument before the Supreme Court. In Lewin's words the story went like this:

> He [Willkie] began sententiously, referring to his client, "This boy was born in Russia in 1905 and came to this country in 1908."
>
> He paused to let that sink in, took a sip of water and repeated for emphasis, "This boy was born in Russia in 1905 and came to this country in 1908."
>
> Whereupon Mr. Justice Murphy looked up and inquired, "How old was he when he came to this country?"[30]

Lewin was a prodigious reader and connoisseur of Shakespeare. In one of his arguments with John Wilson in the *Hutton* case the latter misquoted a passage from *Hamlet* only to find himself corrected in open court. Edmund Dandridge, who frequently accompanied him to New York for depositions in that case, observed that his bedside reading would be Shakespeare, George Eliot, or some other classic, but never *Time* or a modern novel.

Although a regular participant in the Judicial Conference of the United States Court of Appeals for the Fourth Circuit, held at the Greenbrier in White Sulphur Springs, W. Va. or at the Homestead in Hot Springs, Va. and at annual meetings of the Maryland State Bar Association, held in those days in Atlantic City, N.J., Lewin was not active in bar association politics. He was, however, for many years a member of the Wranglers, one of the oldest Baltimore law clubs.

In his waning years Lewin waged a long battle with cancer, but those privileged to visit him in the den of his home in Ruxton, converted to a hospital room, witnessed a vibrant and ever cheerful spirit. His second wife, "Tippy," the former Mary Caroline Hood-Mohr, supported her devoted "Johnny" until this gifted advocate passed to his reward on September 9, 1983.

Endnotes to Part II, Chapter 10:

1. *West v. C&P Telephone Co.*, 295 U.S. 662, 55 S. Ct. 894, 79 L. Ed. 1640 (1935).

2. *United Railways v. West*, 280 U.S. 234, 50 S. Ct. 123, 74 L. Ed. 390 (1930).
3. Lewin on the brief in: *Ethyl Gasoline Corporation v. United States*, 309 U.S. 436, 60 S. Ct. 618, 84 L. Ed. 852 (1940); Lewin as lead counsel and oral advocate in: *United States v. Socony Vacuum-Oil Co.*, 310 U.S. 150, 60 S. Ct. 811, 84 L. Ed. 1129 (1940); *American Medical Association v. United States*, 317 U.S. 519, 63 S. Ct. 326, 87 L. Ed. 434 (1943).

4. *United States v. Standard Oil Company*, 23 F. Supp. 937 (D. WD Wisc. 1938).

5. *United States v. Socony-Vacuum Oil Co., Inc.*, 105 F.2d 809 (7th Cir. 1939).

6. *Supra* note 3.

7. 310 U.S. at 150.

8. *Id.* at 265.

9. *Id.* at 266.

10. *Id.* at 242.

11. *Supra* note 3.

12. *Reminiscences* at 4, an address by John Henry Lewin to the partners and associates of Venable, Baetjer and Howard on October 4, 1972 (hereafter cited as the "Reminiscences").

13. *Id.* Arthur W. Machen, the father of the author, later withdrew from Hershey, Machen, Donaldson & Williams to form Armstrong, Machen & Allen, and Lewin went with him.

14. *Pennsylvania Water & Power Co. v. Consolidated Gas, Electric Light & Power Co.*, 184 F.2d 552 (4th Cir. 1950); Supplemental Opinion 186 F.2d 934 (4th Cir. 1951); *Consolidated Gas, Electric Light & Power Co. v. Pennsylvania Water & Power Co.*, 194 F.2d 89 (4th Cir. 1952); *Pennsylvania Water & Power Co. v. Consolidated Gas, Electric Light & Power Co.*, 209 F.2d 131 (4th Cir. 1953). *Certiorari* was denied in each of these cases.

15. *Johns Hopkins University v. W. E. Hutton & Co.* Plaintiff's motion for summary judgment was granted by the U.S. District Court for the District of Maryland (Kaufman, J.), 297 F. Supp. 1165 (D. Md. 1968); on appeal to the Court of Appeals for the Fourth Circuit, the judgment was affirmed in part and reversed in part, the case being remanded for further proceedings. 422 F.2d 1124 (4th Cir. 1970); on remand the District Court again granted summary judgment for Plaintiff, 343 F. Supp. 245 (D. Md. 1972); and on the second appeal the Circuit Court once again affirmed in part and reversed in part, 488 F.2d 912 (4th Cir. 1973). At this juncture, ten long years after Dandridge's file was opened on October 28, 1963, the fatigued parties settled the case.

16. *Hammett v. Times Herald, Inc.*, 227 F.2d 328 (4th Cir. 1955).

17. *Reminiscences* at 12.

18. *Id.*

19. *Id.* at 13.

20. *Supra* note 11.

21. *Parks v. International Brotherhood of Electrical Workers*, 203 F. Supp. 288 (D. Md. 1962). The firm was forced to give up its representation of IBEW in 1970 when it acquired the firm of labor law specialists, Cook & Cluster, which represented only management.

22. *Parks v. International Brotherhood of Electrical Workers*, 314 F.2d 886 (4th Cir. 1963).

23. Paraphrased from *Reminiscences* at 16.

24. *Id.*

25. *Id.*

26. An expanded version of the *Reminiscences* delivered five years later on November 21, 1977. See *supra* note 7.

27. *Armco Steel Corporation v. State Tax Commission*, 221 Md. 33 (1959).

28. *State Tax Commission v. Armco Steel Corporation*, 226 Md. 533 (1961).

29. *Armco Steel Corporation v. State Department of Assessments and Taxation*, 236 Md. 168 (1964). The brevity of the summary of this case in the text belies its complexity, the record containing "extensive testimony" and "innumerable exhibits." The record extract alone contained 546 pages. 236 Md. at 173.

30. *Reminiscences* at 1.

Top: *H. Vernon Eney signing the draft Constitution at the State House, January 10, 1968*

Bottom: *Benjamin R. Civiletti at the swearing-in ceremony, August 16, 1979 in the presence of Gaile L. Civiletti and Chief Justice Warren E. Burger*

PART III

The Innovators

THE FORTY YEARS since the arrival of H. Vernon Eney at Venable, Baetjer and Howard in 1951 have witnessed an explosive growth in the size of the firm, coupled with significant changes in the make-up of its personnel, the range of its practice, its firm governance, its geographical presence and its institutional personality.

In size, it has grown from 12 lawyers (10, not counting Eney and the author) to 273.

In the make-up of its personnel, it has been transformed into a heterogeneous group of lawyers of different races, creeds and color. Women lawyers, non-existent in 1951, now account for 25% of the roster of attorneys.

In its legal practice, the firm has expanded the range of its Founders and Caretakers, (primarily corporations, finance, creditors' rights, trusts and estates, and general litigation) into specialty fields such as taxes, employee relations, immigration, family relations, pension and retirement benefits, hospital and health care, environmental matters, government contracts, franchises, patents and other aspects of intellectual property, and international trade.

In firm governance, it has been changed from a triumvirate into a structured organization embodying a Management Committee, a

Firm Committee, a chief executive officer known as the managing partner, a chief administrative officer known as the executive director, and a plethora of committees, each with assigned duties and areas of responsibility.

In geographical presence, the firm has expanded from one floor in the old Mercantile Trust Building on Baltimore and Calvert Streets to eight and one-half floors in the building of the same name in the revitalized Hopkins Plaza, plus other offices in Washington, D.C., Tysons Corner, Va., and Towson, Bel Air and Rockville, Md.

In the area of institutional personality the firm has undergone changes that may be the least conspicuous but the most significant, i.e., those resulting from the transformation of the practice of law from a profession into a business. No longer may its partners indulge, as did the Founders and Caretakers, in the luxury of unlimited legal services free of charge to charitable institutions; no longer may they calculate a fee based solely on their subjective assessment of what the services were worth, but rather must base it (or be excused by a billing committee for not basing it) on posted time charges. These and many other changes that have come about in the legal profession over the last four decades have necessarily affected the attitudes of its members towards the institution in which they practice. As law firms grow in size, the forces that divide become stronger than those that unite, a fact reflected in the increasing number of lawyers who change their affiliations after years of association with one firm. All these developments have found expression in varying degrees at Venable, Baetjer and Howard.

The three lawyers, here denominated as the Innovators, who have led the firm during these metamorphoses have been H. Vernon Eney, Jacques T. Schlenger and Benjamin R. Civiletti. The three chapters of this Part III are devoted to their careers in this period of dramatic change.

VENABLE, BAETJER AND HOWARD
ATTORNEYS AT LAW
1409 MERCANTILE TRUST BUILDING
BALTIMORE & CALVERT STS.
BALTIMORE-2, MD.

January 25, 1955

Mr. C. Maynard Wagner
Wagner's Food Stores, Inc.
2313 Homewood Avenue
Baltimore 18, Maryland

Dear Maynard:

(text of letter omitted)

Sincerely,

H. Vernon Eney

HVE:MH
Encs.

1955 letterhead after the 1951 arrival of H. Vernon Eney and before the population explosions of the 1960's, 1970's and 1980's.

H. Vernon Eney, 1908-1980.

H. Vernon Eney

ERNON ENEY WAS born on August 16, 1908, his family then residing in a section of Baltimore County known as Valley View on Belair Road.[1] While he was still an infant, or perhaps a toddler, the family moved to North Monroe Street in Baltimore City, and his parents continued to live in three different houses on that street until 1940 when they moved to suburban Anneslie.

Vernon's father, William Irvin Eney, was a carpenter by trade, later a foreman — or construction supervisor, as the job description is known today. He and his wife, Minnie Florence, were wise in the ways of rearing children and produced a family of achievers: Vernon, whose accomplishments as a lawyer speak for themselves; his youngest brother, Donald, a specialist in pediatric allergies on the staff of Johns Hopkins School of Medicine; an elder brother, Gilbert, a musician who played the bass viol in the Baltimore Symphony Orchestra, the National Symphony and, at the peak of his career, in the Philadelphia Symphony; and another elder brother, William Joseph, a professor of Engineering at Lehigh University. A younger sister, Alice, and a half-brother, Irvin Nimrod, the manager of a radio station, rounded out the family.

After the Eneys had moved to Monroe Street and Vernon had graduated from Junior High at Public School No. 78, he entered Baltimore Polytechnic Institute, completing his studies in February, 1926. It was then that he decided that he wanted to become a lawyer.

His family scoffed at the idea. He had never been to college and had no chance of entrance into an accredited law school that would provide an entree into a learned profession. But coincidentally in that spring of 1926 another important event occurred in the life of Vernon Eney — he met his future bride and wife of nearly 50 years, Margaret F. Davis. They had attended Public School No. 78 at the same time but had never met until that day in April, 1926. There ensued a courtship that lasted five years until their marriage on April 24, 1931. During that period it was she, the ever loyal and devoted Peg, who more than anyone encouraged Vernon to persevere in his ambition to become a lawyer. Without that support in those days and without the same support over nearly half a century thereafter, one may question whether such a career at the bar would have materialized.

After graduating from high school, Eney was employed as a clerk by the Chesapeake & Potomac Telephone Company and in the fall of 1926 enrolled in the night school of the University of Baltimore School of Law. Only a few weeks later on October 26, 1926 and while still working for the telephone company in the daytime, he applied for a job as a clerk with the law firm of Armstrong, Machen & Allen, legal counsel for his father's employer, Frainie Brothers, Inc., a building contractor.

To the young law student it must have been a source of disappointment (to one of lesser ambition it would have been a source of disillusionment) that his letter went unanswered, not even acknowledged, for five months. One may, therefore, imagine his thrill on receiving Wendell Allen's letter of March 30, 1927 inviting him to come in for an interview. The letter is preserved among the Eney family archives.

Allen's letter implies that Armstrong, Machen & Allen did not expect to offer much in the way of compensation, thus dampening expectations with the caveat: "I do not feel, however, that it would be advantageous to you to give up a good position for a position such as the one we have to offer at this time."

That was not enough to cool the ardor of H. Vernon Eney. He attended the interview and made such an impression on Alexander Armstrong and his partners that a few days later they offered him employment as a clerk for a handful of dollars per week. He accepted with alacrity and gave up his daytime job with the telephone company. Then only nineteen years old, Eney entered into his new vocation with gusto. John Henry Lewin, then the only associate at Armstrong, Machen & Allen, described Vernon's early work attitudes in these words: "My, oh my, how eager to please!"

Graduating from law school in the spring of 1929 and passing the bar examinations, Eney was ineligible to become a practicing lawyer because he was under the age of twenty-one. He had to wait until November 7, 1929 to be sworn in.

Even before his admission to the bar, he had become an invaluable associate at Armstrong, Machen & Allen. His innate gift for the law was stimulated by exposure to the scholarship of the two senior partners, by the trial expertise of Wendell Allen and, perhaps most significantly, by intimate contact with John Henry Lewin, whose training and experience on the Harvard *Law Review* had equipped him with an aptitude for research and analysis. Vernon Eney absorbed these talents and they became his own.

In 1933, less than four years after his admission to practice before the Court of Appeals, Vernon Eney became a partner at Armstrong, Machen & Allen. Between 1938 and 1940 he served as assistant attorney general of Maryland under Attorney General William C. Walsh, and three years after his return to full-time private practice the firm's name was changed to Armstrong, Machen, Allen & Eney, the senior partner, Alexander Armstrong, having died in the meanwhile.

With the outbreak of World War II, Eney assisted the war effort by doing volunteer work for the draft board but fidgeted at not being where the action was. Because of his age and parental status he was immune from the draft, but that only intensified his discomfiture. He applied to the Army and was offered a commission as a major, but it would have entailed a desk job in Washington, something for which he had no taste. Then, he turned to the Navy which offered him a 90-day training course in Quonset, Rhode Island leading to a Lt. (j.g.) commission as an Air Combat Intelligence Officer. He left for Quonset in August, 1943, and after receiving his commission and spending Christmas leave with his family in Baltimore, set out for the West Coast on January 10, 1944. Another Maryland lawyer, J. Gilbert Prendergast, later a judge on the Supreme Bench of Baltimore City, was in the same class with Eney at Quonset and on the same train as they departed for the war zone.

After further training at sea, Eney shipped out for the South Pacific aboard the USS *Sargeant Bay*, a small aircraft carrier converted from a Merchant Marine ship. These were ungainly vessels, notoriously fair game for the Japanese Kamikaze brigade. Eney's ship saw action in the Iwo Jima and Okinawa operations and, after the war, returned to the States unscathed.

Back to Armstrong, Machen, Allen & Eney after his discharge, Vernon Eney resumed the practice of law in Baltimore. With Allen's withdrawal in 1946, the firm name was changed to Armstrong, Machen & Eney, my father and Vernon Eney being the only partners. Upon the former's death on May 27, 1950, Eney found himself with a burgeoning practice but no partners with whom to share the load. He was pursued by every major firm in town.

After many discussions and much thought, he settled on Venable, Baetjer and Howard as the assembly of lawyers whose traditions and outlook seemed closest to those to which he was accustomed, and the merger of the two firms took place on June 27, 1951. Eney entered as a partner and I as an associate. Robert M. Thomas, an assistant attorney general, was slated to join the firm as an associate upon his return to private practice, and the only other associates on the roster at the time were Edmund P. Dandridge, Jr. and André W. Brewster.[2]

At the time of Vernon Eney's arrival, Venable, Baetjer and

Howard was a stodgy institution, deeply mired in the long-standing ways of its Founders and Caretakers. In the 51 years since its formation only nine new partners had been added — Harry N. Baetjer some time before 1917, Joseph France in 1929, the Five Juniors in 1939, John Henry Lewin in 1944, and Richard W. Emory in 1951. Not exactly a growth record.

On the operational side it was also antediluvian, geared to the lifestyles of lawyers of independent means with little concern for a partner's need to subsist on professional earnings. Thus, each partner, regardless of seniority, received a monthly draw of $500. Since the firm had no cash capital account and each year's working capital was derived from the previous year's undistributed profits, no distribution from the current year's earnings, other than the $500 monthly draw, would customarily be made until some time in the fourth quarter of the year. So, if a partner lacked investment income or accumulated savings, he might be hard pressed to pay the rent, mortgage, tuition bills or what-have-you.

Tax information was also slow in arriving in those days, generally only a day or so before income tax returns were due. Thus, no opportunity was provided for sensible tax planning. No time sheets were kept, and there was no firm-wide schedule of hourly rates.

Horrified as he was at these unbusinesslike methods, Vernon Eney displayed his wisdom in sublimating his urge to change things. Harry Baetjer was the undisputed head of the firm and was content in having things done exactly as they had been done for the last 40 years. Joseph Kerr, the firm's office manager, who was also in charge of opening all files and maintaining the file docket, had been doing everything the same way for almost the same length of time. A palace revolution would have erupted if Eney had barged in with changes designed to bring the firm's operations into the 20th century. He bided his time.

An opportunity presented itself on Kerr's death. Eney engineered his replacement with Rudolph Bolard, previously Mr. Baetjer's secretary, and employed Miss Irma Bienemann to satisfy Mr. Baetjer's limited secretarial needs. Under the watchful eye of Vernon Eney, Rudolph Bolard overhauled the firm's bookkeeping system, and monthly statements started making their appearances at firm meetings. Quarterly tax data were presented to partners, and with the cooperation of the firm's accountants, annual audited statements were produced in early February or late January instead of mid-March. Eney was beginning to leave his fingerprints on the way things were done at Venable, Baetjer and Howard.

By January 1, 1959, still eight years before Harry Baetjer stopped coming to the office on a regular basis, Vernon Eney had become the dominant executive. In this capacity he positioned the firm for the acquisition of Schlenger & Steinmann in 1963 and Cook & Cluster in 1970, two of the major events of the Eney era.

Eney had a keen perception of the evolutionary changes taking place in the practice of law, leading to a realization that certain specialties could not be effectively homegrown. In particular, the fields of tax and labor law seemed to him areas in which a little learning is a dangerous thing and that, if the firm were to move forward both efficiently and safely in these areas, it needed a cadre of experts who were undeniably qualified as specialists. The firm had so far held its own in both fields in a modest way, but Eney perceived that this would not be enough if the firm were to survive as a major regional institution in the years ahead.

As a first step, he negotiated in 1963 the acquisition of the firm of tax specialists known as Schlenger & Steinmann, the senior partner, Jacques T. Schlenger, becoming a partner at Venable, Baetjer and Howard, and Frederick Steinmann coming in as an associate. These two formed the nucleus of a tax department which, twenty-seven years later in 1990, boasted 48 lawyers. In 1970 Eney managed the acquisition of Cook & Cluster, a firm of labor specialists, the principals, A. Samuel Cook and Raymond Cluster becoming partners and Lawrence S. Wescott coming in as an associate. Twenty-one years later the firm had 25 lawyers in its labor department.

Another change that occurred during Vernon Eney's regime as the firm's chief executive officer had to do with its ethnic and social make-up. Before his arrival in June, 1951 every partner was a subscriber to the Bachelors Cotillon, this being the emblem of male aristocracy in old Baltimore society. The fact that Vernon Eney had not been born into this stratum was a matter of indifference to the other partners who welcomed him into their midst because of his stature at the bar and his reputation as a scholar and a gentleman. Still, his advent brought about a change in attitudes at Venable, Baetjer and Howard.

It is idle to speculate whether ancestry had anything to do with the partnership selection process before 1951, although the record would suggest that it probably did; suffice it to say that thereafter only professional excellence and integrity were the watchwords. Thus, Venable, Baetjer and Howard became the first elitist firm in Baltimore to admit Jewish partners, and by the time of Eney's death in 1980 there were 10. Women and black lawyers were also first admitted as associates during Eney's tenure, the first woman being Arlene R. Bernstein in 1966 and the first black being Ralph A. Ford in 1972. Although Eney was not a starry-eyed liberal in the field of race relations (he once delivered a law club paper defending Maryland's miscegenation statute), his prejudices mellowed with the times, and innovations made in his regime bore fruit in future years. Thus, by January 1, 1991 the firm had 17 women and four black partners, one of the latter and several of the former having been with the firm since the beginning of their careers.

Vernon Eney was also instrumental in introducing businesslike methods into the firm's record-keeping and billing procedures. In 1959 all lawyers except Harry Baetjer were required to maintain daily time sheets, and it was then up to each secretary to transcribe that information onto forms in each individual client's file. It was a primitive system but at least a partner would know how much time had been spent on a particular matter when he prepared a bill. It would then be up to him to apply whatever hourly rate he thought appropriate. Later, the sheets were routed to a clerk in the bookkeeping office who posted the time records to each individual client, but it was still a cumbersome manual system. In 1973 the firm promulgated a schedule of hourly rates for each lawyer and, through the agency of a computer service bureau in Philadelphia, was enabled for the first time to produce electronically a suggested fee based on time charges. In 1982, after Eney's death, the firm acquired its own computer so that this information could be generated in-house.

Shortly after Eney's admission to Venable, Baetjer and Howard as a lateral entry partner, he joined Harry Baetjer and Crossan Cooper in a triumvirate that exercised all managerial functions. By the end of 1959 Eney was running the show although he always deferred to Mr. Baetjer as the firm's father figure, and most memoranda on administrative matters, even if prepared by Eney, went out over the initials "H.N.B." In 1969, upon Baetjer's death, Jacques Schlenger filled the vacancy, an arrangement that continued only for a year or so until Richard W. Emory was added to the group. This was the genesis of the Operating Committee (now the Management Committee), consisting of both permanent and rotating members.

In 1971 the firm was divided into seven departments according to legal specialties, and in 1978 Eney appointed Thomas J. Kenney, Jr. as the firm's full-time administrative partner, an office which later evolved into that of the professional executive director, filled since 1983 by Richard A. Mackey. Eney also inaugurated a system for building up the firm's cash capital by withholding from each partner a percentage of each year's earnings. It was a painful process and would have been much less so had it been started many years before — as it should have been. Eney was playing catch-up ball.

In the decade between Harry Baetjer's death in 1969 and 1979 when Eney transferred to Schlenger the chairmanship of the Operating Committee, the firm grew from 44 lawyers to 82. Many executives would have found the administration of an enterprise of that size a full-time job but, time-consuming though it was for

Vernon Eney, it represented only a fraction of his work product. Consider the following litany:

From 1946 to 1959 he had been a member of the Court of Appeals Permanent Committee on Rules; he was a member of the Permanent Commission on Municipal Courts from 1959 to 1969; he was a member of the Higher Education Corporation from 1972 to 1976; from 1971 to 1979 he was a member of the General Assembly Compensation Commission; for many years he was a member of the American Law Institute as well as its Council; he was the Maryland chairman of the Fellows of the American Bar Foundation, and one of the founders and the first president of the Fellows of the Maryland Bar Foundation; he was a member of the American College of Trial Lawyers and the American Judicature Society; from 1963 to 1964 he was president of the Maryland State Bar Association and a member of the House of Delegates of the American Bar Association.

One of the significant accomplishments of his year as president of the state bar was the drafting of a bill to put into effect the Clients' Security Trust Fund. This was a concept initiated in the prior administration of Judge Kenneth C. Proctor and came into fruition in the subsequent administration of Judge J. DeWeese Carter, with the enactment of the Acts of 1965, ch. 779. To these bar leaders, credit must be given for one of the most important reforms affecting the legal profession in many decades.

Eney's major extracurricular activity related to the Maryland Constitutional Convention of 1967. He served as chairman of the Constitutional Convention Commission which, over a two-year span from 1965 to 1967, prepared an exhaustive and scholarly analysis of Maryland's existing Constitution of 1867 with a preliminary draft of a new Constitution in parallel columns. He was then elected a member of the convention and thereafter the convention's president. The final version of this State Constitution has been hailed as the best of its kind in the country, but it went down to overwhelming defeat at a special election on May 14, 1968.[3] The contents of that Constitution and the reasons for its defeat are beyond the scope of this history, but a few observations are necessary to complete this word picture of H. Vernon Eney.

The first reaction of many delegates was one of amazement as they became exposed to Eney's capacity for work, the breadth of his scholarship, his gift for assembling and organizing masses of detail, his capacity for executive leadership, and his abiding good humor and sense of fair play. The camaraderie that pervaded the convention, even during times of sharp disagreement, was largely the product of Eney's personality. As an example of that corporate spirit, there is reproduced below a "Memo to All Delegates" disseminated in good fun just before the Christmas recess in December, 1967:

MEMO

TO: ALL DELEGATES

FROM: SANTA CLAUSE (WITH APOLOGIES TO CLEMENT C. MOORE)

DATE: DECEMBER 19TH, 1967

A VISIT FROM ST. VERNON

Twas the night before Christmas
When all through the caucus
Not a delegate was stirring, not even a Malkus,
The proposals were hung by the chimney with care,
In hopes that St. Vernon soon would be there;

The delegates were nestled all snug in their beds,
While visions of recess danced in their heads,
And Koss in her kerchief and I in my cap,
Had just settled our brains for a long winter's nap:

When up in the dome there arose such a clatter,
I sprang from my bed to see what was the matter,
Away to the bill-room I flew like a flash,
Tore open the notebook and threw up the sash.

The moon on the breast of the new fallen papers,
Gave the luster of midday to Weidemyer's capers,
When what to my wondering eyes should appear,
But a miniature sleigh, and eight tiny reindeer;

With a little old driver, so full up with learnin',
I knew in a moment it must be St. Vernon.
More rapid than stenotype his coursers they came,
And he whistled, and shouted, and called them by name:

"Now, Dorsey!, now, Della! now Bennett and Rollins!
On Chabot!, on Darby! on Powers and Sollins!
To the top of the balcony, to the top of the dome!
Now dash away! dash away! dash away home!

As amendments before the wild hurricane fly,
When they meet with debate, mount up the sky,
So up to the State House the coursers they flew,
With a sleigh full of data, and St. Vernon too.

And then, in a twinkling, I heard the debate,
The snarling and snapping of each delegate -
As I drew in my head - and was plugging my ears,
Down the chimney St. Vernon came, eyes full of tears.

He was wrapped in amendments, from his head to his foot,
And his garments were covered with ashes and soot;
A bundle of hopes he had flung on his back,
And he looked like a peddler just opening his pack;

His eyes - how they twinkled! his dimples how merry!
Through the demeanor severe never did vary!
His schedule was tight as the string of a bow
And the delays en route caused all kinds of woe;

The remains of a draft by a commission he headed,
Lay round his feet, the provisions were shredded;
He had many sections of a new constitution,
Most of them new, but no real revolution.

He was battered and beaten, but a jolly old elf,
And I laughed when I saw him in spite of myself;
Months of debate had not hurt his head,
So I thought I was sure I had nothing to dread.

He spoke not a word, but went straight to his work,
Rephrasing amendments to clear up the murk,
And laying aside the good he did spawn,
He flew up the chimney - like a flash he was gone.

He sprang to his sleigh, to his team gave a shout,
And home they all flew, as if school was just out.
But I heard him exclaim as he vanished from sight,
"Happy Christmas to all, and to all a good night."[4]

As for the reasons for the Constitution's defeat, it is this writer's view that a principal cause was Eney's unflinching refusal to compromise with political expediency, a judgment which, if valid, would raise questions as to his capacity to wage effective battle in the political arena. The Constitution presented the hostile pols with three issues, none essential to the overall effectiveness of the document but each tailor-made to appeal to voter resistance to change, *viz*: (1) the lowering of the voting age to eighteen; (2) the abolition of the Orphans' Courts and other elected offices; and (3) the provisions for regional metropolitan government. Without these controversial changes, the opponents might have been forced to confine their attacks to the provision for removal of circuit court judges from partisan elections. It may be questioned whether this would have been enough to enable them to carry the day. Judge William C. Walsh, Eney's mentor in the Attorney General's office, besought him to yield to practical politics on some of these issues, but he refused. His intransigeance was his Achilles' heel. Throughout his career as a practicing lawyer he had a reputation of being an intractable negotiator.

Despite its defeat at the polls, a number of important provisions of the Eney Constitution have been engrafted by amendment onto Maryland's crazy quilt Constitution of 1867, and they stand as a memorial to the work of the convention which labored under his leadership.

Vernon Eney's last major venture into public service following the rejection of the 1968 Constitution was as Chairman of the first Prosecutor Selection and Disabilities Commission of Maryland from 1977 until his death in 1980. He had previously served as a member of the Maryland State Bar Association's Special Committee to Study the State Prosecutorial System that looked into the problem and fashioned its solution. After approval of constitutional amendments by the voters at the 1976 election, there was created the office of State Prosecutor whose duty it would be to investigate violations of election laws, political corruption, bribery, and political malfeasance and misfeasance in office. After providing local State's Attorneys the opportunity to prosecute, if so inclined, the State Prosecutor would himself be empowered to take action after a 45-day notice period. The new office filled a void in the state's system for the prosecution of white-collar crime.

The State Prosecutor Selection and Disabilities Commission not only makes nominations to the governor for the office of State Prosecutor but also serves as a disabilities commission with functions patterned after those of the federal Judicial Disabilities Commission.

Participation in this reform was a fitting climax to Vernon Eney's dedication to the improvement of our system of justice. Upon his death, he was succeeded as chairman by another prominent Maryland lawyer, Eugene M. Feinblatt.

During Vernon Eney's 51 years at the Maryland bar, he served on many other boards and commissions in addition to those previously mentioned. He had been on the Maryland Tax Revision Commission of 1939 (the Rawls Commission), and the Maryland Tax Survey Commission of 1949 (the Case Commission); for 24 years from 1954 to 1978 he was a member of the board of trustees of Goucher College and in 1968 received an honorary LL.D. degree from that institution; at one time or another he had been a director of Central Savings Bank, USF&G Corporation, Mercantile-Safe Deposit and Trust Company, Mercantile Bankshares Corporation, Mercantile Mortgage Corporation, and Fidelity & Guaranty Life Insurance Company; and from 1979 until his death the following year he was chairman of the Greater Baltimore Committee. He was a member of two law clubs, the Rule Day Club and the Lawyers' Round Table, and his pet charity was the Maryland Institute for the Blind.

In 1970 the offices of Venable, Baetjer and Howard were moved from the Mercantile Trust Building on the corner of Baltimore and Calvert Streets, their home for 70 years, to the Mercantile Bank & Trust Building in the revitalized Hopkins Plaza. During the period of construction and fitting out of the new floors every item received the careful attention of H. Vernon Eney. He could read a set of drawings as readily as any architect or engineer and no deviation escaped his attention. For example, after the lighting system had been installed, he checked each office and secretarial station with a light meter to confirm its adequacy. The architect, Parker Matthai, shook his head in disbelief.

Every detail of the move was directed by Eney as a general would direct the movement of troops, the principal lieutenants being Stuart H. Rome and Thomas J. Kenney, Jr. Alan Yarbro was in charge of the telephone installation and periodically reported progress to the commander-in-chief. After several postponements, October 15,

1970 was set as moving day and prompted the following exchange of doggerel from Eney to the firm at large followed by a response from Yarbro:

FLASH!!!

If Fate does smile with face benign
And no more goofs do say us nay
And stars with full benevolence shine,
Come ten-fifteen we're on our way.

Yarbro, skeptical as to whether the telephone equipment would be operational by October 15, replied:

MEMORANDUM TO MR. ENEY

Ten-fifteen seems soon to me.
With but one thought do I atone:
How very pleasant it would be
To practice law without a phone.

In 1975 the associates of Venable, Baetjer and Howard suffered a widespread deterioration in morale that could have been disastrous had it not been neutralized. As so often in disrupted personal relationships, a breakdown in communications was the root cause. The associates believed they had not been adequately and fairly informed of their progress (or lack of it) in the development of their careers and felt threatened by the uncertainty as to whether they would achieve the coveted status and tenure of partner or would be asked to leave after eight years or so in the service of the firm. The traditional one-person blackball rule in effect at partners' meetings was especially galling.

Vernon Eney's solution to this crisis was to expose it. He organized a two-day seminar at Cross Keys Inn on March 7-8, 1975, the first day being devoted to matters of interest to the partners (such questions as incorporation of the firm, sabbaticals, *pro bono* and public service, payments on death or retirement of partners, and the structure of firm management), and the second day being exclusively given over to the associates to plan and present the program as they saw fit.

The five topics they selected for discussion were *Development and Training of Associates, Partnership Selection, Evaluation of Associates, Communications,* and *Direction of the Firm.* The five keynote speakers on these subjects were, respectively, Harvey R. Clapp, III, Benjamin Rosenberg, Robert Briskin, Paul F. Strain, and Alexander I. Lewis, III. The lead-off speaker and master of ceremonies was J. Frederick Motz (later U.S. District Judge) whose poise, maturity, and common sense left an indelible impression on the partners.

The discussion on that Saturday in March, 1975 was long and lively, and everyone was ready for cocktails at the witching hour of 5:00 p.m.

Many of the ideas that evolved from this seminar were expeditiously implemented, most importantly the adoption and circulation to all lawyers in the firm of a "Statement of Policy Re Selection of Partners." This document, the work product of a committee headed by Norwood B. Orrick, articulated the criteria to be followed in the partnership selection process and called for the creation of a screening committee to make annual recommendations for new partners. The one-person blackball rule at partnership meetings was replaced with a requirement for at least four "no" votes in order to reject any candidate proposed by the committee. These measures, coupled with better lines of communications through the agency of the Associates Committee, eventually dispelled the miasma of discontent that had threatened the harmony of the firm, and it became once more a pleasant place in which to work. Vernon Eney had skillfully steered the ship through troubled waters.

We now turn to some of the highlights of Vernon Eney's career as a practicing lawyer.

Eney's first oral argument in the Court of Appeals took place when he was only twenty-five years old,[5] although he had been "on the brief" in two earlier cases, the first of which was argued when he was twenty-two.[6] On his first appearance as an oral advocate he successfully defended the owner of a piece of vacant land in a wrongful death case arising out of the death of a child who, while playing on the premises, was suffocated by the collapse of a tunnel caused by the operations of a steam shovel. The case, one of first impression, established the principle that the law of attractive nuisance does not apply in Maryland.

In 1937 at the age of twenty-nine, Eney made his first appearance in the Supreme Court of the United States. The case is reported *sub nom. Smyth v. United States*,[7] and the oral argument for the Petitioners (Eney's client was a Respondent) was equally divided between Eney and Robert A. Taft of Cincinnati, the son of Chief Justice Taft, later a senator from Ohio and several time presidential aspirant. The issue was whether the United States, having gone off the gold standard in accordance with the Presidential Proclamation of January 31, 1934 issued under authority of an Act of Congress, and having called for redemption its Liberty Bonds which provided for payment in gold, could thereby avoid paying subsequently accruing coupons. The case turned on the validity of the notice of call as an effective means of stopping the running of interest. Eney lost the case before Judge William C. Coleman in the United States District Court but won a reversal by a unanimous decision of the Fourth Circuit Court of Appeals.[8] This victory set up a conflict with Taft's loss in the Court of Claims, and the Supreme Court granted a writ of *certiorari*.[9]

The case was argued on November 18 and 19, 1937, the Solicitor General (later Justice) Stanley Reed speaking for the Government with Taft and Eney on the other side. By a sharply divided court, the Government prevailed, four Justices agreeing with Mr. Justice Cardozo's majority opinion and two others concurring. Three Justices dissented. Eney's oral argument was, however, the talk of the town in Washington legal circles. Mr. Justice Brandeis is reported to have said that it was one of the best he had heard, and some years later Professor Paul A. Freund made the same observation to me when I was a student at the Harvard Law School.

Eney's only other appearances in the Supreme Court were on behalf of the state of Maryland while he was serving as assistant attorney general.[10] His other cases in the state and lower federal courts are so numerous that most of them must be consigned to an endnote,[11] but a few others of special interest are briefly summarized.

In 1949, in *Gray v. Harriet Lane Home for Invalid Children*[12] Eney teamed up with Stuart S. Janney, Jr. of Venable, Baetjer and Howard to fashion a doctrine dubbed in the parlance of the probate bar as "judicial *cy pres.*" The Maryland cy pres statute, enacted in 1945,[13] permits a court to divert to another charitable purpose funds given in trust for an object for which there is no longer a demonstrable need. However, this legislative remedy had no application to estates created before 1945. Thus, it could not be invoked as to a trust created in 1921 by a will which left a substantial estate for the support of free patients in two wards at Johns Hopkins Hospital, one for diphtheria and the other for scarlet fever. Medical science had virtually eradicated these diseases and, at the behest of Eney and Janney, the court rose to the occasion by decreeing that the funds could be used to advance the donor's broad charitable purpose, in this case the support of indigent sick children. The decision is a good example of the elasticity of the Common Law.

An early case that helped establish Eney's reputation as an expert on constitutional law was *Redwood v. Lane*[14] concerning the validity of a $50 million state bond issue for school construction. Eney was engaged by the state to bring a test case defended by Attorney General Hall Hammond, later Chief Judge of the Maryland Court of Appeals, and his Deputy, Harrison L. Winter, later Chief Judge of the United States Court of Appeals for the Fourth Circuit. The bill enacting the bond issue, SB. 442, had passed both houses of the legislature, but the Clerk erroneously recorded it in the *Journal* as HB. 442, a measure that had died in committee. Sustaining Eney's contention, the Court of Appeals held this to be a fatal flaw that could not be cured by the courts.

Another victory in the constitutional law field was *Board of Regents of University of Maryland v. Trustees of the Endowment Fund of the*

University of Maryland[15] declaring unconstitutional a bill passed over the governor's veto which would have amended the charter of the Trustees of the Endowment Fund in such a way as to alter its fundamental purposes. Analyzing the *Dartmouth College* case[16] and other constitutional authorities, the court held that this statute was not within the reserved power of the legislature to amend corporate charters of private corporations.

A case of widespread interest in the field of probate law was the *Mullikin Will* case,[17] upholding the mental capacity of an eccentric testator who left the bulk of his $7 million estate to charity. Eney's clients included Goucher College, St. John's College, the First Presbyterian Church, the Johns Hopkins Hospital, and the Johns Hopkins University. The caveator was one of the testator's first cousins who would have been happy to share in the estate by intestacy. The testimony showed that Addison E. Mullikin, an unmarried lawyer, had taken as a legal fee about 25 years before his death some 60,000 shares of stock in a company which prospered extravagantly, those shares being worth approximately $6,800,000 at the time of his demise. The testator's eccentricities were also spread on the record: he was a fresh-air fiend who kept his room in the Southern Hotel unreasonably cold; he slept under mounds of pongee coverings instead of blankets; he was imprecise in speech and sometimes mumbled or slurred his words; he spilled cigar ashes and food on his clothing; he drooled and towards the end was incontinent; most of his waking hours were spent in front of three television sets, each tuned to a different Baltimore station but with the audio on in only one. The Court of Appeals, agreeing with Eney, held that these oddities, neither alone nor together, were sufficient to establish Mullikin's incapacity and that the nurses and chauffeur-valet were not qualified to express an opinion on his mental state. It was a big win for the charitable remaindermen.

A case with an ironic twist was *Black v. Board of Supervisors of Elections*[18] in which Eney represented the Republican State Central Committee in a suit to compel the listing on the ballot of the name of Hyman Λ. Pressman as its party's candidate for Comptroller in the city-wide general election of 1963. Pressman had been defeated in the Democratic primary by Henry R. Hergenroeder by a narrow margin of 104,949 to 99,002, whereupon the Republican candidate, A. Rae Dempsey, withdrew, and the State Central Committee replaced him by naming Pressman in his stead. Judge J. Gilbert Prendergast, Eney's old Navy chum, ruled that the resignation was valid but the replacement illegal since Pressman was a registered Democrat. The appeal was heard on an expedited basis by the Court of Appeals.

In a 4-3 decision Eney prevailed. Thus, Pressman was enabled to run against and to defeat Hergenroeder in the general election, the same man who had bested him in the primary. Eney's court victory in 1963 set in motion Pressman's long political career, but five years later Pressman was one of the most strident opponents of the Eney Constitution that went down to defeat at the polls. Ironic, to say the least.

One of Vernon Eney's last cases, one that dragged on for seven years, was *Madden*. In the first stage, in which Eney did not participate, a young man named Peter Madden sought to have declared invalid his grandmother's Reno divorce, with the object of establishing the illegitimacy of her two daughters born of her second marriage and their resulting ineligibility as remaindermen of a trust under their mother's will. The Court of Appeals dismissed this contention,[19] thus setting the stage for an assault on the Mercantile-Safe Deposit and Trust Company (formerly Safe Deposit & Trust Company of Baltimore) for an alleged breach of trust in having, over 30 years before, sold Pimlico Race Track for a price said to be inadequate.[20] On two separate occasions Judge David Ross of the Circuit Court for Baltimore City directed a verdict for the trustee at the end of the plaintiff's case, and on the second time around he was affirmed by the Court of Special Appeals.[21] With the denial of *certiorari* by the Court of Appeals and the Supreme Court of the United States this bizarre case was finally concluded. Over the seven-year stretch it had consumed many thousands of hours of lawyers' time, and the total fees to the firm stood at $638,390.

Madden was a case that should never have been brought, but once brought it left the trustee no alternative except to defend itself. It is an example of the tragic economic waste resulting from the high cost of fruitless litigation.

Eney's last case in the Court of Appeals was *Maryland Action for Foster Children, Inc. v. State*[22] in which he appeared as *amicus curiae* on behalf of the President of the Senate and Speaker of the House, acting as a policy committee of the legislature. The nub of the case was a dispute between the legislative and executive branches as to whether a statute[23] required the governor to include, in his executive budget, funds for the minimum payments for foster care specified in the legislation. The governor contended that in the absence of a supplementary appropriations bill enacted by the legislature the funding was within the executive's discretion. Eney's brief supported the legislative side, but in a 4-3 decision the Court of Appeals sustained the governor. Chief Judge Murphy led the dissent in an opinion in which Judges Smith and Digges concurred, quoting at length from Eney's scholarly analysis of the budget-making process. Judges Eldridge, Singley, Levine, and Gilbert (specially assigned) could not be persuaded, and the case was lost.

A catalogue of Eney's numerous other cases in the state and federal courts is contained in an endnote[11]. They cover a wide range of subjects including constitutional law, labor relations, securities regulation, patents, federal procedure, and civil rights.

For the better part of the first half of their married life the Eneys lived in a masonry house on a corner lot in Stoneleigh, a suburban development in southern Baltimore County. However, in December, 1955 they fulfilled a long-standing dream for a place in the country. They bought a 17-acre farm on Belfast Road in Butler with a charming house nestled in the hillside, the oldest part of which was built in colonial times. Eney played the role of gentleman farmer, even to the point of mowing the fields and raising a herd of sheep. Visitors to this homestead saw a side of Vernon Eney that was quite different from the workaholic visible at the office. Instead, they saw a man full of humor and genial hospitality. He loved young children and enjoyed taking them for rides on his tractor and showing them around the place — the barn, the greenhouse, and the ha-ha that penned the sheep. In this setting Eney had the opportunity to unwind, to put out of sight and out of mind the pressures of the office. Although the farm in Butler must have added a good many minutes to his daily commuting time to Baltimore Street, it probably added years to his life in providing an essential outlet for rest and relaxation from his workaday world.

Although Eney accepted as inevitable the introduction of business methods into the operations of the modern-day law firm, he never lost sight of what he perceived to be the real fun of practicing his profession — the satisfaction one derives from helping those in need. Mrs. Eney recalls a case in point.

One late Saturday afternoon, as was his wont, he was working alone in the office at the old Mercantile Building when he heard a rap on the door. On opening it, he was greeted by a sailor from a ship that had just docked at the inner harbor. The man spoke broken English but could make it understood that he had a serious legal problem and needed the services of a lawyer. He had walked up Calvert Street, headed into the first office building he could find and was told by the guard that he could probably find H. Vernon Eney still at work on the fourteenth floor.

The fortunate sailor then laid bare his difficulties and, whatever they were, it took several hours for Eney to unravel them — after, of course, putting aside the other work on which he had been engaged. The problem once resolved, Eney sent the sailor back to his ship and made his own way back to Belfast Road, late again for dinner. Explaining the delay to his ever patient wife, Vernon made the point that she has never forgotten: This, as he put it, "is the real fun of practicing law," i.e., to take on one's shoulders the cares and woes of someone else and discharge them through the application of common sense and sound legal judgment. This is lawyering in its highest and best form. This, not just making money, is what it is all about.

By January 1, 1979 when Eney turned over to Jacques Schlenger the leadership of Venable, Baetjer and Howard, he had been debilitated by a steadily worsening case of emphysema and by 1980 had to carry around a portable oxygen tank during all waking hours and to sleep with the help of an oxygen converter. Finally, in desperation and against the advice of his physicians he submitted to an operation designed to give him more breathing capacity, but too much damage had been done to his lungs and he lived only a few days thereafter. He died on December 4, 1980 survived by his wife, Margaret F. D. Eney, their two daughters, Joan E. Kuehn and Margaret E. Richmond, six grandchildren, and one great-grandchild.

The first of the firm's Innovators, Vernon Eney was also one of the finest lawyers in Maryland's history.

Endnotes to Part III, Chapter 1:

1. The name, Valley View, has no connection with the popular home and garden shop now located on York Road in Baltimore County, known as Valley View Farms.

2. Brewster withdrew from Venable, Baetjer and Howard in 1957 and joined Piper & Marbury where he later became its managing partner. Another associate, Raymond S. Clark, withdrew shortly before the merger with Armstrong, Machen & Eney. He later became president of the Canton Railroad Company.

3. The state-wide vote was 284,033 for and 367,101 against. The new Constitution was rejected in Baltimore City and every county save two.

4. Although distributed anonymously, this parody was known to have been written by C. William Gilchrist, a lawyer and delegate from Cumberland. According to other delegates, Gilchrist was an able member of the convention and one who also contributed much to its lighter moments.

5. *State To the Use of Lorenz v. Machen*, 164 Md. 579 (1933).

6. *Harlan v. Simering*, 163 Md. 609 (1933), argued and won by Alexander Armstrong with Eney on the brief, a case involving a dispute over real estate commissions; *McCrory Stores Corp. v. Bennett*, 159 Md. 568 (1930), argued and lost by Armstrong and John Henry Lewin with Eney on the brief, a case holding that the statutory right of redemption in a tenant under a lease for more than 15 years does not apply to a lease by a trustee without power of sale.

7. 302 U.S. 329, 58 S. Ct. 248, 82 L. Ed. 294 (1937).

8. *Machen v. United States*, 87 F.2d 594 (4th Cir. 1937).

9. 302 U.S. 672, 58 S. Ct. 28, 82 L. Ed. 519 (1937).

10. *Fidelity Assurance Society v. Sims*, 318 U.S. 608, 63 S. Ct. 807, 87 L. Ed. 1032 (1943); *Pittman v. Home Owners' Land Corporation*, 308 U.S. 21, 60 S. Ct. 15, 84 L. Ed. 11 (1939). Other cases in the federal and state courts argued by Eney on behalf of the state while he was in the Attorney General's office are not tabulated in this history.

State Court Cases:

11. *Potomac Edison Co. v. State To the Use of Hoffman*, 168 Md. 156 (1935), and *State To the Use of Hoffman v. Potomac Edison Co.*, 166 Md. 138 (1934), two wrongful death cases argued by Eney and Armstrong; *Darden v. Bright*, 173 Md. 563 (1938), and *Grace v. Thompson*, 169 Md. 653 (1936), two will construction cases; *Engle v. United States Fidelity & Guaranty Company*, 175 Md. 174 (1938), a case involving the law of suretyship which Eney lost to Charles McHenry Howard; *Sugar v. Hafele*, 179 Md. 75 (1941), a personal injury case which Eney won; *Taggart v. Wachter, Hoskins & Russell, Inc.*, 179 Md. 608 (1941), a case in which Eney successfully achieved the reversal of an assessment on the policies of an insolvent cooperative insurance organization — his last appellate appearance before he went to war; *Ridgely v. Pfingstag*, 188 Md. 209 (1946), a complicated will construction case in which Eney on behalf of the defendants won a partial reversal; *County Commissioners of Anne Arundel County v. Buch*, 190 Md. 394 (1948), upholding the right of a taxpayer to complain about the underassessment of the property of others; *Wharton v. Fidelity-Baltimore National Bank*, 222 Md. 177 (1960), a loss for Vernon Eney, holding that a director is not an "employee" entitled to exercise stock options; *Giardina v. Wannen*, 228 Md. 116 (1962), where Eney successfully upheld the mental capacity of a testatrix; *Panamerican Consulting Co., Inc. v. Broun*, 238 Md. 438, reh. den. 238 Md. 548 (1965), a complicated case involving corporation and contract law which Eney won for the appellant; *First National Bank v. White*, 239 Md. 289 (1965), a victory for Eney in the field of probate law; *Goucher College v. DeWolfe*, 251 Md. 638 (1968), a zoning case which Eney lost on appeal; *Randolph Hills, Inc. v. Shoreham Developers, Inc.*, 266 Md. 182 (1972), a case involving the right of vendor and purchaser in a real estate contract, a loss for Eney on appeal; *American Structures v. City of Baltimore*, 278 Md. 356 (1976), in which Eney filed a brief as *amicus curiae* on behalf of Baltimore Contractors, Inc. explaining the application of sovereign immunity to the state in contract claims and its nonapplication to counties and municipalities if the subject of the contract is within their municipal power.

Federal Cases:

Atlantic Coast Line Railway Co. v. B.&O. Railroad Co., 12 F. Supp. 711 (D. Md. 1935), and 16 F. Supp. 647 (D. Md. 1936), two wins for Eney in disputes involving the division of rates between carriers; *Tait v. Safe Deposit & Trust Co.*, 74 F.2d 851 (4 Cir. 1935), a victory for Eney in the federal estate tax field; *Conviser v. Simpson*, 122 F. Supp. 205 (D. Md. 1954), involving question of corporate law and the Investment Company Act of 1940; *Carter Products v. Colgate-Palmolive Company*, 130 F. Supp. 557 (D. Md. 1955), the first salvo in a long and losing battle that lasted for four years dealing with the patent for aerosol shaving cream, other federal decisions in this case being reported at 230 F.2d 855 (4th Cir. 1956), 151 F. Supp. 427 (D. Md. 1957), 243 F.2d 163 (4th Cir. 1957), 164 F. Supp. 503 (D. Md. 1958), 269 F.2d 299 (4th Cir. 1959), and 214 F. Supp. 383 (D. Md. 1963); *Robinson v. Board of Education of St. Mary's County*, 143 F. Supp. 481 (D. Md. 1956), an early segregation case which Eney won for the Board of Education on the ground that administrative remedies had not been exhausted; *Chesapeake Motor Lines v. United States*, 153 F. Supp. 812 (D. Md. 1957), involving interstate motor tariffs; *Groves v. Board of Education of St. Mary's County*, 164 F. Supp. 621 (D. Md. 1958), aff'd in Board of Education of *St. Mary's County v. Groves*, 261 F.2d 527 (4th Cir. 1958), a school segregation case that Eney lost on the authority of the Supreme Court's landmark decision in *Brown v. Board of Education; Hart v. Board of Education of Charles County*, 164 F. Supp. 501 (D. Md. 1958), another segregation case which was dismissed as moot since the plaintiff had been admitted to a desegregated bus; *District 50, United Mine Workers of America v. Revere Copper & Brass, Inc.*, 204 F. Supp. 349 (D. Md. 1962), a labor relations case in which Eney prevailed on summary judgment; *In re Food Town, Inc.*, 208 F. Supp. 139 (D. Md. 1962), reporting a skirmish in a long drawn-out bankruptcy proceeding; *Cummins Engine Co. v. General Motors Corp.*, 299 F. Supp. 59 (D. Md. 1969), a patent case; *Hare v. Family Publications Service, Inc.*, 334 F. Supp. 953 (D. Md. 1971), and 342 F. Supp. 678 (D. Md. 1972), reporting two federal rules skirmishes; *Goodman v. Poland*, 395 F. Supp. 660 (D. Md. 1975), involving state and federal securities laws; *Baumel v. Rosen*, 412 F.2d 571 (4th Cir. 1969), a major Rule 10-b-5 securities case in which Eney was brought in by other counsel for the appeal, a major economic victory for Eney's client who was ordered to pay money damages instead of the disastrous rescission ordered by the District Court; *Appalachian Power Co. Environmental Protection Agency*, 477 F.2d 495 (4th Cir. 1973), a case involving the newly emerging environmental law; and Eney's last argument in the federal courts, another securities law victory, *Healey v. Catalyst Recovery of Pennsylvania, Inc.*, 616 F.2d 641 (3d. Cir. 1980).

12. 192 Md. 251 (1949).

13. Acts of 1945, ch. 727.

14. 194 Md. 91 (1949).

15. 206 Md. 559 (1955).

16. 4 Wheat (U.S.) 518 (1819).

17. *West v. Fidelity-Baltimore National Bank*, 219 Md. 258 (1959).

18. 232 Md. 74 (1963).

19. *Madden v. Cosden*, 271 Md. 118 (1974).

20. The *Madden* saga had started in 1972 when the Trustee instituted proceedings for instructions as to how its trust estate should be distributed. These proceedings were suspended while the first round went forward, i.e., Peter Madden's case to determine the legitimacy of his aunts.

21. On the first appeal the case was sent back for further proceedings, *Madden v. Mercantile-Safe Deposit and Trust Company*, 27 Md. App. 17 (1975), and on the second Judge Ross was affirmed, 41 Md. App. 519 (1979), cert. den. 285 Md. 732 (1979), 444 U.S. 941 (1979).

22. 279 Md. 133 (1977).

23. Acts of 1974, ch. 867, codified in Art. 88A, §60(b).

VENABLE, BAETJER AND HOWARD

ATTORNEYS AT LAW

A PARTNERSHIP INCLUDING PROFESSIONAL CORPORATIONS

CHARD M. VENABLE (1839-1910)
DWIN G. BAETJER (1868-1945)
HARLES McH. HOWARD (1870-1942)

RTHUR W. MACHEN, JR., P. C.
DBERT M. THOMAS, P. C.
SAMUEL COOK, P. C.
DBERT R. BAIR, P. C.
CQUES T. SCHLENGER, P. C.
HARLES B. REEVES, JR.
LLIAM J. McCARTHY, P. C.
JSSELL R. RENO, JR., P. C.
HOMAS P. PERKINS, III, P. C.
ERALD M. KATZ, P. C.
KE MARBURY
VAN LEUVEN STEWART, P. C.
WRENCE S. WESCOTT, P. C.
EORGE C. DOUB, JR., P. C.
HN HENRY LEWIN, JR., P. C.
AN D. YARBRO, P. C.
DBERT A. SHELTON
COB L. FRIEDEL
ARRY D. SHAPIRO
TANLEY MAZAROFF, P. C.
E M. MILLER, P. C.
HOMAS J. KENNEY, JR., P. C.
TER BARNES, P. C.
PETER LAREAU, P. C.
DUGLAS D. CONNAH, JR., P. C.
HOMAS J. MADDEN*
LLIAM L. WALSH, JR., P C.**
ENJAMIN ROSENBERG, P C.
DBERT G. SMITH, P. C.
MES D. WRIGHT, P. C.
E A. SHULL**
RARD F. TREANOR, JR., P. C.**
DBERT E. MADDEN*
NNETH C. BASS, III**
UL F. STRAIN, P. C.
EXANDER I. LEWIS, III, P. C.
AX STUL OPPENHEIMER, P. C.
LLIAM D. DOLAN, III, P. C.**
RRY F. HALL

CRAIG E. SMITH
BRYSON L. COOK, P. C.
CHARLES M. KERR, P. C.
BENSON EVERETT LEGG
ROBERT G. AMES
WILLIAM G. MURRAY, P. C.**
NELL B. STRACHAN
J. PHILLIP JORDAN
RICHARD L. WASSERMAN, P. C.
JOHN W. SCHEFLEN
BARBARA E. SCHLAFF
RONALD B. SHEFF
JAMES K. ARCHIBALD
G. STEWART WEBB, JR.
GEORGE W. JOHNSTON, P. C.
JEFFREY D. KNOWLES*
F. DUDLEY STAPLES, JR.
EDWARD L. WENDER, P. C.
DAVID M. FLEISHMAN
JANA HOWARD CAREY, P. C.
JEFFREY A. DUNN
CONSTANCE H. BAKER
ROBERT C. GOMBAR
STEPHEN L. OWEN
PETER P. PARVIS
JAMES L. SHEA
MITCHELL KOLKIN
JEFFREY P. AYRES, P. C.
KENNETH R. HOFFMAN
BRIGID E. KENNEY
BRUCE R. SPECTOR
JOHN H. MORRIS, JR.

COUNSEL
NORWOOD B. ORRICK
RICHARD W. EMORY
EDMUND P. DANDRIDGE, JR.
NEAL D. BORDEN, P. C.

1800 MERCANTILE BANK & TRUST BUILDING

2 HOPKINS PLAZA

BALTIMORE, MARYLAND 21201

(301) 244-7400

WASHINGTON, D. C. OFFICE
SUITE 1200
1301 PENNSYLVANIA AVENUE, N. W.
WASHINGTON, D. C. 20004
(202) 662-4300

VIRGINIA OFFICES

PLAZA SUITE THREE
4141 NORTH HENDERSON ROAD
ARLINGTON, VIRGINIA 22203
(703) 243-5000

SUITE 500
2000 CORPORATE RIDGE
MCLEAN, VIRGINIA 22102
(703) 749-3500

---

*ADMITTED IN DISTRICT OF COLUMBIA
NOT ADMITTED IN MARYLAND

**ADMITTED IN DISTRICT OF COLUMBIA AND
VIRGINIA-NOT ADMITTED IN MARYLAND

***ADMITTED IN VIRGINIA
NOT ADMITTED IN MARYLAND

WRITER'S DIRECT NUMBER IS

DAVID B. IRWIN
SUSAN K. GAUVEY
MAURICE BASKIN*
ELIZABETH C. HONEYWELL
ROBERT B. GREEN
M. LUCINDA MOTSKO
AMY S. BERMAN*
PETER S. SAUCIER
ELLYN L. BROWN
CHRISTOPHER R. MELLOTT
MARIANNE SCHMITT HELLAUER
W. ROBERT ZINKHAM
KATHLEEN MORRIS McDONALD
DAVID E. RICE
JOHN B. WATKINS, X
ELIZABETH R. HUGHES
JAMES A. DUNBAR
RONALD W. TAYLOR
WILLIAM T. FITZGERALD, JR.
STEPHEN P. CARNEY
ROBERT L. WALDMAN
THOMAS D. WASHBURNE, JR.
ELIZABETH S. ROESE
FRANCIS R. LAWS
HERMAN EUGENE FUNK, JR.
BERT BLACK
KATHLEEN FLYNN RUSSELL
ROBERT J. PROUTT
ROBERT J. BOLGER, JR.
ERNEST A. CROFOOT
NANCY LARK SCHULZE
RICHARD B. MORROW*
JEFFREY J. PECK*
LAWRENCE H. NORTON
LESLIE B. COHEN*
CLAYTON H. PATERSON
M. LANE HOWELL*
PATRICK J. STEWART
DAVID A. SOLEY
NINA A. PALA***
VICKI L. DEXTER
CALLA B. SAMUELS*
GEORGE BRENT MICKUM, IV**
PAUL A. SERINI

SUSAN E. KEHOE
CYNTHIA A. BERMAN
ARIEL VANNIER
HAROLD NUSSENFELD
CLEMENT D. ERHARDT, III
MARYRUTH VOLLSTEDT
JANET BRANDT MAJEV
JAMES H. SCOTT
THERESE M. SCHMITT
VERNA H. GLASS
GARY M. HNATH
NEIL C. KAHN
ANITA R. ELEY
RICHARD B. LEHMANN
DOUGLAS M. TOPOLSKI
KEVIN L. SHEPHERD
GEOFFREY R. GARINTHER
WILLIAM F. HOWARD
MICHAEL A. DUFF
H. HAYWOOD MILLER, III
JAMES R. MOXLEY, III
ALLEN F. LOUCKS
NEWTON B. FOWLER, III
GEORGE B. MERRILL
MICHAEL J. BAADER
JAMES E. CUMBIE
GARRETT A. PFEIFER
WAYNE M. ZELL
KENNETH R. APPLEBY
DARRELL R. VANDEUSEN
MARC R. ENGEL
CHERI L. CANNON
DENISE L. SPEER
VIRGINIA A. ZRAKE
THOMAS L. PATZ
DAVID G. LAROCHE
FREDERICK C. LEINER
ROBIN L. ZIMELMAN
LAWRENCE S. STERN
ANTHONY J. FERRISE
TERRI L. TURNER
BRUCE M. LUCHANSKY
MARCIA E. GOTTESMAN
JANET S. HANKIN

The last engraved letterhead with the names of all lawyers. Because of turnovers in personnel, these letterheads were usually obsolete before their release.

Their use was discontinued in 1987.

Jacques T. Schlenger, 1927 -

Jacques T. Schlenger

A LTHOUGH THE WORD "History" in the title of this book may include a record of recent developments, this author finds it difficult to play the role of historian in describing them. These events have not been polished by the sands of time and cannot be placed in perspective. Also, the writer is torn by conflicting motives, on one hand a desire to be candid (as promised in the Preface) and, on the other, a concern that the written word might cause offense to people still living.

The easy way out of this dilemma would be to end this account with the chapter just concluded. However, so many incidents of importance, some with substantial public interest, have befallen the firm in the 1980's that it would be disingenuous to ignore them. Accordingly, the story continues, but the reader must be aware that the material that follows cannot be taken as a complete and objective record of contemporary developments. That task must await the attention of some future historian who writes the sequel to this book, perhaps on the firm's 150th birthday in 2050.

So said, the penultimate chapter in the current history of the firm begins on January 1, 1979 when Jacques T. Schlenger, the second Innovator, succeeded Vernon Eney as chairman of the Operating Committee and as chief executive officer.

Schlenger was born on October 11, 1927 and graduated with honors from the University of Virginia in 1948. He received his LL.B. degree from Yale Law School in 1951 and for the next two years was associated with a sole practitioner in tax work in the District of Columbia. For three years thereafter, 1952-55, he served as Special Attorney in the Interpretative Division of the office of Chief Counsel of the Internal Revenue Service, an excellent training experience for a budding tax specialist. Then he hung up his shingle in Baltimore, later joined by Frederick Steinmann, in a firm of tax lawyers. In 1963 the pair joined Venable, Baetjer and Howard as the nucleus of a tax department, Schlenger coming in as partner and Steinmann as associate.

From the beginning, Schlenger displayed an aptitude for management and was the logical successor to Harry Baetjer as a member of the threesome that governed the firm in those days.

When Eney retired in 1979, Schlenger was also the logical successor for the post of chief executive officer of the firm, although Eney sought the advice of his partners before announcing the appointment. These one-on-one confabs were something of a charade since Eney had made up his mind before they began, but that was his style of establishing a consensus.

During the eight years of his term as managing partner Schlenger introduced many innovations in the firm's operations, notably the acquisition of its first in-house computer for the maintenance of accounting and time records, the installation of electronic word processing equipment at each secretarial station, the opening of a popular lawyers' dining room on the fifteenth floor (appropriately dubbed Chez Jacques), the expansion of office space to several new floors, a wider use of paralegals, the regularization of distributions to partners in order to permit better individual financial planning, a revamping of the firm's policies for payments on death, retirement or incapacity, the organization of investment opportunities for partners seeking tax shelter, and the engagement of the first full-time non-lawyer executive director in the person of Richard A. Mackey.

In 1981 partners were permitted to incorporate as professional associations, and in 1982 Nell B. Strachan became the first woman to be admitted into the partnership. John H. Morris, Jr. became the first black associate to make the grade in 1986.

Although from the earliest days of the Founders the partners of Venable, Baetjer and Howard had involved themselves deeply in public and charitable causes, the firm itself remained more or less aloof as an institution in the community. A move away from this posture had been inaugurated in the Eney era with the pledge of a substantial corporate gift to the University of Maryland School of Law in memory of Harry N. Baetjer. It was, however, during the Schlenger era that the firm discarded its traditional reticence and became openly involved in the support of charitable and eleemosynary organizations. The firm joined the "Five Percent Club" whereby it agreed to devote to charitable causes in the community at least five percent of its previous year's earnings. In order to facilitate this commitment and provide a vehicle for making matching gifts, the Venable, Baetjer and Howard Foundation was formed and has made substantial long term commitments to such institutions as the Peabody Institute, the Baltimore Symphony, the Baltimore Museum of Art, the University of Maryland School of Law, the GBMC Foundation, the University of Baltimore School of Law, the Community Foundation of Greater Washington, Inc., and others. Since his retirement as managing partner Jacques Schlenger has remained in charge of this program.

Between 1979 and 1987 the firm grew in size from 82 lawyers to 160, but even more significant than the population explosion were the opening of the Washington office in 1981 and the entree into northern Virginia in 1985, *viz*:

When President Jimmy Carter lost his bid for reelection in 1980, his Attorney General, Benjamin R. Civiletti, could have written his ticket for admission to almost any major law firm in the country. Although Civiletti had been a home-grown product of Venable, Baetjer and Howard, having risen from the associate ranks to partner in 1969, there were few who harbored much hope of luring him back. Jacques Schlenger thus accomplished a major coup in negotiating Civiletti's return on January 20, 1981 to head up a Washington office that opened its doors on April 1 under the name Venable, Baetjer, Howard & Civiletti. At first, there were mixed feelings about the enlargement of the firm name, but these were dissipated when it was pointed out that this has been done before when the D.C. office of a regional firm brings in as a partner a celebrity from government service.[1]

Initially, the Washington office was staffed by a few expatriates from Baltimore, but on September 1, 1984 their ranks were swelled by the merger into Venable, Baetjer, Howard & Civiletti of the firm of McCarthy, Shull & Knowles. Its members consisted of Charles R. McCarthy, Jr., Joe A. Shull, and Jeffrey D. Knowles whose ranks were augmented at the time of the merger by the addition of Thomas J. Madden and Jeffrey A. Dunn, two other experienced practitioners in the fields of government contracts and litigation. Thus, there were brought into the firm five new D.C. partners with a diversified and established client base. After a modest beginning in 1981, the expanded Washington office was established as a solid profit center.

The expansion into northern Virginia in February, 1985 was also significant. This was accomplished by the acquisition of the firm of Dolan, Treanor, Murray & Walsh, headquartered in Arlington, Virginia, whose offices were moved six months later to new and expanded space at Tyson's Corner in McLean. William D. Dolan III, the senior partner in the acquired firm, was at the time of the merger the president of the Virginia State Bar Association. The other new partners resulting from this merger were William L. Walsh, Jr., Gerard F. Treanor, and William G. Murray. This combination, another accomplishment of the Schlenger era, accorded the firm a presence in one of the fastest growing business communities in the northeast.

The picture thus far painted of Schlenger's early years as managing partner may suggest that everything was beer and skittles. It was not. There were headaches, not the least of which occurred during the first four years of his term when two partners were asked to leave, one of whom was later disbarred by the Court of Appeals.

The 1982 incident involved the only partner in the firm's history to lose his license — Gary Z. Nothstein who had been caught padding his expense account by approximately $40,000, his machinations having been detected by the firm's administrative partner, Thomas J. Kenney, Jr. Almost all of the defalcations were at the expense of the firm, but a few which had been billed to clients were, of course, promptly refunded. Responding to its ethical duty to report to the Attorney Grievance Commission any violation of the disciplinary rules, the firm laid the matter before Bar Counsel. The Court of Appeals, rejecting the respondent's contention that he was suffering from a mental disorder that controlled his actions, ordered disbarment.[2]

The partner who was asked to leave a year or so later will remain nameless, even in the endnotes, because there is no public record of his peccadillos. His problem was plagiarism; in an article written for one of the firm's circulars on current developments in the law, he quoted extensively, without attribution, the product of another law firm on the West Coast. It was spotted by a partner in the other firm who was catching up on his reading while flying across the country. Hardly so serious as padding an expense account, this was still conduct unbefitting a partner at Venable, Baetjer and Howard, and the gentleman was asked to move along.

We turn now to a review of some of Jacques Schlenger's accomplishments as a practicing lawyer. They might be summarized in the watchword, "Big is Beautiful!" Many of Schlenger's clients have been rich people who would rather pay legal fees than taxes, and his major successes have been in big cases. This predilection to the big is reflected in his book, published by the Michie Company in 1988 entitled LARGE WEALTH — Strategic Tax and Estate Planning which defines a "wealthy" person as one with a net worth of twenty-five to fifty million dollars. A mini-millionaire worth only five million dollars or so may have achieved "some security" and a "badge of achievement" but is not "wealthy." In order to meet the definition of "rich" one has to cross the one-hundred million dollar threshold.

In 1957 Schlenger acquired a client who satisfied that test, Donaldson Brown, a vice-chairman of the board of General Motors and said to be the most affluent citizen in Maryland. His family company, Broseco, was engaged in widespread oil exploration in Louisiana and Texas, and the Internal Revenue Service proposed a tax deficiency of many millions of dollars on the grounds that it had unreasonably accumulated earnings. After a year of labor Schlenger produced a mammoth brief containing not only decided cases but also extensive reports from geologists and economists, all supporting his argument that, if Broseco were to strike oil on only a few of its exploratory wells, its retained capital would be inadequate. After oral argument before the Appellate Division the Service conceded the larger part of its claim, and Mr. Brown was so pleased that he awarded Schlenger a substantial voluntary bonus.

In 1965 both Mr. and Mrs. Brown died, and Schlenger, who by this time had joined forces with Venable, Baetjer and Howard, was engaged as counsel for both estates aggregating more than $150,000,000, believed to be the largest in the State's history. Tax questions of enormous complexity were presented and Schlenger spent five years of labor on the engagement. After a favorable tax audit, the firm was awarded a fee of approximately one million dollars, at that time the largest in its 70-year life.

In the early 1960's Schlenger took on the representation of another wealthy Marylander, Carroll Rosenbloom, the owner of the Baltimore Colts who had established his reputation in the financial community as an early corporate takeover artist (Warner Brothers, American Totalisator, Philadelphia & Reading, etc.). The first item of business was an audit of the football club involving an exposure of millions of dollars for disallowed deductions for travel, entertainment, business gifts, etc. After several years of work Schlenger was successful in knocking out all penalties and was able to negotiate a settlement for a relatively small amount. Thus, he picked up another satisfied client.

In 1972 Rosenbloom became disenchanted with his native Baltimore after having been mercilessly needled by the sports media, particularly John Steadman of the *News-American*, for having raised ticket prices. Rosenbloom consulted Schlenger as to how best to sell the club for $10,000,000, a mere pittance compared with the present-day price of an N.F.L. franchise. After no Baltimore buyers were willing to step forward, Schlenger devised a plan whereby the Baltimore club would be swapped in a tax-free exchange for the Los Angeles Rams, a team that was on the market because of the recent death of its owner, Dan Reeves. The plan called for a two-step transaction, telescoped into one: first, a purchaser, Mr. X, would buy the Rams and simultaneously exchange that stock for stock in the Baltimore Colts. An heir of the Johnson wax fortune had been lined up as Mr. X.

At the last minute the prospective purchaser of the Rams withdrew, whereupon a little known businessman from Skokie, Illinois named Robert Irsay stepped forward as a willing substitute. Thus, when the Schlenger's swap was over, Irsay wound up owning the Colts and Rosenbloom the Rams. This was precisely what Rosenbloom wanted, but it was bad news for Baltimore football fans, worse yet when Irsay moved the Colts to Indianapolis in 1984.

Schlenger was criticized by the tax bar for having proceeded without an advance ruling — he explains that to do so would have killed the deal. It was, nonetheless, as sportswriters would put it, "a gutsy call." When a public outcry erupted over the tax-free nature of the exchange, the Service sent in auditing agents to look into the transaction even before the tax returns had been filed, an almost unheard-of procedure. After extensive examinations in Baltimore and Washington, the IRS upheld the tax treatment that Schlenger had developed, and his call was sustained.

In addition to Donaldson Brown and Carroll Rosenbloom whose affairs have received widespread publicity, Schlenger has represented many other wealthy clients whose names are withheld in the interests of privacy. His clientele has also included a wide spectrum of public officials, educators, financiers, professional people, and sports figures, among them some colorful characters. His major court appearances are summarized in an endnote.[3] He once represented in a criminal tax case a defendant who confessed to maintaining three separate sets of accounting records; at the sentencing he wore a dark blue suit with a golden stickpin inscribed, "In God We Trust." He is said to have enjoyed his sojourn in jail because he lost a lot of weight and had ample time to read the Bible.

This leads us to a review of some of Schlenger's activities in the area of large ideas.

One of his most innovative was a private developer's use of tax-free government financing for the construction or improvement of government facilities by means of their sale to a private limited partnership and their lease-back to the city of Baltimore. The purchase price would be covered by a loan to the purchaser of the proceeds of industrial revenue bonds. The object was to obviate the provision of Article XI, Section 7 of the Constitution of Maryland that no debt of the city may be created unless approved by an act of the legislature and ordinance of the City Council, submitted to and ratified by the voters of the city. The scheme developed by Schlenger was upheld by Judge Martin B. Greenfeld of the Circuit Court of Baltimore City, and the Court of Appeals, bypassing the Court of Special Appeals, affirmed.[4] Robert A. Shelton of Venable, Baetjer and Howard was the successful oral advocate for the appellee.

The essence of Chief Judge Murphy's majority opinion was that the transaction, as structured by Schlenger, did not create a "debt" subject to the constitutional proscription. Speaking in dissent for himself and Judge Dudley Digges, Judge Marvin Smith borrowed a phrase from Gertrude Stein in asserting that "a debt is a debt is a debt." Despite this rhetoric, the five-judge majority carried the day, and Schlenger's creative financing stood approved. The technique was later copied widely and Schlenger lectured about it nationally.

In 1977 Timonium Fair, officially the Maryland State Fair & Agricultural Society, faced a crippling assessment proposed by the Internal Revenue Service based on the contention that its racing revenue constituted "unrelated business income." Richard W. Emory, it will be remembered, had earlier won an important case upholding Timonium's right to an exemption from local real property taxes.[5] But this new onslaught from the IRS was another matter. The only effective way to win this one was through legislation.

Thus, Schlenger prepared an amendment to the Internal Revenue Code to exempt such income, retroactively, on the basis of its derivation from "entertainment or recreational activity traditionally conducted at fairs or expositions promoting agricultural and educational purposes."[6] Schlenger testified in favor of the bill before the House Ways and Means Committee under the chairmanship of Representative Wilbur Mills, and — when the IRS committed the mistake of auditing, on the same theory, a state fair in Louisiana, the home of Senator Russell Long, Chairman of the Senate Finance Committee — Schlenger's bill was quickly enacted into law. For the second time in 16 years Timonium Fair had been saved by the lawyers of Venable, Baetjer and Howard.

In 1977 Schlenger was separately approached by the Baltimore Chamber of Commerce and the Greater Baltimore Committee to determine whether he would be willing to attempt to combine them. Agreeing, Schlenger spent over a year on a *pro bono* basis meeting with the officers and staff of the two organizations, culminating in a merger between the 2,000-member Chamber and the 100-member GBC. Vernon Eney later became president of the reorganized Greater Baltimore Committee, and following Eney's death Schlenger became a member of the GBC Board.

One of the projects of which Schlenger is proudest is his role in helping establish the Baltimore Leadership Program, a plan designed to train young people in the business and professional world for service on boards and commissions of civic and charitable agencies and institutions. Richard Sullivan, president of the Greater Baltimore Committee, appointed a blue ribbon committee of civic leaders, including Jacques Schlenger, to study the workings of such a program in Cleveland, and they were so impressed that a similar one was established in Baltimore. It became quite an honor to be chosen for training in the program, and the firm of Venable, Baetjer and Howard distinguished itself by having three of its associates so selected, Constance H. Baker, Peter S. Saucier, and Ellyn L. Brown. Although not aimed directly at blacks and women, the program has had the desirable side-effect of bringing into positions of leadership a wider circle of people from these groups.

Schlenger's own service on boards and commissions has been extensive. Among the more important have been the Greater Baltimore Committee, the board of trustees of the Johns Hopkins University, president of the Five Percent Club of Baltimore, chairman of the Advisory Council of the Peabody Institute, a member of the board of managers of the Children's Aid and Family Service, a member and vice-chairman of the board of trustees of Bryn Mawr School, a member of the board and vice-president of the Baltimore Symphony, a member of the executive board of Yale Law School, a member of the board and counsel to CPHA, a member of the board of trustees of the Maryland Historical Society, chairman of the Zoning Revision Committee of Baltimore County, and chairman of the Baltimore County Revenue Authority. Other areas of service too numerous to list in the text are consigned to an endnote.[7] He has also been a prolific contributor to professional journals in addition to writing his book, *Large Wealth*.

Over a six-month period in 1990 Schlenger headed a major fund-raising campaign which may prove to be the salvation of the Peabody Institute as a viable cultural ornament in Baltimore. Earlier that year, the legislature by the Acts of 1990, Ch. 67 pledged $15 million in state aid to the Peabody on condition that it raise a like account from private sources by September 15. This was a tall order, since most of the work would have to be done during the summer doldrums.

Jacques Schlenger, nevertheless, accepted the challenge and went about the task with unbridled energy. As the deadline approached with more than $12 million committed, the trustees of the Johns Hopkins University guaranteed the balance. It is safe to say that never before in Maryland has so much money been raised for a charitable cause in such a short period of time.

This chapter concludes with a report of two pieces of litigation in which the firm was involved, one a libel case instituted in 1971 claiming $5,000,000 in damages and the other a $450,000,000 malpractice case filed against the firm in 1986 as a result of the collapse of the savings and loan industry.

The libel case was brought in the United States District Court for the Southern District of Florida by a Miami attorney who was aggrieved by a statement, alleged to be defamatory, in a letter dated May 6, 1971 from Venable, Baetjer and Howard's correspondent Florida counsel. A copy of the letter was sent by Schlenger to other parties, and this was said to constitute a republication. The offending words were that the plaintiff "may be in some financial trouble which could result in personal judgments against him and also possibly in disciplinary actions by the bar."[8]

Each partner and associate in the firm was personally named as a defendant and served with process. To those who had never been sued it was an eerie feeling and enabled them to empathize with clients who receive a knock on the door from a process server or a registered letter from the clerk of a court. Francis D. Murnaghan, Jr., one of the firm's leading litigators and an expert on the law of defamation, was put in charge of the case.

The outcome was a dismissal for want of jurisdiction, and the suit was never refiled in Maryland. Although the result was gratifying, the experience was unpleasant since it was not clear that damages in a defamation suit would have been covered by malpractice insurance. The individually owned assets of the partners might have been at risk.

Many times more unpleasant was the huge malpractice case filed by the Maryland Deposit Insurance Fund of the State of Maryland on July 3, 1986, an event that did little to enhance the enjoyment of the Fourth of July holiday.[9] And, speaking of insurance, the firm had a $30 million malpractice insurance policy which clearly applied to the acts complained of in this case — except perhaps, for the irresponsible third count that sounded in "fraud." However that may be, since the state was asking for $450 million, at least $420 million remained uninsured. One wondered whether the family jewels might be on the bargaining table. Understandably, therefore, the eventual settlement within policy limits prompted deep sighs of relief.

The saga began in May, 1985 when depositors at a number of state chartered savings and loan associations began a run on these institutions amid rumors of mismanagement and financial problems at Old Court Savings & Loan Association (Old Court). It became apparent that if the problems at Old Court were not isolated, as later proved to be the case, then the assets held by Maryland Savings-Share Insurance Corporation (MSSIC), the corporation formed by the legislature to insure the deposits in state-chartered S & L's, would be inadequate. In response to the crisis, Governor Harry Hughes, then on a trip to Israel, beat a hasty retreat to Annapolis and called a special session of the legislature.

At that session the Maryland Deposit Insurance Fund (MDIF) was created,[10] unmistakably a state agency as MSSIC had not been, despite the latter's colorful logo which closely resembled the Great Seal of Maryland. MSSIC was folded into MDIF, assuming all its rights and obligations, and the 102 state-chartered S & L's were told to secure federal insurance, merge with some federally insured institution or be taken over by MDIF for liquidation. It was strong medicine but the patient was very sick.

As part of the legislative package adopted at the special session in May, 1985, the legislature created the office of Special Counsel, charged with the duty of investigating all phases of the S & L collapse and directing him to submit his report by January 8, 1986. That date coincided with the arrival in Baltimore of thousands of attorneys from all over the country to the midwinter meeting of the American Bar Association. His report,[11] sharply critical of Venable, Baetjer and Howard, was widely publicized in the local press and made juicy reading for the out-of-town lawyers.

The Special Counsel appointed by Governor Hughes was Wilbur D. Preston, Jr., the senior partner in the firm of Whiteford, Taylor & Preston. Preston was a well-respected trial lawyer who applied his litigating instincts by going after potential defendants with deep pockets instead of concentrating on the public officials, both elected and appointed, who were primarily responsible for allowing the debacle to occur. Although the *Preston Report* was critical but not rhetorical in its characterizations of Venable's behavior, the complaint filed on July 3, 1986 brings to mind the purple prose of Simon Sobeloff's report of December 31, 1935 on the activities of the directors of the Baltimore Trust Company.[12] Sobeloff used such expressions as "a profligacy that now seems incomprehensible," and "a reckless abandon that is perfectly shocking," and the 1986 complaint against Venable gave vent in the first paragraph to the expression "gross, flagrant and repeated violations of the most minimal ethical standards and legal duties." Both outbursts were more calculated to inflame than to inform and both were widely reproduced in the news media.

Since an analysis of the 457-page *Preston Report* and the 65-page complaint would take us far afield, this discussion will be confined to the accusations of ethical lapses and the assault on the integrity of Schlenger's advice in his letter of August 17, 1976.

On the ethical front, the criticisms were addressed principally to the activities of two Venable partners, Gerald M. Katz and Terry F. Hall.

Katz, the head of the tax department who succeeded Schlenger when he became managing partner, had, on occasion, provided tax advice to Old Court and some of its affiliated companies, but never in connection with any regulatory matters involving MSSIC. He was also one of many attorneys who had represented Old Court's president, Jeffrey Levitt, who later went to jail on conviction of his criminal mismanagement of the association's affairs for his personal benefit. Also sent away was another Katz client, Jerome S. Cardin, an old friend and sometime client of Jacques Schlenger's. In retrospect, these relationships seem incompatible with the traditions of Venable, Baetjer and Howard, but the fact remains that no scintilla of criminal conduct was ever charged against anyone at the firm, this at a time when public resentment was running at fever pitch.

Later, when the dust had settled, Katz had his day in court on charges of ethical improprieties brought by Bar Counsel on behalf of the Attorney Grievance Commission, and he was exonerated.[13] Yet, before and after this decision, there remained a cadre of partners who harbored and sometimes expressed resentment that "he got us into this mess" and had epitomized an insensitivity to propriety that had ruptured the fabric of the partnership. Perhaps in response to this sentiment, Katz resigned on October 31, 1986. It was a sad day for him and for the firm. Katz was a brilliant lawyer and had many admirers within the firm and outside.

Crucial to the resolution of the ethical question was the conduct of Terry F. Hall. This junior partner at Venable, Baetjer and Howard had worked under my tutelage in the Corporate and Securities group before his move to the Real Estate Department, and I vouch without reservation for his integrity. During the period of the developing S & L crisis, Hall had been assigned to MSSIC as its corporate counsel, a task for which he seemed well trained because of his corporate and real estate background. However, since MSSIC was represented by Terry Hall while Levitt and Old Court had been represented in some instances by Hall's partner, Jerry Katz, Preston raised the question whether this gave rise to a conflict of interest.

Its answer depended on the credibility of Hall's testimony that he had explained Venable's posture to Charles C. Hogg, the chairman of MSSIC, in a telephone conversation on January 11, 1983, confirmed by an entry in Hall's time sheets, and had secured Hogg's consent. Hogg could neither confirm nor deny the conversation but had no recollection of it. Hall also claimed that he had later explained the matter to the full board but none of its members could recall the event and it was not recorded in the minutes. However, when the issue of credibility later came before the Circuit Court for Baltimore

City in the proceedings brought by the Grievance Commission, Judge David Ross believed Terry Hall, and the Court of Appeals, on motion of Bar Counsel, accepted Judge Ross's analysis.[14]

This answer to the ethical question leaves open the practical question, "Could this 'mess' have been avoided?" Of course, the answer is "Yes." Using 20-20 hindsight, there are many things that could have been handled differently — the Ethics Committee could have scheduled regular meetings *en banc* instead of meeting in panels on an *ad hoc* basis; it could have been required to submit regular reports to the Operating Committee, and written confirmation of any waivers from clients could have been made mandatory; Terry Hall, honest and able though he was, could have profited from closer supervision by a partner with more maturity of judgment; warning signals about Levitt's questionable conduct could have been heeded and acted upon; as skippers of the ship both Eney and Schlenger could have maintained a closer watch over other members of the crew; and individual partners could have been less concerned with legal business and more with the abyss of conflicts. To borrow an overused adage, there was "enough blame to go around," or, as other lawyers were saying, "There but for the grace of God go we."[15]

If the case against Venable had not been settled, the charges of ethical improprieties, even if established, would have presented MDIF with a difficult problem of proof, i.e., the task of connecting the alleged lapses with any loss to MSSIC.

Putting it differently: however gratifying was the vindication in the grievance process, the fact that charges had been brought against some Venable partners was a bitter pill to swallow, but even if the charges had been proved, it is difficult to perceive how they could be causally connected with any loss to the client. Not so, however, with Preston's charge that Schlenger's so-called "opinion" of August 17, 1976 constituted "ineffective legal advice" which, according to the Special Counsel, enormously enlarged the risks that MSSIC had assumed by sanctioning "per account" insurance coverage, rather than "per depositor." This charge was echoed in the complaint, and if plaintiff had been able to get to a jury on this issue, the exposure could have been substantial. It was, therefore, the linchpin of the state's case and, more than anything else, led to the settlement. It was also unfair because the advice was sound and, even if it had not been, the state was estopped from repudiating it. These two points require some analysis.

The advice was sound because it characterized as defensible a MSSIC bylaw that reproduced *verbatim* the critical language of the MSSIC statutory charter. This reasoning was founded on the cardinal rule of statutory construction that statutes are to be construed as having the plain meaning of the words used.[16]

MSSIC's statutory charter required its board of directors to adopt rules and regulations establishing a limit on the amount of insurance that might be provided to the holders of accounts in member associations. In relevant part the legislature had provided as follows:

> As one of such rules and regulations the board of directors from time to time shall establish a limit on the amount of insurance which may be provided *for each separate share account* of an association; and this limit may not exceed by more than the sum of $10,000.00 the amount of prevailing insurance available from the Federal Savings and Loan Insurance Corporation or its successor instrumentality from time to time. [Emphasis added].[17]

In 1976 MSSIC's board of directors amended its bylaws to read as follows:

> The limit of insurance liability for which the Corporation may be required to pay *for each separate share account* of any association may not exceed by more that $10,000 the amount of prevailing insurance available from the Federal Savings and Loan Insurance Corporation or its successor instrumentality from time to time. [Emphasis added].[18]

Wisely or unwisely (and subsequent events would indicate the latter) the MSSIC board took advantage of the plain words of the statute which permitted limits to be set *for each separate share account.* The tie-in to the federal rules applied only to the dollar amount of coverage that might be extended, the $10,000 differential being intended to provide a competitive advantage over federal associations. There was no tie-in with the so-called "$100,000 per depositor" rule of FSLIC unless it was to be implied from extrinsic evidence, and courts do not do that where the words used in a statute are plain and unambiguous.[19] Besides, the federal standards defining a depositor were themselves an elastic yardstick, as witness a FSLIC brochure entitled: *Know How a Small Family Can Have $400,000 to $1,400,000 of Insured Savings.*[20] This promotion of multiple accounts on the federal level, despite its "per depositor rule," is at variance with the allegation in the complaint that "FSLIC treated various types of accounts with common ownership interests as single accounts for insurance purposes."[21] Also, the multi-billion dollar scandals that have plagued the federal savings and loan industry in the late 1980's and early 1990's have established that FSLIC was not the Rock of Gibraltar it was perceived to be in Maryland in 1985.

Having made the business decision to avail itself of the latitude permitted by the Maryland statute, the MSSIC board asked Schlenger for Venable's blessing of the action. His reply of August 17, 1976 was more a comfort letter than an opinion or, as one commentator put it, "a distinction akin to preventive medicine as opposed to corrective surgery."[22] Schlenger concluded that there were "strong arguments" supporting the board's position but warned that if the new policy produced abuses, there might be some danger that a court could be persuaded to upset it. In short, it was the statute, not Schlenger's letter, that facilitated the change in MSSIC policy.

However, the factor that puts the issue to rest as to Schlenger's letter is the long-standing acquiescence by the legislature in MSSIC's per account rule. In an opinion dated February 27, 1986 Attorney General Stephen H. Sachs conceded that "the per account rule was not unknown at various levels of government" and that in 1984 there had been a "proposed amendment that would have set a limit on total loss coverage for each depositor."[23] This prior knowledge by the legislature of MSSIC's policy and especially its rejection of an amendment that would have reversed it constituted legislative acquiescence. If any validation of Schlenger's letter was needed, this provided it.

The settlement of the MDIF case takes us out of the Schlenger era but, in the interest of continuity, it would be better to complete the saga in this chapter, even though it was Benjamin R. Civiletti who played the leading role in this critical event in the firm's history. We begin with the adage that settlements take place only when all parties want them, and that was the case here.

The state wanted to settle for at least three reasons: first, it wanted as much immediate cash as it could lay its hands on to help in the bailout of depositors; second, it had engaged the Washington offices of Latham, Watkins & Hills as trial counsel, and legal fees were mounting steadily; and third, even if it were successful in winning a verdict before an Anne Arundel County jury, there could be no assurance that the verdict would stand up on appeal. After years of expensive litigation MDIF might wind up with nothing from this source.

Venable wanted a settlement because the steady barrage of bad publicity was fraying the nerves. Also, confident though we were of our legal position, the appellate process might have taken years to complete, and the outcome could not be predicted with certainty. Some partners would have liked to take the high road and press for vindication as Edwin Baetjer had done when he was sued as a director of the old Baltimore Trust Company, but today no experienced litigator would recommend that tactic if a reasonable settlement is obtainable. The risk of an adverse result to a defendant in a jury trial of an emotionally charged case is rarely worth taking.

And, finally, the insurance company wanted a settlement because litigation expenses were becoming massive, and if an insurer negligently fails to settle within policy limits, there is danger that it may be held liable for a verdict in excess of those limits under established principles of insurance law.

The settlement process began on March 19, 1987 when the state submitted a written offer to settle for $50 million. Although rejected, this communication sent an important signal: no longer was the state pressing for the $450 million in the *ad damnum* clause in the complaint. Instead, the word had been put out that the case could be disposed of for an amount that would allow Venable to survive and still provide a tidy sum for depositors.

Negotiations began in earnest a month later on April 20, 1987 at a meeting in Governor Schaefer's office where the general parameters of a settlement agreement were fashioned. The governor made it clear that the state would not agree to any indemnification of Venable against depositors' suits.

A week later on April 26, 1987 the lawyers hammered out a tentative agreement for the payment of $25 million. This was a dramatic break-through since theretofore the state had insisted that Venable must be punished by the exaction of a substantial payment by the partners over and above their insurance coverage. The abandonment of this position was a major catalyst in the settlement process. Yet, the indemnification issue remained unresolved. Venable was not worried about depositors' suits but wanted protection against private parties who might try to relitigate the malpractice case after the settlement with the state.[24]

The next significant date was May 4, 1987 when the state offered to accept $27 million, reflecting a $2 million increment over its prior offer in return for partial indemnification, i.e., against claims other than those of depositors. Still striving for better terms, Civiletti rejected this offer on May 6, 1987, whereupon Attorney General J. Joseph Curran, Jr. replied that unless the offer were accepted, the trial date set for January 11, 1988 would be strictly adhered to. Thus, the case would be put on the fast track, to be tried ahead of all other civil suits filed by MDIF, and Venable would be held out as the arch-villain. The firm's outside counsel advised that the choice was to accept the state's offer or proceed to trial.

On May 8, 1987 Civiletti agreed to present the offer to the partnership, and at a meeting on May 11 it was accepted. Governor Schaefer announced it the next day, and on June 10 the $27 million was wired into the state's bank account from the carrier in London. It was said to be the second largest malpractice settlement in the nation's history.[25]

After the settlement had been announced, the hostility of the press continued. An editorial in *The Sun* on the morning of May 14, 1987 chastized the state for failure to exact a penalty from the individual Venable partners, concluding that "the wrongdoer ought to suffer some pain." To those to whom the S & L lawsuit had seemed like a year-long nightmare, this was the most unkindest cut of all.

In retrospect, credit must go to Jacques Schlenger and his administrative partner, Thomas J. Kenney, Jr., for their good judgment in carrying $30 million of insurance. Whether a lesser sum would have been sufficient to achieve a settlement within policy limits is debatable, but the fact remains that Schlenger and Kenney must be given kudos for having provided enough insurance to get the job done.

It is a quirk of history that leaders are often remembered more for events that caused them embarrassment than for their achievements. The closing years of Schlenger's tenure as chief executive officer of Venable, Baetjer and Howard were so overshadowed by the S & L crisis that many may have been blinded to his stature at the bar, to his contributions to the life of the community and to the innovations he brought about in the operation of the firm. Those achievements were substantial and lasting.

Jacques Schlenger and his wife, the former Suzanne Johnson, have lived for a number of years in the Fox Chapel community west of Dulaney Valley Road in Baltimore County. They have three daughters, Lynda Sue Winter, Martha J. Rabicoff, and Kirsten Schlenger. A bibliophile and connoisseur of wines, Schlenger has an extensive library and wine cellar. The library contains a number of rare first editions and a remarkable collection of the works of Anthony Trollope while the wine cellar boasts over 1,600 bottles. Most wines, like old books, improve with age and these collections are getting better all the time. They are a reflection of the sophisticated taste of their owner.

At a firm seminar in 1984 Schlenger announced that he would step down as managing partner in his 60th year. In keeping with that promise he turned over the leadership of the firm to Benjamin R. Civiletti on January 1, 1987. So began the era of Benjamin R. Civiletti, the third of the Innovators at Venable, Baetjer and Howard.

Endnotes to Part III, Chapter 2:

1. For example, the New York firm of Fried, Frank, Harris, Shriver & Jacobson was known in the District of Columbia as Fried, Frank, Harris, Shriver & *Kampelman*, recognizing the Washington presence of Max M. Kampelman, the distinguished scholar and diplomat; and the Los Angeles firm of Latham & Watkins was known in the District as Latham, Watkins & *Hills*, recognizing the Washington presence of Carla A. Hills, former Secretary of HUD and Roderick Hills, former Chairman of the SEC. However, the practice seems to have been a passing fad, and both firms now use the same name in the District as in their home states.

2. *Attorney Grievance Commission v. Nothstein*, 300 Md. 667 (1984). Another former Venable partner, Jacob L. Friedel, was disbarred for unprofessional conduct occurring after he had left the firm. *Attorney Grievance Commission v. Friedel*, Court of Appeals of Maryland, Misc. Docket (Subtitle BV) No. 37, September Term 1989, unreported *per curiam* opinion filed September 26, 1990.

3. The following tax cases of interest were argued by Schlenger over the years:

Williams v. United States, 378 F.2d 693 (U.S. Ct. Claims 1967), upholding the availability of a gift tax exclusion for the present value of a life interest of a minor in a gift in trust for his benefit, coupled with a discretionary power in the trustee to invade principal for his needs if the income proved insufficient therefor. The deed of trust had been drafted by another lawyer at Venable, Baetjer and Howard, and Schlenger undertook its defense for the honor of the firm at no expense to the client. Other counsel of record for the plaintiff were Frederick Steinmann, Theodore W. Hirsh, Gerald M. Katz, and Robert C. Embry.

Ellis v. United States, 280 F. Supp. 786 (D. Md. 1968), holding that property subject to a general power of appointment which had been effectively released in part before the statutory deadline of November 1, 1951 escapes the federal estate tax. Also listed as counsel of record for the plaintiff were Theodore W. Hirsh and Edmund P. Dandridge, Jr.

Estate of Edmund S. Hoskins v. Commissioner of Internal Revenue, 71 T.C. 379 (1978), where Schlenger unsuccessfully attempted to establish a charitable deduction from federal estate tax for an appointed estate in remainder which did not qualify as an annuity trust, a unitrust or a pooled income trust. Harry D. Shapiro and Bryson L. Cook were also counsel of record for the petitioner.

Henry J. Knott v. Commissioner of Internal Revenue, 67 T.C. 681 (1977), a very important victory for one of Schlenger's wealthy clients, holding that a bargain sale of real estate to Mr. Knott's foundation was a deductible charitable gift and that the subsequent resale of the property by the foundation did not constitute constructive income to the donor. Theodore W. Hirsh and Harry D. Shapiro also appeared in the case.

Howard Construction, Inc. v. Commissioner of Internal Revenue, 43 T.C. 343 (1964), holding that no part of the consideration received on the sale of stock was to be attributed to a covenant not to compete. Frederick Steinmann was co-counsel for the successful petitioner.

Other cases in which Schlenger's appearance is entered "on the brief" but not as oral advocate include:

Electronic Modules Corporation v. United States, 695 F.2d 1367 (4th Cir. 1982), a victory for Harry D. Shapiro in a case upholding as bona fide loans a corporation's advances to its wholly owned subsidiary; *Maryland Savings Share Insurance Corporation v. United States*, 644 F.2d 16 (Ct. Cl. 1981), where Shapiro was unsuccessful in upholding MSSIC's deduction for its reserve for bad debts since it had never been called upon to pay a claim and no event had occurred during the tax year to indicate a potential liability — an ironic result in the light of the disaster soon to befall MSSIC; *Maryland National Bank v. United States*, 609 F.2d 1078 (1979), where Shapiro was unsuccessful in upholding the application of the $3,000 annual exclusion from gift tax for an estate said to represent a future interest; *Ramsay-Scarlett & Co., Inc. v. Commissioner of Internal Revenue*, 521 F.2d 786 (4 Cir.1975), where Hirsh was unsuccessful in sustaining a deduction for theft loss, absent a showing that there was no reasonable prospect of recovery; *Loyola Federal Savings & Loan Association v. United Sates*, 390 F. Supp 1375 (D. Md. 1975), where Hirsh was unable to sustain the deductibility of a reserve for bad debt on a construction loan absent proof of realistic risk of default in the tax year.

4. *Eberhart v. Mayor and City Council of Baltimore City*, 291 Md. 92 (1981).

5. *Maryland State Fair & Agricultural Society v. Supervisor of Assessments*, 225 Md. 574 (1961), *supra* Part II, Ch. 8, note 17.

6. I.R.C. Sec. 513(d)(2)(a): "The term 'public entertainment activity' means any entertainment or recreational activity of a kind traditionally conducted at fairs or expositions promoting agricultural and educational purposes, including, but not limited to, any activity one of the purposes of which is to attract the public to fairs or expositions or to promote the breeding of animals or the development of products or equipment."

7. In addition to the offices enumerated in the text, Schlenger has been a member of the Johns Hopkins University National Council for Medicine, a trustee of United Way of Central Maryland, trustee of the Schaeffer Institute of Public Policy of the University of Baltimore, a member of the Financial Advisory Council of Baltimore County, Chairman of the Pension Review Committee of Baltimore City, a member of the Board of Center Stage, Chairman of the GBMC Foundation, and a director of Merry-Go-Round, Inc. He was the first elected chairman of the Tax Section of the Maryland State Bar Association and has served on numerous committees of the State and American Bar Associations. He has also been a frequent lecturer on tax questions.

8. *David E. Graham v. Jacques T. Schlenger, et al.*, Civil Action No. 711545 Civ-PF, United States District Court for the Southern District of Florida, Miami Division.

9. *The Maryland Deposit Insurance Fund Corporation v. Venable, Baetjer & Howard, et al.*, C.A. No. 1112919 in the Maryland Circuit Court for Anne Arundel County, the Complaint being hereinafter cited as the "Complaint."

10. State Government Article of the Annotated Code of Maryland, Section 9-1204, enacted by Ch. 11 of the Acts of the General Assembly, 1st Special Session, 1985.

11. Report of Wilbur D. Preston, Jr., Special Counsel, dated January 8, 1986 addressed to Governor Harry R. Hughes, Senator Melvin A. Steinberg, President of the Maryland State Senate, and Delegate Benjamin L. Cardin, Speaker of the House of Delegates, hereinafter cited as the *Preston Report*.

12. Part I, Ch. 2, note 7.

13. *Attorney Grievance Commission of Maryland v. Terry F. Hall and Gerald M. Katz*, Case No. 89107053-DP in the Circuit Court for Baltimore City, Findings of Fact and Conclusions of Law of the Hon. David Ross, entered July 19, 1989, concluding that there were no violations of the disciplinary rules of professional conduct by either Respondent. On recommendation of Bar Counsel, the petition for disciplinary action was dismissed by order of the Court of Appeals, September 8, 1989, Misc. Docket, Subtitle BV, No.3, September Term 1989 (not reproduced in Maryland *Reports*).

14. Judge Ross's judicial findings, supplementing the stipulated facts, included the statement, "All of Hall's testimony regarding the conversation is believed and is accepted as accurate." *Id.* at 25.

15. An article in the *Daily Record* of March 8, 1986 analyzed the new ethics procedures implemented by Venable, Baetjer and Howard, and in a sub-article, *Other Firms Examine In-House Procedures*, the reaction of other lawyers was discussed.

16. *Comptroller v. John C. Louis Company*, 285 Md. 527, 538-9 (1979) and numerous cases therein cited.

17. Annotated Code of Maryland (1957), Art. 23, 161 SS; Acts of 1962, Ch. 131, 1; repealed by Acts of 1980, Ch. 33.

18. Quoted in letter dated August 17, 1976 from Jacques T. Schlenger to Mr. Harry B. Wolf, Jr., Executive Vice-President of MSSIC.

19. *Hunt v. Montgomery County*, 248 Md. 403, 414-15 (1968).

20. A question-and-answer article in *The Sun* of February 5, 1986 by Jesse Glasgow, Financial Editor, entitled *Different Account Titles Allows investor to Push FDIC Coverage Over $100,000*, addresses primarily the question under FDIC rules but cites also the FSLIC brochure mentioned in the text. Both sets of federal rules were "elastic yardsticks."

21. Complaint, Paragraph 35.

22. Ray Jenkins, *Venerable Law Firm Finds Itself in Unaccustomed Role*, op-ed article in the *Evening Sun*, May 12, 1986 correctly analyzed the Schlenger "opinion," but most news stories, editorials and commentaries accepted unquestioningly the *Preston Report* of "ineffective legal advice." Particularly galling was a lead editorial in *The Sun* of January 13, 1986 that regurgitated the charge that the Schlenger "opinion" had "allowed the agency to give virtually unlimited insurance coverage . . . . . contrary to the intention of the legislature." It did no such thing. With knowledge of MSSIC's "per account rule," the legislature acquiesced in it for over eight years.

23. Opinion letter, February 27, 1986, from the Hon. Stephen H. Sachs, Attorney General of Maryland to Senator Howard A. Denis and Mr. William S. Ratchford, II, page 8, fn. 8.

24. Among the various defenses to the depositors' claims was the well settled principle that depositors are creditors and, as such, have no right to file derivative suits against their corporate depositary's agents or attorneys. Hanks, *Maryland Corporation Law* (1990) at 114,§ 4.16.

25. The largest at the time was a $40 million settlement by Rogers & Wells, a Wall Street firm, according to an article in the *Sunday Sun* of June 14, 1987 and numerous other news accounts of the Venable settlement. These records, of dubious distinction, have since been broken by much larger settlements, notably one for $55 million in 1990 paid on behalf of a Philadelphia firm in a case arising out of the failure of a federal savings and loan institution.

Benjamin R. Civiletti, seventy-third Attorney General of the United States, from a photograph of the portrait by William F. Draper in the Department of Justice.

Reproduced with permission of the artist.

Benjamin R. Civiletti

I F THE PREVIOUS CHAPTER was difficult to write because of nearness in time, this one is even more so because it deals not with history but with current events. Once more the call goes out to a future chronicler to put in proper perspective the material that follows.

Benjamin R. Civiletti was born in Peekskill, New York on July 17, 1935 and graduated from the Johns Hopkins University in 1957. After receiving his LL.B. degree from the University of Maryland School of Law in 1961, he began his legal career as a law clerk for Judge W. Calvin Chesnut of the United States District Court for the District of Maryland, a jurist about whom much has been written in the chapter on John Henry Lewin. In 1962 Civiletti was named an Assistant United States Attorney for the District of Maryland, and, as a twenty-eight year-old prosecutor, he teamed up with fellow Assistant United States Attorney Stephen H. Sachs (later Attorney General of Maryland) to investigate the 1959 collapse of several state thrift institutions in Maryland; this resulted in the successful prosecution of D. Spencer Grow, a financier from Utah, C. Oren Mensik, a banker from Chicago, and A. Gordon Boone, Speaker of the Maryland House of Delegates, among others. In 1964 he joined the firm of Venable, Baetjer and Howard as an associate. Five years later he was elected a partner and only two years after that was named the head of the firm's litigation department, specializing in commercial litigation, both civil and criminal.

During the 1970's Civiletti assisted two of his senior partners in their trial of cases of widespread interest, *viz*:

First, in one of Vernon Eney's *Madden* cases[1] he conducted the cross-examination of an expert witness for five days after 30 days of direct testimony on the fair market value of Pimlico Race Track which had been sold in 1949. On retrial, another judgment for the defendant was rendered, this one being affirmed on appeal.

Second, in one of Norwood Orrick's *Robb Tyler Landfill* cases[2] the question was whether Tyler had for more than 15 years illegally filled with refuse a 200-acre tract owned by plaintiff. A jury verdict for the defendant was rendered after a seven-week trial. Civiletti used muskrat trappers from Patapsco River as expert witnesses on the accretion and losses of soil in tidal or marshlands.

A turning point in Civiletti's career occurred in 1972 when Orrick enlisted his help in an antitrust case, *Lanier Business Products v. Graymar Company*,[3] an engagement that had been forwarded to Orrick by Charles H. Kirbo of the Atlanta firm of King & Spalding. Kirbo was the personal attorney for Governor, later President, Jimmy Carter. Civiletti's handling of the *Lanier* case made such an impression on Kirbo that when the President's first Attorney General, Griffin Bell, was casting about for qualified lawyers to fill his staff, Kirbo recommended Civiletti for consideration. When similar endorsements came in from various federal judges whom Bell had also consulted, he summoned Civiletti. The result was his appointment as Assistant Attorney General in charge of the Criminal Division.

Thus, when President Carter took office in January, 1976 Civiletti became the lawyer in charge of all federal criminal investigations in the land. Three of the most interesting were:

1. Koreagate involved alleged briberies of members of Congress by Tong Sun Park, a Korean rice merchant and suave Washington

partygoer. Park fled to Korea where Civiletti pursued him. Despite the absence of an extradition treaty with that country, after two visits to Korea and prolonged negotiations Civiletti was able to get Park returned to the United States where he testified before Congress and at successful prosecutions of several defendants involved in the scandal.

2. Civiletti inherited from the Ford administration the investigation of top members of the FBI for alleged unlawful break-ins in pursuit of underground Weathermen. After three years, the former deputy Director of the FBI and the assistant director were prosecuted and convicted in the United States District Court for the District of Columbia.

3. Civiletti directed an investigation leading to the guilty plea of Richard Helms, former director of the CIA, for misleading Congress in testimony concerning the CIA's involvement in the election of President Augusto Pinochet in Chile.

A little over a year after his move to Washington, Civiletti's rise continued, as he assumed the job of Deputy Attorney General after having twice been offered and twice declined a nomination to be director of the FBI. On August 16, 1979 following Griffin Bell's resignation, Civiletti was sworn in as the 73rd Attorney General of the United States. Six other Marylanders, William Pinkney (1811-14), William Wirt (1817-29), Roger B. Taney (1831-33), John Nelson (1843-45), Reverdy Johnson (1849-50) and Charles J. Bonaparte (1906-09), had previously held that office.

During the ensuing 17 months of 1979-80 until the end of Carter's administration, Civiletti participated actively in litigation on behalf of the government instead of delegating that function exclusively to the Solicitor General. Traditionally, at least in recent history, Attorneys General have occupied themselves with administrative matters, leaving to subordinates all court appearances. Not so Attorney General Civiletti.

He represented his country before the International Court of Justice at The Hague, arguing on behalf of the American hostages in Iran.[4] (During that crisis he had repeatedly restricted, on constitutional grounds, the proposals of the White House staff to impose reprisals on Iranian students resident in the United States). He also represented the government in a significant case in the Supreme Court upholding the government's right to denaturalize Nazi war criminals who had falsified their past in the naturalization process.[5] He successfully defended in the Court of Appeals for the District of Columbia President Carter's wage and price guidelines.[6] Other personal court appearances during his tenure as attorney general are collected in an endnote.[7]

During his administration as attorney general, Civiletti was responsible for the Justice Department's promulgation of guidelines for open trials and for the use of informants and the conduct of undercover agents. Several significant departmental publications were also issued in his regime, notably *National Priorities for the Investigation and Prosecution of White-Collar Crime*, *Principles of Federal Prosecution*, and *National Prison Standards*. Those years also saw two of the most sensational undercover investigations in departmental history — ABSCAM and Operation GREYLORD. ABSCAM was the investigation of congressional bribery by the F.B.I. posing as Mid-Eastern sheiks. Operation GREYLORD placed an undercover agent as the defense lawyer in a state criminal court system to catch corrupt judges. Fifteen Chicago jurists either resigned or were convicted as a result of GREYLORD.

Upon returning to private practice, Civiletti's first assignment was the organization of the Washington office at 1301 Pennsylvania Avenue, N.W. Although the quarters were limited, they commanded an excellent view of the inaugural parade in January, 1985, and the firm played the role of host to friends and clients who enjoyed the occasion in convivial surroundings. When the operations outgrew the Pennsylvania Avenue location, the Washington office was moved to its present quarters at 1201 New York Avenue, N.W.

During Civiletti's career in private practice he has participated in a wide variety of litigation in many fields, including statutory construction,[8] antitrust,[9] federal jurisdiction,[10] contracts,[11] condemnation,[12] patents[13] and labor relations.[14] A few of his significant engagements are summarized below.

The *Burning Tree* saga in the late 1980's ranks among his most celebrated, although the final chapter ended in defeat. Burning Tree Club is an all-male country club in the Washington suburbs of Maryland. Under a 50-year agreement with the state it enjoyed special tax treatment for the "open space" it provided in the form of its golf links — this despite the fact that only its male members could walk on the open space, others being required to enjoy its vistas, if at all, from the public highways. The arrangement was challenged as a violation of the anti-discrimination law enacted by the legislature in 1974, sometimes known as the Equal Rights Act or E.R.A.[15]

In *Burning Tree I*,[16] the Court of Appeals held unconstitutional and non-severable the "principal purpose" exemption in the E.R.A., i.e., the provision permitting discrimination if the primary purpose of the club is to "serve or benefit members of a particular sex." Accordingly, Civiletti prevailed, and the whole statute was struck down, the court never reaching the other exemption permitting "periodic discrimination," i.e., the provision permitting the exclusion of members of one sex on specific dates or at specific times. This second exemption would, for example, have sanctioned the exclusion of women from the golf course on Saturday mornings.

The legislature reacted to *Burning Tree I* by reenacting the E.R.A., this time omitting the "primary purpose exemption" but retaining the "periodic discrimination exemption."[17]

In *Burning Tree II*[18] the Court of Appeals agreed with Civiletti's contention (or strategic concession) that the "periodic discrimination exemption" was bad but, *mirabile dictu*, held it severable so that the rest of the amended E.R.A. could stand. The majority of the court, speaking through Judge Eldridge, relied on the "dominant purpose" rule to uphold severability; i.e., they looked at the broad social objectives sought to be achieved by the statute in order to uphold its constitutionality. The dissent (McAuliffe and Murphy, J. J.) argued that the invalidity of an exemption in a scheme of statutory regulation compels a holding of non-severability on the rationale that the legislature would not have passed the regulation at all without the exemption's inclusion.

Civiletti invoked the authority of *Burning Tree I* to invalidate an exemption which, if held non-severable, would have invalidated the whole statute. The majority's refusal to go along with his contentions on severability had the effect of undercutting this strategy, but it was a noble effort.

The story of *Burning Tree* is an example of an attorney's espousal of a client's cause with which he may not be in sympathy. One need only peruse the many awards that Civiletti has received in the field of race relations[19] to perceive that he is not one who accepts discrimination in any form; yet his client, Burning Tree Club, had a legal point worthy of assertion, as witness its victory in the first round in the Court of Appeals and the two dissents it garnered in the second. Vernon Eney followed the same precept of a lawyer's calling in his rearguard actions against the integration of the public schools.[20] The courts are designed to hear all disputes that have merit on both sides, not just those that represent causes in vogue.

In 1983 Civiletti was involved as counsel for a number of Toyota distributorships in a complicated piece of multi-district antitrust litigation, the settlement of which was finally approved by the Federal District Court after protracted negotiations.[21] Several years later he represented a Toyota distributorship in a long and bitter dispute over the construction of an employment contract, a case which went to the Court of Special Appeals twice and the Court of Appeals once.[22] The opinions fashion some new law on the standard of proof required to sustain a case of negligent misrepresentation. Paul Strain argued the first appeal and Civiletti the other two. Eventually, the case was settled.

A 1971 case that reflects Civiletti's high standing with the Federal bench is *Bundy v. Cannon*[23] where he and Herbert Belgrad were appointed by the Court as *amici curiae* to help resolve a dispute between the state penal authorities and 82 inmates of the Maryland Penitentiary who challenged the constitutionality of their transfer from other institutions. The court expressed its "great appreciation" to the *amici* for their diligent work in fashioning a stipulation of facts which materially expedited the resolution of the case.

Civiletti's first appearance before the Supreme Court was in 1974 when he was invited by the court to brief and argue a case in support of the holding below dealing with the construction of the Bankruptcy Act and the Consumer Credit Protection Act.[24] The lower appellate court had held that an income tax refund is "property" under 70(a) of the Bankruptcy Act and that the provision of the Consumer Credit Protection Act limiting wage garnishments to not more than 25% of a person's "disposable savings" does not apply to a tax refund. The Supreme Court affirmed.[25]

Another engagement of public importance after Civiletti's return to private practice was his representation of the Rhode Island House of Representatives in connection with the institution of impeachment proceedings against Chief Justice Joseph A. Bevilacqua of that state's Supreme Court in 1986. Robert A. Shelton, Gerard F. Treanor, Jr., Kenneth C. Bass, III, and Newton B. Fowler, III assisted Civiletti in the preparation for a two-week televised impeachment hearing after which Justice Bevilacqua resigned. Accordingly, no Bill of Impeachment was ever issued for trial in the State Senate, but the result has the familiar ring of another impeachment proceeding on the federal level which also resulted in a resignation.

Beginning in December, 1984, Civiletti and five other Venable lawyers represented Lakewood Hospital, located in the western suburbs of Cleveland, Ohio, in defending against an attempt by the local Blue Cross entity to drive the hospital out of business. The members of the Venable team lived in Cleveland for four months during the winter of 1984-1985, and simultaneously tried a four week jury trial as well as a state court administrative proceeding. Lakewood Hospital prevailed. It was granted an injunction against Blue Cross's efforts to terminate its existence, and a $4.25 million damage award.

Jeffrey Dunn and James A. Dunbar were among those who assisted Civiletti in this achievement.

In 1985, a committee of the board of directors of Ashland Oil Company retained Civiletti to conduct an internal investigation into allegations that Ashland had made improper payments to foreign officials in violation of the Foreign Corrupt Practices Act in order to obtain contracts assuring a continued supply of crude oil. The company, including its current and former chief executive officers and in-house counsel, were the focus of a Securities and Exchange Commission criminal investigation and a shareholder derivative suit based on these allegations.

A team of attorneys from Venable, Baetjer and Howard under Civiletti's supervision conducted a 16-month investigation across three continents. James L. Shea journeyed to London and Abu Dhabi to pursue whether improper payments had been made to officials of the Emirate of Abu Dhabi. Thomas P. Perkins, III and Jeffrey D. Knowles braved the African bush country in Zimbabwe to investigate whether a $25 million acquisition by Ashland of a chrome mine had been a bona fide investment or a disguised payment to an alleged foreign official of Oman.

Jeffrey Dunn and James A. Dunbar had less rigorous duty in London, Paris, Zurich, and Geneva untangling the legal and accounting labyrinth which accompanied many of the transactions.

The derivative suit and the SEC proceedings were settled without the need for a formal report of the findings of the investigation, a subject which remains confidential. The abrupt ending of the engagement gave rise to concern as to what would keep these lawyers busy, but there proved to be life after Ashland as other business appeared on the scene and the firm continued to prosper.

A *cause celebre* in which Civiletti was involved in 1989-90 centered around the embezzlement by an attorney, Edward S. Digges, Jr., of some $3.6 million from his client, Dresser Industries, Inc., and over $1 million from his law firm, Digges, Wharton & Levin. A former partner at Piper & Marbury, Digges was the scion of one of Maryland's best known family of lawyers, his uncle and grandfather both having been judges of the Court of Appeals. Digges had established himself as an outstanding advocate in the field of product liability defense, and the news of his padded time sheets and false disbursements came as a surprise to those who knew him. On behalf of Dresser and with the assistance of Douglas D. Connah, Jr. and David J. Heubeck, Civiletti obtained in a malpractice suit against Digges and his firm a summary judgment[26] for the bulk of the loss. When brought to the bar of justice in the criminal case, Digges was ordered to pay $1 million in restitution and to serve 30 months in jail. The case has been an ongoing saga, the malpractice insurance carrier for the Digges firm having so far been successful in avoiding responsibility for damages resulting from the proved fraud. As this book goes to press, this issue is on appeal to the Fourth Circuit Court of Appeals.

True to the traditions established by the Founders and the Caretakers, Civiletti has participated in a wide range of civic, charitable and public causes in addition to his active professional practice and service as the firm's chief executive. Thus, on the appointment of Governor Hughes he served as chairman of a two-year task force, known as the "Civiletti Commission," to study the funding of public education in Maryland, resulting in a $600 million increase in that budget item. He has served as chairman of the board of visitors of the University of Maryland School of Public Affairs and also the Johns Hopkins School of Arts & Sciences advisory committee. He was the first chairman of the Maryland Legal Services Corporation which implemented an innovative program to assist in the delivery of legal services to the poor. In 1986 he was chairman of the University of Maryland Task Force on Drug Abuse which developed a model program for colleges and universities for the reduction and prevention of substance abuse on our campuses.

In service to his profession outside the state of Maryland, Civiletti has been chairman of the litigation section of the American Bar Association and a member of the Special Coordinating Committee on Professionalism and the Advisory Committee on Governmental

Affairs and the Commission on Minorities. He is a Fellow of the American College of Trial Lawyers and a member of its Committee on Special Problems in the Administration of Justice. He is a past vice-president and director of the American Judicature Society and member of its executive committee.

On the local front, Civiletti has been a director of the Maryland National Bank and also a member of the board and chairman of the executive committee of its parent, MNC Financial, Inc. He has been a member of the Public Policy Council of the Greater Baltimore Committee and a member of the Economic Club of Washington. Like the Founders, Civiletti has served as a trustee of the Johns Hopkins University. He has been a member of three Baltimore law clubs, Serjeants' Inn, the Wranglers and the Lawyers' Round Table. Other activities and awards of honor are listed in an endnote.[27]

In the firm's long history the only event that has challenged its existence was the S & L crisis of 1985-1987, described in the previous chapter. A word of tribute must yet be added to extoll Civiletti's handling of the settlement of this case. He was the point man who dealt with an inquisitive and hostile press, the cheerleader who bolstered the morale of the partners amid a barrage of inflammatory publicity, and the strategist who directed the course of settlement and the ultimate survival of the firm. He played each of these roles with skill and dedication.

Upon his assumption of the office of managing partner on January 1, 1987, Civiletti introduced some innovations in the mechanics of firm operations, notably the replacement of the old Operating Committee by a new one called the Management Committee, coupled with the formation of an entirely new group which acts somewhat like a Board of Overseers and is known as the Firm Committee. He also abolished regular monthly meetings of the entire firm, since they had outlived their usefulness. Instead meetings were scheduled on a quarterly basis to be supplemented by special ones to handle special matters. With no reflection on the prior regimes of Vernon Eney and Jacques Schlenger, it may be said that Civiletti has introduced a new style of management with clearer lines of executive authority and a more streamlined structure designed to meet the needs of a partnership of steadily increasing size.

While the Schlenger years had witnessed a dramatic expansion of the firm into Washington and Northern Virginia, the first four years of the Civiletti era saw an equally significant Maryland expansion into Rockville, Towson and Bel Air.

The incursion into Rockville was made possible by the acquisition of Titus & Glasgow, one of the leading firms in that rapidly growing suburban area of Montgomery County. The senior partner, Roger W. Titus, then president of the Maryland State Bar Association, and his partner, Paul T. Glasgow, joined forces with Venable, Baetjer and Howard on July 1, 1988.

The move into Towson, the county seat of Baltimore County, and Bel Air, the county seat of Harford County, was achieved by the merger into the firm of Cook, Howard, Downes & Tracy on June 1, 1989, adding 16 new partners to the firm's ranks. Thus, Venable, Baetjer and Howard became a regional firm with a presence running through the metropolitan sections of Maryland and into Washington and Virginia.

James H. Cook, the senior partner in Cook, Howard, Downes & Tracy, is a former president of the Maryland State Bar Association and the acknowledged dean of the Towson bar, while his partner John B. Howard is known as one of the leading local real estate lawyers. The Bel Air office, headed by Frank F. Hertsch, has given the firm an entree into Harford County and other sections of northeast Maryland.

In June, 1988 the firm expanded into the area of high-tech international trade matters with the lateral entry of John C. Dibble as a partner in the Washington office. Formerly a partner in the firm of Weaden, Dibble & Rehm, Dibble was joined by Thomas J. Cooper and Barbara L. Waite, also formerly with the Weaden firm. This group specializes in handling the legal aspects of commodities under export controls as well as international and domestic commodities laws. These additions have provided the firm with an infusion of expertise in the rapidly growing field of international practice.

On February 1, 1990 another addition occurred with the merger of Robbins & Laramie into Venable, Baetjer, Howard & Civiletti in Washington. Frank E. Robbins and James R. Laramie, are specialists in the law of patents, copyrights and intellectual property and add an important dimension to the range of services offered by the firm. In addition to the two seniors, John E. Holmes, Jeffrey L. Ihnen and James R. Myers joined the ranks of Venable's partners and have brought with them a cadre of nearly 45 lawyers and staff.

During the years of the Civiletti regime, the managing partner has been on the alert for the lateral entrance of lawyers from other firms who were seeking new associations and who could bring a wider range of service. These additions are so numerous that the names of these attorneys are consigned to an endnote,[28] but their importance to the growth and development of the firm cannot be overstated.

As of January 1, 1991 Civiletti spearheaded a reorganization of the firm into three divisions — Business, headed by Bryson L. Cook, Government, headed by Thomas J. Madden and Labor-Litigation, headed by Paul F. Strain. This reorganized structure is designed not only to improve the quality of legal service but also training procedures and business development.

On September 1, 1991 the firm had 127 active partners, 14 lawyers holding the titles Senior Of Counsel or Of Counsel, 132 associates, 394 legal assistants, secretaries and other staff, or a total personnel complement of 667. A tabulation of the partners as of September 1, 1991 according to their assigned divisions and location of principal office is contained in an endnote.[29]

Civiletti is married to the former Gaile L. Lundgren, and they have three children, Benjamin H., Andrew S., and Lynne T. Their home on a farm in Monkton in upper Baltimore County has been the scene of annual parties for the partners and spouses, events which have become legendary.

The conclusion of this Part III, *The Innovators*, is not to suggest that the process of innovation at Venable, Baetjer and Howard has been concluded. On the other hand, it is difficult to believe that the changes over the next forty years will be ratably comparable to those of the last forty; were it so, the firm would have 36 offices by the year 2031 and 5,938 lawyers. That seems unlikely. But who knows? An office in London? Paris? Brussels? Berlin? Singapore? Tokyo? Moscow? Or maybe even New York?

Perhaps.

Endnotes to Part III, Chapter 3:

1. See Part III, Chapter 1, *infra*, for a discussion of the saga of the *Madden Cases*.

2. See Part II, Chapter 7, *infra*, for a discussion of Orrick's representation of Robb Tyler.

3. *Lanier Business Products v. Graymar Company*, 342 F. Supp. 1200 (D. Md. 1972).

4. *United States Diplomatic and Consular Staff in Iran, Judgment, I.C.J. Reports 1980, p. 3.* [The official report of this case erroneously lists Roberts B. Owen of the Department of State as the advocate for the United States. At the insistence of President Carter, the case was actually argued by Civiletti.]

5. *Fedorenko v. United States*, 449 U.S. 490, 101 S. Ct. 737, 66 L. Ed. 2d 686 (1981).

6. *American Federation of Labor and Congress of Industrial Organizations v. Kahn*, 199 U.S. App. D.C. 300 (1979).

7. *Missouri-Kansas-Texas R. Co. v. United States*, 632 F.2d 392 (5th Cir. 1980), a case involving administrative law; *Prapavat v. Immigration and Naturalization Service*, 638 F.2d 87 (5th Cir. 1980).

8. *American Hospital Association v. NLRB*, 899 F.2d 651 (7th Cir. 1990), a loss for Civiletti on appeal, the question being whether the NLRB could be enjoined from recognizing only eight bargaining units for employees of acute care hospitals; the injunction obtained in the lower court, 718 F. Supp. 704 (N.D. Ill. 1989) was vacated. *McClelland v. Goodyear Tire & Rubber Co.*, 735 F. Supp. 172 (D. Md. 1990), where Civiletti obtained summary judgment on his contention that a parent corporation has no liability for a workers' compensation claim of an employee of a subsidiary; *Northeast Community Organization v. Weinberger*, 378 F. Supp. 1287 (D. Md. 1974), Civiletti appearing for the Health and Welfare Council of Central Maryland in an unsuccessful attempt to challenge the denial of assistance under the Emergency School Aid Act.

9. *Call Carl, Inc. v. B. P. Oil Co.*, 403 F. Supp. 568 (D. Md. 1975), where a new trial was granted unless the defendant filed a *remittitur* for excessive damages. For an earlier skirmish where defendant's motion to dismiss was demised, see 391 F. Supp. 367 (D. Md. 1975).

10. *Paturzo v. Home Life Insurance Co.*, 382 F. Supp. 357 (D. Md. 1974), a victory for Civiletti in a case holding no federal jurisdiction in a suit against the insurer on a life insurance policy.

11. *Westinghouse Electric Co. v. Garrett Co.*, 437 F. Supp. 1301 (D. Md. 1977), a victory for Civiletti in a case construing a complicated commercial contract.

12. *Stewart v. Baltimore City*, 250 Md. 569 (1968), a win for Civiletti as Appellant, the Court finding error in instructions to the jury where its award was less than half the amount supported by testimony.

13. *Kaehni v. Diffraction Co.*, 342 F. Supp. 523 (D. Md. 1972), where Civiletti not only won the defense of an infringement suit but was also successful in recovering attorney's fees, a very rare result in the patent field; *Chemithon Corporation v. Proctor & Gamble Co.*, 287 F. Supp. 291 (D. Md. 1968), a loss for Civiletti and forwarding counsel from Chicago in an unsuccessful patent infringement case.

14. *Meola v. Bethlehem Steel Co.*, 246 Md. 226 (1967), a successful defense of a wrongful discharge case.

15. Acts of 1974, Ch. 870.

16. *Burning Tree Club, Inc. v. Bainum*, 305 Md. 53 (1985). In an earlier case, *State v. Burning Tree Club, Inc.*, 301 Md. 9 (1984), the court held (Civiletti prevailing) that the Attorney General had no standing to question the constitutionality of a Maryland statute.

17. Acts of 1986, Ch. 334.

18. *State v. Burning Tree Club, Inc.*, 315 Md. 254 (1989).

19. See *infra*, note 27.

20. *Groves v. Board of Education of St. Mary's County*, 164 F. Supp. 621 (D. Md. 1958), aff'd in *Board of Education of St. Mary's County v. Groves*, 261 F.2d 527 (4th Cir. 1958); *Hart v. Board of Education of Charles County*, 164 F. Supp. 501 (D. Md. 1958).

21. *In re Mid-Atlantic Toyota Antitrust Litigation*, 564 F. Supp. 1379 (D. Md. 1983).

22. *Weisman v. Connors*, 76 Md. App. 488 (Md. App. 1988); *Weisman v. Connors*, 312 MD. 428 (1988); *Weisman v. Connors*, 69 Md. App. 732 (Md. App. 1987).

23. 328 F. Supp. 165 (D. Md. 1971).

24. *Kokoszka v. Belford*, 417 U.S. 642, 94 S. Ct. 2431, 41 L. Ed. 374 (1974).

25. *In re Kokoszka*, 479 F.2d 990 (2 Cir. 1973).

26. *Dresser Industries, Inc. v. Digges*, U.S. District Court for the District of Maryland, Court Action No. JH-89-485 (1989).

27. In addition to the posts mentioned in the text, Civiletti has been a director of the National Institute Against Prejudice & Violence; chairman of the board of Maryland Healthcorp, Inc.; a member of the Washington/Baltimore Regional Association; a fellow of the American Bar Foundation, the American Law Institute and the Maryland Bar Foundation; and a member of the Advisory Committee of the National Workshop on Christian-Jewish Relations.

Among his awards and honorary degrees have been: the Herbert H. Lehman Ethics Award from the American Jewish Theological Seminary; degrees of Doctor of Laws from the University of Baltimore, New York Law School, St. John's University, Tulane University, Notre Dame University and the University of Maryland; a degree of Doctor of Public Service from the University of Maryland, and a degree of Doctor of Humane Letters from Towson State University. He has been a prolific contributor to articles in professional journals and has been a frequent lecturer on many aspects of the legal profession.

28. Between January 1, 1987 and September 1, 1991 the following lateral entrants have joined Venable, Baetjer and Howard as partners, excluding those who have left in the meanwhile:

Name	Former Firm	Specialty
Joel Z. Silver	Thomas & Fiske	Real Estate
Michael B. McGovern	Sole Practitioner	Real Estate
Ellen F. Dyke	Thomas & Fiske	Real Estate
Jan K. Guben	Shapiro & Olander	Real Estate
David G. Lane	Lewis, Mitchell & Moore	Litigation
Kevin A. Gaynor	Department of Justice	Environmental
James A. Cole	Niles, Barton & Wilmer	Real Estate
John C. Dibble	Weaden, Dibble & Rehm	International Law
George F. Pappas	Melnicove, et al. (1)	Litigation
Roger W. Titus	Titus & Glasgow	Litigation

Name	Former Firm	Specialty
Paul T. Glasgow	Titus & Glasgow	Litigation
Paula M. Junghans	Melnicove, et al. (1)	Tax
L. Paige Marvel	Melnicove, et al. (1)	Tax
Mikol S. Neilson	Steptoe & Johnson	Tax
Judson W. Starr	Department of Justice	Environmental
Daniel J. Kraftson	Lewis, Mitchell & Moore	Litigation
Andrew A. Caffey	Kaufmann, et al. (2)	Franchising
Mark Muedeking	Hogan & Hartson	Employee Benefits
H. Russell Frisby, Jr.	Melnicove, et al. (1)	Corporate
Michael Schatzow	Melnicove, et al. (1)	Litigation
James H. Cook	Cook, et al. (3)	Litigation
John B. Howard	Cook, et al. (3)	Litigation
David D. Downes	Cook, et al. (3)	Real Estate
Daniel O'C. Tracy, Jr.	Cook, et al. (3)	Real Estate
John H. Zink, III	Cook, et al. (3)	Litigation
Joseph C. Wich, Jr.	Cook, et al. (3)	Litigation
Herbert R. O'Conor, III	Cook, et al. (3)	Litigation
Frank F. Hertsch	Cook, et al. (3)	Real Estate
Thomas L. Hudson	Cook, et al. (3)	Corporate
C. Carey Deeley, Jr.	Cook, et al. (3)	Litigation
M. King Hill, III	Cook, et al. (3)	Litigation
Robert A. Hoffman	Cook, et al. (3)	Real Estate
Cynthia M. Hahn	Cook, et al. (3)	Litigation
Kathleen G. Cox	Cook, et al. (3)	Litigation
John J. Klusaritz	Sidley & Austin	Tax
Frank E. Robbins	Robbins & Laramie	Corporate
James R. Laramie	Robbins & Laramie	Corporate
John E. Holmes	Robbins & Laramie	Corporate
Jeffrey L. Ihnen	Robbins & Laramie	Corporate
James R. Myers	Robbins & Laramie	Litigation
Thomas B. Hudson	Willkie, et al. (4)	Consumer Banking
Robert A. Cook	Willkie, et al. (4)	Consumer Banking
Mary E. Pivec	Frank, et al. (5)	Labor, Immigration
Nathaniel E. Jones, Jr.	Miles & Stockbridge	Corporate
William D. Coston	Winston & Strawn	Litigation
Ronald R. Glancz	Drinker, Biddle (6)	Corporate

(1) Melnicove, Kaufman, Weiner, Smouse & Garbis, P.A.
(2) Kaufmann, Caffey, Gilden, Rosenblum & Schaeffer, P.C.
(3) Cook, Howard, Downes & Tracy
(4) Willkie Farr & Gallagher
(5) Frank, Bernstein, Conaway & Goldman
(6) Drinker, Biddle & Reath

The following attorneys joined Venable, Baetjer and Howard as "Of Counsel" between January 1, 1987 and September 1, 1991, excluding those who left in the meanwhile:

Name	Former Firm	Specialty
Thomas J. Cooper	Weaden, Dibble & Rehm	International Law
Herbert R. O'Conor, Jr.	Cook, et al. (3 above)	General Corporate
Ilona Modly Hogan	Hogan & Hogan	International Law
Edward F. Glynn, Jr.	Federal Trade Commission	International Law
Emried D. Cole, Jr.	CSX Transportation	Tax/Estates & Trusts
John J. Pavlick, Jr.	U.S. Army	Government Contracts
Keith G. Swirsky	Clary & Moore	Taxation

29. Partners as of September 1, 1991 according to their assigned divisions and location of principal office were:

BUSINESS

Baltimore

Constance H. Baker
Robert J. Bolger, Jr.
Neal D. Borden
James A. Cole
Bryson L. Cook
Robert A. Cook
David M. Fleishman
H. Russell Frisby, Jr.
Jan K. Guben
Marianne Schmitt Hellauer
Elizabeth R. Hughes
Nathaniel E. Jones, Jr.
Thomas J. Kenney, Jr.
Mitchell Kolkin
N. Peter Lareau
Alexander I. Lewis, III
Luke Marbury
William J. McCarthy
Lee M. Miller
M. Lucinda Motsko
Mark Muedeking
Mikol S. Neilson

Max Stul Oppenheimer
Stephen L. Owen
Peter P. Parvis
Thomas P. Perkins, III
Charles B. Reeves, Jr.
Russell R. Reno, Jr.
David E. Rice
John W. Scheflen
Barbara E. Schlaff
Jacques T. Schlenger
Nancy Lark Schulze
Paul A. Serini
Robert A. Shelton
F. Dudley Staples, Jr.
Robert L. Waldman
Thomas D. Washburne, Jr.
Richard L. Wasserman
Edward L. Wender
James D. Wright
Alan D. Yarbro
W. Robert Zinkham

Washington
Andrew A. Caffey
Ellen F. Dyke
Ronald R. Glancz
Joel J. Goldberg
John E. Holmes
Thomas B. Hudson
Jeffrey L. Ihnen

John J. Klusaritz
James R. Laramie
Michael B. McGovern
William S. Oshinsky
Frank E. Robbins
Joe A. Shull
Joel Z. Silver

Towson
David D. Downes
Robert A. Hoffman
John B. Howard

Thomas L. Hudson
Daniel O'C. Tracy, Jr.

Bel Air
John J. Gessner

Frank F. Hertsch

Tysons Corner
Robert E. Madden

GOVERNMENT

Baltimore
Anthony M. Carey
Brigid E. Kenney

Robert G. Smith

Washington
John C. Dibble
Kevin A. Gaynor
Jeffrey D. Knowles

Thomas J. Madden
Judson W. Starr

Tysons Corner
William L. Walsh, Jr.

LITIGATION/LABOR

Baltimore

James K. Archibald
Jeffrey P. Ayres
Jana Howard Carey
Benjamin R. Civiletti
Douglas D. Connah, Jr.
A. Samuel Cook
George C. Doub, Jr.
James A. Dunbar
Susan K. Gauvey
David J. Heubeck
Elizabeth C. Honeywell
George W. Johnston
Paula M. Junghans
Francis R. Laws
John H. Lewin, Jr.

L. Paige Marvel
Stanley Mazaroff
Christopher R. Mellott
John H. Morris, Jr.
George F. Pappas
Mary E. Pivec
Peter S. Saucier
Michael Schatzow
James L. Shea
Craig E. Smith
Nell B. Strachan
Paul F. Strain
Ronald W. Taylor
G. Stewart Webb, Jr.
Lawrence S. Wescott

Washington

Robert G. Ames
Maurice Baskin
William D. Coston
Jeffrey A. Dunn

Amy Berman Jackson
James R. Myers
William D. Quarles
Gerard F. Treanor, Jr.

Towson

James H. Cook
Kathleen G. Cox
C. Carey Deeley, Jr.
Cynthia M. Hahn

M. King Hill, III
Herbert R. O'Conor, III
Joseph C. Wich, Jr.
John H. Zink, III

Tysons Corner

Kenneth C. Bass, III
William D. Dolan, III
Daniel J. Kraftson

David G. Lane
Bruce E. Titus

Rockville

Paul T. Glasgow

Roger W. Titus

VENABLE, BAETJER AND HOWARD

ATTORNEYS AT LAW

A PARTNERSHIP INCLUDING PROFESSIONAL CORPORATIONS

1800 MERCANTILE BANK & TRUST BUILDING

2 HOPKINS PLAZA

BALTIMORE, MARYLAND 21201-2978

(301) 244-7400

FAX (301) 244-7742

TELEX 898032

WASHINGTON, D. C.
McLEAN, VA
ROCKVILLE, MD
TOWSON, MD
BEL AIR, MD

RICHARD M. VENABLE (1839-1910)
EDWIN G. BAETJER (1868-1945)
CHARLES MCH. HOWARD (1870-1942)

WRITER'S DIRECT NUMBER IS

The formal letterhead in use in 1991 in all offices except Washington, D.C.

VENABLE, BAETJER, HOWARD & CIVILETTI

ATTORNEYS AT LAW

A PARTNERSHIP INCLUDING PROFESSIONAL CORPORATIONS

SUITE 1000

1201 NEW YORK AVENUE, N. W.

WASHINGTON, D. C. 20005-3917

(202) 962-4800

FAX (202) 962-8300

BALTIMORE, MD
McLEAN, VA
ROCKVILLE, MD
TOWSON, MD
BEL AIR, MD

RICHARD M. VENABLE (1839-1910)
EDWIN G. BAETJER (1868-1945)
CHARLES MCH. HOWARD (1870-1942)

WRITER'S DIRECT NUMBER IS

The formal letterhead in use in 1991 in the Washington, D.C. office

PART IV

Epilogue

T HIS PICTURE OF Venable, Baetjer and Howard has been developed from profiles of its Founders, Caretakers and Innovators, but a few words must be added about the staff, the partners and associates who have engaged in public service, and some of the engagements of other lawyers that stand out in the firm's life.

The Staff

Few organizations have been blessed with a more loyal and dedicated corps of secretaries and other employees. Mention will be made of a few who have contributed much to the amiable work environment.

One who left an indelible impression is the late Seymour Larabee, known to all as "Larry." When asked, "What do you do around here?," he replied, "What do I do around here? I do everything from picking up the mail to driving Mr. Eney's Cadillac." On the occasion of John Lewin's marriage, Larry was given the task of delivering flowers to the bridal suite at the Belvedere Hotel. He seized the opportunity to see that the furnishings were rearranged to his liking for a wedding night and, upon his return, proudly announced what he had done. With a twinkle in his eye, Lewin replied, "Quick thinking, Larry. Quick thinking."

Miss Irma Fowler, who retired in 1988 after many years of service as a secretary but continues to work part-time, has a bounce in her step and a contagious spirit of good humor. An ardent baseball fan, she left the office early one balmy April afternoon to take in Opening Day at Memorial Stadium, leaving as her excuse that she was attending her grandmother's funeral. Some years before, Crossan Cooper had lodged the same explanation with Miss Porsinger at the switchboard as he, too, took off for the afternoon. Both times the alibi was taken in all seriousness by some, much to the amusement of others who were quick to calculate how old "grandmother" would have been.

Speaking of Miss Porsinger, mention must be made of the other switchboard operators over the years. Her successor was Frieda McEnaney, followed by Carolyn Collins and Dolores Rosier. Their gracious manners have done much to project the pleasant image of the firm in the community.

Some people rise to the top by good luck, others by innate talent; more often it is a combination of both. So it was with the ascendancy of Nancy M. Looker who began her career at Venable, Baetjer and Howard as secretary for Robert R. Bair. When Vernon Eney found himself bereft of secretarial help as a result of the retirement of Mary K. Harrison and Ethel Hall Price (both alumnae of Armstrong, Machen & Eney), Bair stepped forward and offered his secretary to the managing partner. She filled that role until 1978 when Eney named her Secretarial Coordinator. Her present title is Director of Personnel, supervising more than 200 people.

In 1987 Benjamin R. Civiletti inaugurated the "H. Vernon Eney Award," given annually to members of the staff whose attitudes, diligence, professional excellence and esprit de corps have contributed to the life of the firm. It has been given to 74 staff members whose names are catalogued alphabetically in an endnote,[1] the presentations having been made at the annual holiday party at which Mrs. H.

Vernon Eney has been an honored guest. The award consists of a gold pin inscribed with the donee's initials and a bonus check (in addition, of course, to any regular bonus) in the amount of $1,000. The H. Vernon Eney Award has promoted an awareness of the ultimate in work ethic that he exemplified and has encouraged others to emulate that example.

Public Service

Many former partners and associates of Venable, Baetjer and Howard have been involved in public service, the most notable being Benjamin R. Civiletti, the 73rd Attorney General of the United States. The highest judicial office of a former partner is held by Francis D. Murnaghan, Jr. on the bench of the United States Court of Appeals for the Fourth Circuit. On the state appellate level, Alan M. Wilner, a former associate, has been a long-time Associate Judge of the Court of Special Appeals, now its Chief Judge.

Among state *nisi prius* judges, Judge Joseph H. H. Kaplan, a former partner, stands out as the Administrative Judge of the Circuit Court for Baltimore City and has been in the forefront of many cases of public interest, notably the litigation arising out of the Savings & Loan crisis in the 1980's. On the federal side Judge J. Frederick Motz, another former partner, has similarly lent distinction to the United States District Court for the District of Maryland since his assumption of that office on July 22, 1985 following a four-year stint as United States Attorney. On May 14, 1991, still another Venable partner, Benson Everett Legg, was appointed by President Bush to fill the latest vacancy on the local federal bench.

So many lawyers in the firm have served as assistant attorneys general and assistant United States attorneys that it would be impracticable to list them all, but it is noteworthy that Richard W. Emory and Paul F. Strain have held the office of Deputy Attorney General, the second highest legal office in the state.

On the political front, the firm of Venable, Baetjer and Howard has spawned two United States Senators — John Marshall Butler,

1950-62, and Paul S. Sarbanes who was first elected in 1982 and reelected to a second term in 1988. Prior to his elevation to the Senate, Sarbanes had served three terms in the House of Representatives and before that had been a member of the Maryland House of Delegates. He was still an associate in the firm when he withdrew to devote full time to public service.

Another former associate, Charles Gilchrist later became County Executive of Montgomery County and is now an Episcopal priest. Still another, Robert C. Embry, Jr., was Assistant Secretary for Community Planning and Development of the Department of Housing and Urban Development during the Carter administration and before that had been a member of the Baltimore City Council and president of the School Board.

In 1974 Robert A. Shelton, a partner, took leave of absence to serve as Associate Special Counsel to the House Judiciary Committee in its impeachment inquiry into the activities of President Nixon. In that capacity, he became associated with John Doar who later teamed up with him in the *Federal Leasing* litigation discussed hereafter.

In academe, the firm's stellar performer has been a former associate, Robert J. Martineau, now a professor of law at the University of Cincinnati and noted jurisprudential scholar.

Other Engagements

This section deals with other engagements denominated as "The Incomparable Sam Cook," "Corporate Finance," "The Federal Leasing Case," "G. D. Searle" and "Times Mirror."

The Incomparable Sam Cook

One of the most colorful and aggressive lawyers at Venable, Baetjer and Howard has been the head of its labor department, A. Samuel Cook. Boasting that he never achieved much in the way of scholarship (modestly omitting that he graduated from Gilman School, Princeton University and the University of Maryland School of Law and claiming that he only did so "*magna cum difficultate*"), he embarked on a legal career in 1947 as an associate with a sole practitioner in Baltimore and a year later talked his way into Piper, Watkins, Avirett & Egerton, a forerunner of Piper & Marbury. He says that the late William L. Marbury was disdainful of accepting in the merger a lawyer of such limited academic attainments, but by this time the issue was itself academic because Cook had decided to become a labor lawyer. In those days firms such as Piper & Marbury and Venable, Baetjer and Howard did not practice in the grimy field of labor relations, preferring to refer this business to a small group of labor practitioners at the Baltimore bar. Piper & Marbury and Sam Cook thus went their separate ways.

After a stint with the office of general counsel to the National Labor Relations Board and the U.S. Department of Labor and a tour of duty with the industrial relations division of Davison Chemical Company, Cook teamed up with H. Raymond Cluster to form the labor relations law firm of Cook & Cluster. One of their early referrals was the representation of the Johns Hopkins Hospital in its efforts to stave off the unionization of hospital workers by District 1199 E of the Hospital Workers Union. J. Crossan Cooper, Jr. was then the president of the hospital.

As a non-profit hospital, Hopkins was exempt from the federal labor laws, but it could become subject to them if it voluntarily agreed to a certification election by secret ballot. Fred Punch, the pugnacious organizer of 1199 E, embarked on a public relations campaign to compel the hospital to agree to an election. At high noon he staged a walkout of hospital employees with Coretta King and towering members of the Baltimore Bullets marching down Broadway. Then Punch called Cook on the telephone to warn him that the hospital's alternatives were "ballots or bullets." He did not seem to be referring to the professional basketball team.

Although the result of an election was a foregone conclusion, the workers being predominantly black and underpaid, there seemed no reasonable alternative to submission. The result was as expected and the union was certified. A few years later, however, when the

Baltimore City Hospital was merged with Johns Hopkins to form the Francis Scott Key Medical Center, Cook was able to decertify three unions representing nurses, technicians and blue collar staff. Fred Punch remained for a number of years as Cook's arch-rival and once threw a chair across the table at his opponent during a negotiating session at Cross Keys. Punch later switched allegiances and became a management consultant.

Crossan Cooper was so impressed by Cook's handling of the Johns Hopkins labor problems that it led to Venable's invitation to Cook & Cluster to join ranks in 1970.

Unlike customs prevailing in other fields where firms may represent both classes of litigants, it is an unwritten rule that labor lawyers are either pro-management or pro-labor. Venable, Baetjer and Howard is committed to the management side and, for this reason, has even been blacklisted by some activist law students as a firm of "union busters" to be shunned in associate recruitment. This has not deterred its recruiting efforts, and it is unlikely to have any adverse effect in the future. In fact, Cook's rebuttal of the student charge has received national approbation, not just from management circles but also from law school deans and newspaper editorials. There is, after all, a world of difference between legitimate union avoidance and illegal coercion amounting to union-busting.

As of January 1, 1990 the Labor and Employment Law Department at the firm acquired a new chairman, Stanley Mazaroff, and in the reorganization of 1991 the department and its 25 lawyers became part of the Labor and Litigation Division.

Corporate Finance

As a business-oriented law firm, Venable, Baetjer and Howard has played a leading role in the field of corporate finance on the Baltimore scene. In the 1960's and 70's the firm represented as general counsel four of the five locally based members of the New York Stock Exchange, Robert Garrett & Sons, Inc., Stein Bros. & Boyce, Inc., Baker, Watts & Co., and John C. Legg & Co., now Legg Mason

Wood Walker, Inc., and did a substantial business with the fifth and largest, Alex. Brown & Sons. In 1971 Venable represented Alex. Brown in the public offering of $125,250,000 of common stock of American General Bond Fund, Inc., at the time the largest equity underwriting exclusively managed by a non-Wall Street investment banker, a record which has since been broken many times. Over the last 20 years the firm has worked on public offerings, private placements and business combinations aggregating several billions of dollars. As the senior Venable partner in what was formerly known as the Securities Department, I was the lead counsel in most of these transactions, often assisted by Alan D. Yarbro, now the head of this group. Other partners on the current team include John W. Scheflen, Thomas D. Washburne, Jr., Elizabeth R. Hughes and Charles B. Reeves, Jr.

The Federal Leasing Case

The case of *Federal Leasing, Inc. v. Underwriters at Lloyd's* is a landmark case in the history of Venable, Baetjer and Howard. It sparked one of the biggest disasters in the life of Lloyd's of London, said to exceed $444 million.[2] Robert A. Shelton, a Venable partner, was the protagonist.

The idea of insurance to guarantee against the cancellation of computer leases by agencies of the federal government had been around for some time before Shelton's client, a small leasing company headquartered in McLean, Virginia, entered the field. The concept is simple: federal agencies (FHA, Social Security, or what have you) need computers for their daily operation; the best way to procure them is by lease or conditional sale; but constitutional or statutory constraints may impede the agency's power to enter into long-term arrangements extending beyond its current budgetary authority. This is where the insurance comes into play. The leasing company buys the equipment from IBM or other manufacturer, leases it or sells it under conditional contract of sale to the agency, coupled with the agency's reservation of its right to cancel, procures an insurance policy guaranteeing against cancellation, and lays off the commercial paper with a financial institution, i.e., assigns the agency's obligation to a bank for cash. So long as the agency pays, the arrangement is a license to make money: the insurer feels secure because it knows of the agency's continuing need for the equipment and its residual value in the event of a cancellation; the bank is protected by the leasing company's obligation, backed up by the insurance; and the leasing company relies both on the insurance and the residual value of the hardware in the unlikely event of a default.

The Federal Leasing scenario involved the adaptation of this concept not only to federal agencies but also to states and local governments. Thanks to the ingenuity of Theodore W. Hirsh, then a Venable partner, the payments from the state or municipal authority could be tax free. What had been a license to make money was now a license to mint.

For a while the money machine worked to the satisfaction of all. Then, suddenly everything that could go wrong did go wrong.

On March 25, 1977 IBM came out with a new generation of lower-priced mainframe computers that rendered obsolete existing equipment and decimated the residual value of hardware then under lease. There was no longer a motive on the part of lessees to renew and, worse yet, the residual values on which the leasing companies, the banks, and the underwriters had relied were sharply reduced. Cancellations of leases and conditional sales contracts abounded, and the leasing companies were called upon to honor guarantees they thought were protected by insurance.

Confronted with staggering claims, Lloyd's (and other insurers, as well) struggled to find a way out of the dilemma, first contending that no claims had to be paid under the policies until the end of the term of the particular sales agreement or lease. This defense was without merit, and eventually American counsel for the underwriters so advised them.

Meanwhile, fearing the domino effect of a lawsuit, Lloyd's entered into settlement negotiations with Federal Leasing, culminating in an

Agreement of March 13, 1978 whereunder the underwriters agreed to continue paying claims as they were filed, and Federal Leasing agreed to remit the proceeds of sales of residuals. Pursuant to the March 13 Agreement, Federal Leasing paid the underwriters some $900,000 from sales, and Lloyd's paid $8,676,918 of claims until February of 1979 when suddenly all payments stopped. There seemed to be no reason other than that the volume of claims was becoming monstrous.

On June 12, 1979 Federal Leasing surprised the insurance world by filing in the United States District Court for the District of Maryland a 168-page complaint against the underwriters at Lloyd's and 17 other British insurance companies claiming an aggregate of $623 million in damages.[3] In the first 23 counts the plaintiff sought recovery of $23 million which it had been forced to cover on notes guaranteeing the non-cancellation of leases and conditional sales contracts; Counts 25 and 26 sought another $100 million in compensatory damages and $500 million in punitive damages.

As general counsel for Federal Leasing, Robert A. Shelton managed the litigation, but the lead litigator was John Doar of New York City whom Shelton had met in connection with the Nixon impeachment hearings. Doar set up shop in an office at Venable, Baetjer and Howard and for the duration devoted himself almost full time to the case. He was assisted by two lawyers from Venable's litigation department, Benjamin Rosenberg, a partner, and G. Stewart Webb. Jr., then an associate.

For a while Federal Leasing paid the regular hourly charges of Doar and the firm, but as time wore on its management realized that the cost of the litigation was becoming prohibitive in the light of Federal Leasing's precarious financial position. At this point Shelton stepped forward with an offer to continue the representation on a contingent fee basis pegged to one-third of any recovery over and above what was necessary to make the banks whole. It was understood that Doar's hourly charges would continue to be paid on a regular basis and would ultimately be deducted from any contingent fee paid to Venable. These arrangements were memorialized in a formal engagement letter dated December 12, 1979.

The first indication of victory occurred on April 17, 1980 when Judge Alexander Harvey, II issued a temporary injunction directing the insurers to abide by the terms of the March 13 Agreement.[4] He stopped short of ordering the insurers to pay the claims involved in the suit, but he directed them to continue processing claims as they had done before the sudden moratorium in February, 1979.

Lloyd's took an appeal to the Court of Appeals for the Fourth Circuit where Judge Harvey was affirmed.[5] A few months later another skirmish occurred in the Court of Appeals when the underwriters sought a *mandamus* order directing Judge Harvey to permit further discovery. This was denied,[6] and the stage was set for a trial on the merits.

On the eve of trial before a Baltimore jury the case was settled by the underwriters' agreement to pay Federal Leasing's legitimate claims under its policies as required by the March 13 agreement and to pay compensatory damages of $10,000,000 on top of that. This resulted in a contingent fee to Venable, Baetjer and Howard of $3.3 million (compared with accumulated time charges in excess of one million dollars), and 1983 was thereby rendered a good year. It is also noteworthy that all Federal Leasing's banks and other institutional investors received 100 cents on the dollar plus accrued interest, whereas in some of the other settlements the banks were forced to accept substantial discounts. This was one of the most gratifying victories in the firm's history.

G. D. Searle

G. D. Searle & Co., a pharmaceutical manufacturer of a wide range of cardiovascular, gastrointestinal and gynecologic drugs, became a significant Venable client in early 1985 when it was faced with 26 cases set for trial before Judge Joseph H. Young in the United States District Court in Baltimore. Previously, the cases had been handled by a small firm that had been unable to keep up with the court's pre-trial discovery schedule, and Searle concluded that it needed a firm with more attorneys to prepare the cases. They were product liability actions involving the Cu-7 intrauterine contraceptive, at that time the most widely used IUD in the United States.

Venable came to Searle's attention through one of its counsel in Chicago who had worked with Douglas D. Connah, Jr. on the editorial board of *Litigation*, the magazine published by the Litigation Section of the ABA. Because he was at the time heavily involved in asbestos cases, Connah recommended as lead counsel Paul F. Strain, who had recently returned to the firm from the Maryland attorney general's office. After interview, Strain was selected to head a team of lawyers to prepare the 26 cases in which almost no discovery had been done and which were scheduled for trial in nine months. Strain organized a team of litigators that included Edmund P. Dandridge, Jr., Nell B. Strachan, James L. Shea, Elizabeth Honeywell, and Maria Howell, at that time a legal assistant in the litigation department.

The team's first task was to learn about the Cu-7 and the disability involved in the claims, i.e., pelvic inflammatory disease. With the help of experts from the Johns Hopkins School of Medicine, the team took a crash course in contraception, reproduction and sexually transmitted diseases. Simultaneously a massive discovery effort began. Because the majority of the plaintiffs were not from Maryland, Venable attorneys were soon traveling all over the United States to take depositions and to meet with experts. Eventually the first, and to this day the only consolidated Cu-7 case in Maryland (17 plaintiffs) began in September of 1985 before Judge Joseph H. Young.

The conclusion did not come quickly, however. After several weeks of trial and days of deliberation the jury was unable to reach a verdict. Months later Judge Young granted judgment in Searle's favor, holding that the plaintiffs had failed to present sufficient evidence for the jury to consider whether the Cu-7 had caused pelvic inflammatory disease. The court's decision was hotly contested in the United States Court of Appeals for the Fourth Circuit which affirmed the District Court.[7]

Despite the result, cases continued to be filed in Maryland, and by 1991 the team had been involved in approximately 100. In addition, Searle expanded Venable's role by asking its help in defending cases pending in Minnesota where Strain became lead counsel in the first Cu-7 case tried in that jurisdiction.

In 1988 G. D. Searle & Co. established regional counsel to supervise its litigation throughout the United States, Venable, Baetjer and Howard being named regional counsel for an area covering New Jersey, Delaware, Maryland, the District of Columbia, Virginia, North Carolina, South Carolina, Georgia and Alabama. As of January 1, 1991 it had been a major engagement for six years and the end was not in sight.

Times Mirror

The corporate client with the longest relationship with Venable, Baetjer and Howard has been the A. S. Abell Company, publisher of *The Sun*. In Volume No. 1 of the firm's file docket, cases numbered 6, 8, 10 and 12, all of which were closed in 1902, involved the defense of suits against this client, and over the years it has provided a steady stream of legal business culminating in its sale to the Times Mirror Company for $600,000,000 in 1986.

William J. McCarthy was the partner in charge of that file and, because of its size and complexity, was assisted by numerous other lawyers in the firm, principally Jacques T. Schlenger, Lee M. Miller, Elizabeth R. Hughes, Paul A. Serini, Robert L. Waldman, John W. Scheflen, Mitchell Kolkin, Stephen L. Owen, Robert A. Shelton, James E. Cumbie and Newton B. Fowler. The Washington firm of Hogan & Hartson participated as special counsel in matters involving federal communications law and the rules and regulations of the FCC. Despite this array of people who were privy to the matter, there were no leaks, and it is a tribute to the professionalism of the working team that not even other Venable lawyers, including the author, were aware of the sale until they read about it in the papers after the public announcement.

There is a saying among business lawyers that big deals differ from small ones only in degree, not in kind. The A. S. Abell Company-Times Mirror transaction is a case in point. In lawyers' lingo, it was structured as a "reverse triangular cash-out merger," a device familiar to any attorney who practices in the field of business combinations; but in layman's terms it was a sale of stock in the A. S. Abell Company for $5,745.97 per share in cash. To be exact, this resulted in a cash payment of $599,999,924.37 in respect of the 104,421 shares outstanding. The price was skillfully negotiated on behalf of the selling stockholders by William E. McGuirk, Jr., Abell's chairman of the board, and by Reg Murphy, its president.

To reduce the transaction to its least common denominator is not, however, to belittle its importance. *The Sun* was one of the last major metropolitan newspapers in the country that had not been acquired by some chain, and the size and complexity of the deal are reflected not only in the dollars involved but also in the 14 boxes of papers containing the closed files at Venable, Baetjer and Howard. William J. McCarthy was the maestro who directed the harmonious interplay of disciplines and sub-specialties that produced a smooth and timely closing on October 27, 1986.

The A. S. Abell-Times Mirror transaction was, dollar-wise, the largest in Venable's 86-year life, but nearly five years later, in February, 1991, there was a closing on another transaction almost double its size, i.e., the sale of the credit card business of MNC Financial, Inc. for 1.1 billion dollars. John W. Scheflen was the partner in charge of that file, representing the selling party. Thus, as the firm approaches its ninety-second birthday, the mantle of leadership has been passed to a new generation of lawyers of whom the Founders would have been justly proud.

Endnotes to Epilogue:

1. Rebecca A. Abbey, Maria T. Adams, Elizabeth A. Anderson, Jennifer P. Armstrong, Timothy S. Bavis, Paula R. Berger, Marsha A. Boyd, Laura E. Braunstein, Renee J. Brinegar, Marion F. Burnett, Linda E. Butta, Patti S. Cockey, Helen N. Currie, Doris P. Duncan, Catherine L. Dunnigan, Joanne M. Edwards, Natalie J. Ely, Donna D. Faecke, Tracey L. Fultze, Carmalene Galaski, Arnez A. Gillis, Linda F. Goodrich, Mary M. Grossman, Kimberly A. Gutridge, Frances Harris, Ann M. Jensen, Ellen L. Karner, Linda E. Kates, Judy A. Lahey, Donna Lannon-Zinser, Michael Lee, Elizabeth A. Lineweaver, Mary Jane Lingner, Mary C. Lovell, Vernita C. Lyes, Judy A. Lynch, Terry M. MacDougall, Mary T. Magee, Tomas A. Mallonga, Tammy D. Martin, Gina M. Miller, Sharon U. Miller, Amy L. Millhouser, Jean L. Moore, Ethel M. Nicholas, Alice A. Norfolk, Sharon C. O'Dunne, Agnes A. Perticone, Donna C. Pieper, Rona A. Polinsky, Pauline J. Raymond, Lynne A. Rhoades, Pearl L. Richmond, Kathleen M. Rifkind, Dolores E. Rosier, Ethel R. Scott, Vince P. Sherlock, Deanna K. Sinclair, Constance R. Smith, Maria T. Spencer, Janet M. Stried, Marilyn Sullivan, Ralph S. Tabler, Jessie J. Thomas, Diane L. Thompson, Betty J. Tiggle, Diane R. Traube, Donna E. R. Trivas, Melinda S. Van Zant, Diane M. Vermette, Kim L. Vinch, Robin A. Welbourn, Jean D. White, Peggy E. White

2. The importance of the case is highlighted in Hodgson, *Lloyd's of London*, (New York, Viking Penguin, Inc., 1984) at 220 et seq.

3. *Federal Leasing, Inc. v. Underwriters at Lloyd's*, United States District Court for the District of Maryland, Civil Action No. H-79-6088.

4. *Federal Leasing, Inc. v. Underwriters at Lloyd's*, 487 F. Supp. 1248 (D. Md. 1980).

5. *Federal Leasing, Inc. v. Underwriters at Lloyd's*, 650 F.2d 495 (4th Cir. 1981).

6. *In Re Underwriters at Lloyd's*, 666 F.2d 55 (4th Cir. 1981).

7. *Marder v. G. D. Searle & Co.*, 630 F. Supp. 1087 (D. Md. 1986), aff'd without op. *sub. nom. Wheelahan, et al. v. G. D. Searle & Co.*, 814 F.2d 655 (4th Cir. 1987).

Appendix I

List of Partners of
Venable, Baetjer and Howard
July 1, 1900 - September 1, 1991
In the Order of their Admission as a Partner

	Year of Admission as Partner	Year of Death (D), Retirement or Resignation (R)
Richard M. Venable	1900	1910(D)
Edwin G. Baetjer	1900	1945(D)
Charles McHenry Howard	1900	1942(D)
Harry N. Baetjer	*	1969(D)
Joseph France	1930	1964(R)
J. Crossan Cooper, Jr.	1939	1980(R)
John M. Butler	1939	1948(R)
Hunter H. Moss	1939	1948(D)
Stuart S. Janney, Jr.	1939	1959(R)
Norwood B. Orrick	1939	1981(R)
John Henry Lewin, Sr.	1944	1983(R)
Richard W. Emory	1951	1982(R)
H. Vernon Eney	1951	1980(R)
Edmund P. Dandridge, Jr.	1952	1983(R)
Arthur W. Machen, Jr.	1957	1989(R)
Robert M. Thomas	1957	1990(R)
Francis D. Murnaghan, Jr.	1957	1979(R)
Robert R. Bair	1960	1990(R)
Jacques T. Schlenger	1963	

*Harry N. Baetjer joined the firm as as associate in 1906 following his graduation from law school earlier that year. The date of his admission as a partner has not been ascertained, but it was sometime before 1917.

Charles B. Reeves, Jr.	1964	
William J. McCarthy	1964	
Russell R. Reno, Jr.	1966	
Frederick Steinmann	1967	1972(R)
Theodore W. Hirsh	1968	1976(R)
Thomas P. Perkins, III	1968	
Joseph H. H. Kaplan	1969	1977(R)
Benjamin R. Civiletti	1969	
Gerald M. Katz	1969	1986(R)
William O. Evans	1969	1970(R)
Luke Marbury	1970	
Stuart H. Rome	1970	1983(D)
C. Van Leuven Stewart	1970	1991(R)
A. Samuel Cook	1970	
H. Raymond Cluster	1970	1972(R)
Lawrence S. Wescott	1970	
Anthony M. Carey	1972	
Wilbur E. Simmons, Jr.	1973	1982(R)
George C. Doub, Jr.	1973	
John Henry Lewin, Jr.	1973	
Alan D. Yarbro	1973	
Neal D. Borden	1973	
Robert A. Shelton	1973	
Jacob L. Friedel	1974	1986(R)
Harry D. Shapiro	1975	1987(R)
Stanley Mazaroff	1975	
Arnold P. Schuster	1976	1978(R)
Lee M. Miller	1976	
Thomas J. Kenney, Jr.	1976	
J. Frederick Motz	1976	1981(R)
N. Peter Lareau	1976	
Douglas D. Connah, Jr.	1976	
Harvey R. Clapp, III	1977	1985(R)
Benjamin Rosenberg	1977	1987(R)

Robert G. Smith	1977	
James D. Wright	1977	
Paul F. Strain	1979	
Edward J. Adkins	1980	1981(R)
Alexander I. Lewis, III	1981	
Max Stul Oppenheimer	1981	
Gary Z. Nothstein	1981	1982(R)
Terry F. Hall	1981	1986(R)
Craig E. Smith	1981	
Bryson L. Cook	1981	
Charles M. Kerr	1981	1988(R)
Thomas S. Martin	1981	1983(R)
Francis T. Coleman, Jr.	1981	1983(R)
Benson E. Legg	1982	1991(R)
Robert G. Ames	1982	
Nell B. Strachan	1982	
Richard L. Wasserman	1982	
John W. Scheflen	1983	
Barbara E. Schlaff	1983	
Ronald B. Sheff	1983	1987(R)
James K. Archibald	1983	
G. Stewart Webb, Jr.	1983	
George W. Johnston	1983	
J. Phillip Jordan	1983	1987(R)
Peter Barnes	1983	1987(R)
F. Dudley Staples, Jr.	1984	
Edward L. Wender	1984	
David M. Fleishman	1984	
Jana Howard Carey	1984	
Thomas J. Madden	1984	
Jeffrey A. Dunn	1984	
Charles R. McCarthy, Jr.	1984	1985(R)
Joe A. Shull	1984	
Jeffrey D. Knowles	1984	

Constance H. Baker	1985	
Robert C. Gombar	1985	1987(R)
Stephen L. Owen	1985	
Peter P. Parvis	1985	
James L. Shea	1985	
William L. Walsh, Jr.	1985	
Gerard F. Treanor, Jr.	1985	
William D. Dolan, III	1985	
William G. Murray	1985	1988(R)
Robert E. Madden	1985	
Kenneth C. Bass, III	1985	
Mitchell Kolkin	1986	
Jeffrey P. Ayres	1986	
Kenneth R. Hoffman	1986	1988(R)
Brigid E. Kenney	1986	
Bruce R. Spector	1986	1988(R)
John H. Morris, Jr.	1986	
Bruce E. Titus	1986	
David B. Irwin	1987	1988(R)
Elizabeth C. Honeywell	1987	
Joel Z. Silver	1987	
Michael B. McGovern	1987	
Ellen F. Dyke	1987	
Michael J. Letchinger	1987	1988(R)
Jan K. Guben	1987	
Robert M. Fields	1987	1988(R)
David G. Lane	1987	
Kevin A. Gaynor	1987	
Maurice Baskin	1988	
Robert B. Green	1988	1988(R)
M. Lucinda Motsko	1988	
Amy Berman Jackson	1988	
William D. Quarles	1988	
Christopher R. Mellott	1988	

James A. Cole	1988	
John C. Dibble	1988	
George F. Pappas	1988	
Roger W. Titus	1988	
Paul T. Glasgow	1988	
Paula M. Junghans	1988	
L. Paige Marvel	1988	
Mikol S. Neilson	1988	
Judson W. Starr	1988	
Daniel J. Kraftson	1988	
Andrew A. Caffey	1988	
Susan K. Gauvey	1989	
Marianne J. S. Hellauer	1989	
David E. Rice	1989	
Peter S. Saucier	1989	
Thomas D. Washburne, Jr.	1989	
W. Robert Zinkham	1989	
Mark Muedeking	1989	
H. Russell Frisby, Jr.	1989	
Michael Schatzow	1989	
James H. Cook	1989	
John B. Howard	1989	
David D. Downes	1989	
Daniel O'C. Tracy, Jr.	1989	
John H. Zink, Jr.	1989	
Joseph C. Wich, Jr.	1989	
Henry B. Peck, Jr.	1989	1991(R)
Herbert R. O'Conor, III	1989	
Frank F. Hertsch	1989	
Thomas L. Hudson	1989	
C. Carey Deeley, Jr.	1989	
M. King Hill, III	1989	
George K. Reynolds, III	1989	1991(R)

Robert A. Hoffman	1989	
Cynthia M. Hahn	1989	
Kathleen G. Cox	1989	
John J. Klusaritz	1989	
James A. Dunbar	1990	
John J. Gessner	1990	
Elizabeth R. Hughes	1990	
William S. Oshinsky	1990	
Rebecca B. Ransom	1990	1990(R)
Ronald W. Taylor	1990	
Robert L. Waldman	1990	
Frank E. Robbins	1990	
James R. Laramie	1990	
John E. Holmes	1990	
Jeffrey L. Ihnen	1990	
James R. Myers	1990	
Thomas B. Hudson	1990	
Robert A. Cook	1990	
Mary E. Pivec	1990	
Nathaniel E. Jones	1990	
Joel Goldberg	1991	
David J. Heubeck	1991	
Paul A. Serini	1991	
Nancy Lark Schulze	1991	
Francis R. Laws	1991	
Robert J. Bolger, Jr.	1991	
William D. Coston	1991	
Ronald R. Glancz	1991	

Appendix II

Armstrong, Machen & Eney

On May 27, 1950, the date of death of the author's father, Arthur W. Machen (1877-1950), the partnership of Armstrong, Machen & Eney was reduced to a sole proprietorship consisting of H. Vernon Eney, the sole surviving partner, and five associates, three of whom made other connections in the ensuing year. On June 27, 1951 Vernon Eney joined Venable, Baetjer and Howard as a partner, and the author and Robert M. Thomas (then on leave with the Attorney General's office) came in as associates.

Founded in 1925 as Armstrong, Machen & Allen, the three original partners were Arthur W. Machen, Alexander Armstrong, a former Attorney General of Maryland, and Wendell D. Allen, a gifted young trial lawyer. Eney became a partner in 1933 and Armstrong died ten years later in 1943. Upon Eney's return from service in World War II, the firm's name was changed to Armstrong, Machen, Allen & Eney, and it became Armstrong, Machen & Eney on Allen's withdrawal in 1946.

Schlenger & Steinmann

Schlenger & Steinmann was formed two years before its affiliation with Venable, Baetjer and Howard in 1963, Schlenger coming in as a partner and Frederick Steinmann as an associate. At the time, Gerald M. Katz had been engaged by Schlenger & Steinmann but had not yet arrived on the scene. He joined Venable, Baetjer and Howard as an associate shortly thereafter. Steinmann withdrew from the firm in 1967 and Katz in 1986. Schlenger & Steinmann formed the nucleus of the firm's tax department, a group that has expanded dramatically in depth and scope over the ensuing 28 years.

Cook & Cluster

The firm of Cook & Cluster was formed on June 15, 1961, the partners being A. Samuel Cook and H. Raymond Cluster, both specialists in labor law representing management. They joined Venable, Baetjer and Howard as partners in 1970 and Lawrence S. Wescott came in as an associate. Cluster withdrew in 1972 to move to Massachusetts to engage in labor arbitration. This group has been the core of the firm's labor department which now provides a wide range of services covering the whole spectrum of employee relations.

McCarthy, Shull and Knowles

McCarthy, Shull and Knowles was formed in 1983, an offshoot from the Washington, D.C. firm of Dunaway, McCarthy & Dye, P.C. The three principals consisted of Charles R. McCarthy, Jr., Joe A. Shull and Jeffrey D. Knowles, all of whom had practiced together in the fields of administrative, corporate, securities and general business law for more than six years. They joined the Washington offices of Venable, Baetjer, Howard & Civiletti as partners in 1984, and McCarthy withdrew the following year. Their clients, comprised of local and national businesses, including publicly held corporations, investment bankers and trade associations, significantly added to the depth and breadth of the firm's practice in the nation's capital.

Dolan, Treanor, Murray & Walsh

This Virginia firm, formed on February 1, 1977, joined forces with Venable, Baetjer and Howard in 1985, thus providing a major presence in the rapidly growing region of northern Virginia. The head of the firm, William T. Dolan, III, was at the time of the merger the president of the Virginia State Bar Association and was well recognized as an accomplished litigator. Gerard F. Treanor, Jr., also a trial lawyer of note, William F. Walsh, Jr., a specialist in the field of government contracts, and William G. Murray, an estate planner and probate counsel, rounded out the Dolan firm. Murray withdrew from Venable, Baetjer and Howard in 1988 and Dolan and Walsh continue to head up the firm's expanded presence at Tyson's Corner in McLean, Virginia, while Treanor is now the partner in charge of the District of Columbia office.

Titus & Glasgow

The firm of Titus & Glasgow was formed in Rockville, Maryland in 1973 and merged with Venable, Baetjer and Howard in 1988. The principals, Roger W. Titus and Paul T. Glasgow, had developed a significant general practice with an emphasis on litigation, land use and administrative matters. Titus was president of the Maryland State Bar Association and his firm was recognized as among the outstanding practitioners at the Montgomery County bar.

Cook, Howard, Downes & Tracy

The firm of Cook, Howard, Downes & Tracy, which merged with Venable, Baetjer and Howard on June 1, 1989, had itself been created by merger 13 years before on June 1, 1976. On that date two prominent Baltimore County firms, Downes & Dietz and Cook, Murray, Howard & Tracy, were combined. The Downes firm had been formed in 1946 by James D. C. Downes and Ralph Dietz, both general practitioners at the Towson bar with special interest in real estate practice. The Cook firm had been the successor by evolution of the firm of Turnbull & Brewster formed in 1954 by John Grason Turnbull, a long time member of the Maryland Senate and later an Associate Judge of the Circuit Court for Baltimore County, and by Daniel B. Brewster, later a member of the United States Senate.

By the time of the merger with Venable, Baetjer and Howard in 1989, Cook, Howard, Downes & Tracy had grown into the largest law firm headquartered in Towson, and James H. Cook, its senior partner, had been president of the Maryland State Bar Association. It enjoyed an excellent client base and provided Venable with an important entree into the Baltimore County and Harford County marketing areas.

Robbins & Laramie

Founded in January 1981 by Frank E. Robbins and James R. Laramie and merged with Venable, Baetjer and Howard on February 1, 1990, the firm of Robbins & Laramie added an important new dimension to the firm's range of services delivered from the Washington office. It was a firm specializing in the law relating to all phases of intellectual property and had a staff well trained and experienced in the technical disciplines. In 1986 the four partners, Frank E. Robbins, James R. Laramie, John E. Holmes and Jeffrey L. Ihnen, added to their ranks James R. Myers, an experienced civil litigator and an expert in space law, but not a patent lawyer. The move proved to be a successful one, and all five partners were folded into the Venable ranks upon the merger. Thereupon, these five headed up the following sub-specialties:

Frank E. Robbins	Chemistry, chemical engineering and food technology
James R. Laramie	International trade and administration
John E. Holmes	Mechanical, electrical, electronic and aerospace
Jeffrey L. Ihnen	Biotechnology and pharmaceutical chemistry
James R. Myers	Litigation, trademarks and general law

Index